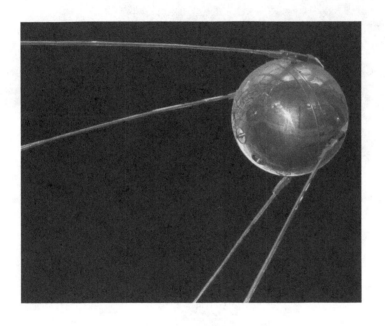

1957

Also by Eric Burns

NONFICTION

Broadcast Blues: Dispatches from the Twenty-Year War Between
a Television Reporter and His Medium

The Joy of Books: Confessions of a Lifelong Reader

The Spirits of America: A Social History of Alcohol

Infamous Scribblers: The Founding Fathers and the Rowdy
Beginnings of American Journalism

The Smoke of the Gods: A Social History of Tobacco

All the News Unfit to Print: How Things Were . . . and
How They Were Reported

Virtue, Valor and Vanity: The Founding Fathers and the Pursuit of Fame

Invasion of the Mind Snatchers: Television's Conquest of
America in the Fifties

1920: The Year That Made the Decade Roar

The Golden Lad: The Haunting Story of Quentin and Theodore Roosevelt

Someone to Watch Over Me: Eleanor Roosevelt and the Tortured Father
Who Shaped Her Life

The Politics of Fame

FICTION

The Autograph: A Modern Fable of a Father and a Daughter
Mid-Strut: A Novel

1957

The Year That Launched the American Future

Eric Burns

ROWMAN & LITTLEFIELD PUBLISHERS, INC.
Lanham • Boulder • New York • London

An imprint of The Rowman & Littlefield Publishing Group, Inc.
4501 Forbes Blvd., Ste. 200
Lanham, MD 20706
www.rowman.com

Distributed by NATIONAL BOOK NETWORK

British Library Cataloguing in Publication Information available

Library of Congress Control Number: 2020940214

ISBN: 978-1-5381-3995-0 (cloth : alk. paper)
ISBN: 978-1-5381-4069-7 (electronic)

♾ ™ The paper used in this publication meets the minimum requirements of American National Standard for Information Sciences—Permanence of Paper for Printed Library Materials, ANSI/NISO Z39.48-1992

To my favorite male companion,
To his favorite female companion,
And to their joint effort

Contents

Contents

Prologue

Sputnik 1

The United States was not at war. Nor was there a threat of war. Or of terrorism. In fact, terrorism was a word seldom uttered in those days. If we heard it at all, it was probably from Douglas Edwards on CBS or Huntley-Brinkley on NBC, and it referred to people behaving violently toward other people in some faraway part of the world. The TV reports never provided causes or details, and as a twelve-year-old eager to watch the program following the news, *Sergeant Preston of the Yukon*, I found that the stories never registered.

Until now. Now all of that changed. Now we Americans felt pangs of terror as we had never known them before, although in a different manner from those victimized abroad. No one was treating anyone else violently at home—not as a matter of policy, at least—but suddenly a threat was overhead, and it would remain there for ninety-three days, every one of them riddled with the same mystery, the same unanswerable questions, the same fear of answers.

Those upon whom we depended for leadership did not lead; they patronized. Or so it seemed. In their press conferences and speeches, they behaved like mothers who coo nonsense syllables to their children as they pat them on their back when they have night frights. Maybe, deep in their hearts, the experts believed that the end of days was coming but did not want to alarm the populace, afraid of rioting in the streets. Maybe they wanted peace until the apocalypse. Maybe they, too, stayed up past midnight wondering how many days we had left.

It was the not knowing that made our lives so tense.

The source of the national angst was the heavens—of all places. Something was up there these days that had not been there before, and if I remember my early lessons in Roman Catholicism correctly, that something should not have been there, *could* not have been there. After all, my faith taught that the empyrean was inhabited by eternal objects, unchanging cycles. Yet now, without warning, an object was soaring above us that we had never seen before, its purpose known only to those who had launched it, an orb with long antennae protruding forward, sensing devices of some sort reaching into the darkness of space. The orb did not move according to the rhythms of the Sun or Moon, but according to rhythms of its own.

Usually, when we looked up, we did not see it. But if our timing was right and the skies over the East Coast were clear, the object would glide into view, passing high overhead and casting shadows of apprehension below. The passage was brief, however, only a few seconds in any given place. Then it was gone, the object having been programmed to make elliptical passages around the world at its own pace. But it would be back over my hometown, returning again and again.

We would soon learn the following about the new addition to the solar system:

It was traveling eighteen thousand miles an hour.

It was visible over the United States between four and six times a day.

It orbited the earth once every ninety-six minutes.

The path of its transit was unevenly shaped, bringing the object as close as 141.7 miles to our planet at times, carrying it as far away as 588 miles at other times.

It was shiny and highly polished. In time we would find out that Sergei P. Korolev, the chief designer of the Soviet Union's Design Bureau, although proud of his device for a number of reasons, was especially proud of its luster. "It is important that the orbit and the optical characteristics of the satellite," Korolev said, "are such that almost all people in the world will be able to watch its flight with their own eyes."

So a satellite; that's what the thing up there was, a satellite made by human beings. It had never been done before.

And we learned that it was perfectly round, except for four protruding antennae, shooting out like unwaveing contrails.

It was about the size of a beach ball.

It was twenty-two inches in diameter.

It weighed 184 pounds.

And it was called Sputnik, an example of wry humor to which I have not heard anyone refer. In Russian, "sputnik" means "fellow traveler," and that was the phrase used by people such as the recently deceased, fire-breathing American commie hunter, the give-no-quarter and take-none senator from

Wisconsin, Joseph McCarthy. A fellow traveler, to this man who already was creating a terror all his own, was a person who, although not a card-carrying member of the Communist Party, supported its goals and in some cases worked for its advancement.

And so Americans wondered: When would Sputnik start dropping bombs on us?

It did not seem a preposterous question at the time.

Three classic novels were published in 1957, and we feared that one of them, Nevil Shute's *On the Beach*, was ominously prescient.

As Shute's tale begins, nuclear bombs have been dropped in the Northern Hemisphere. The radiation is drifting slowly southward, killing everyone in its wake. Thus Australians will be the last to go and will have the most time to consider mortality and its end, inevitably approaching. The beach will be their final place of refuge before they walk like zombies into the ocean.

Shute's book, according to the *New York Times*, was "the most haunting evocation we have of a world dying of radiation after an atomic war." But what is haunting about it is not ghastly scenes of death and destruction, of graphically described violence, misery, and human disintegration; it is, rather, just the opposite: the almost robotic acceptance of doom by scores of Aussies who have, at most, but a few weeks to live. Not much time. Better get ready. So much to do. It is this attitude, the response of the last people on Earth to the most mundane of moments left to them, that so unremittingly unnerves the reader.

Lieutenant Commander Peter Holmes of the Royal Australian Navy, presently assigned to submarine duty but now on shore leave, stops at his pharmacy in Melbourne one day and, as casually as if he were chatting about the flowers his wife is planting but will not see bloom, asks about the symptoms that lie ahead.

" 'Nausea,' the chemist says. 'That's the first symptom. Then vomiting, and diarrhea. Bloody stools. All the symptoms increase in intensity. There may be slight recovery, but if so it would be very temporary. Finally death occurs from sheer exhaustion.' He pauses. 'In the very end, inflection or leukemia may be the actual cause of death. The blood-forming tissues are destroyed, you see, by the loss of body salt in the fluids. It might go one way or the other.'

" 'Somebody was saying it's like cholera.'

" 'That's right,' the chemist verifies. 'It is rather like cholera.'

" 'You've got some stuff for it, haven't you?'

" 'Not to cure it, I'm afraid.'

" 'I don't mean that. To end it.' "

Yes, the chemist replies, he has "medicine" for suicide. Lieutenant Holmes, a good man trying to live a normal life under the circumstances, expects to be at sea in his submarine, the Scorpion, when death wafts in. He will leave behind a wife and daughter, and he wants the best for them. He buys a pill for his spouse to end her life, even though she is not one of those who has accepted her fate with a chilling calm; rather, Mrs. Holmes is hysterical about the prospect of having to use the pill.

Her husband also buys a pill for their daughter.

Being a youngster, the girl will require a more complicated means of bidding farewell to life, the chemist says. So he gives the lieutenant commander instructions to pass along to his wife on how to kill their child.

Why does she have to do it? Holmes wants to know.

Well, can't have your wife slip away first, the chemist says, now can we? If she does, your daughter might be left to suffer for hours, maybe even days, and she'll be going through it all alone.

The logic is ruthless.

Did Americans believe the same fate awaited them in real life? The truth is that we didn't know what to believe, and it is likely that only a few of us chose a vision as grim as Shute's. Besides, the Royal Australian Navy had instruments to prove that clouds of radiation were on their way, and to measure their speed and toxicity. Americans probably had similar instruments, but they gave no evidence that anything unusual was in the air, fatal or otherwise. We had no reason even to believe that the gleaming beach ball posed an immediate threat. It was so tiny, after all. If it did carry a weapon, it could hardly do much damage.

So why was it circling us? What was it looking for? Maybe, because the Soviets were advanced enough technologically to produce a satellite, they also were advanced enough to produce a miniature bomb as destructive as the big ones.

On the day that Sputnik was launched, Nevil Shute's apocalyptic novel was number two on the *Times*'s best-seller list. For the next two months, as the satellite continued to orbit, the book continued to sell, with Americans eventually buying more than four million copies in the volume's first year in the stores. It seemed a grimly appropriate time to be reading so grimly hopeless a tale.

Just as eerie as the sight of the object in the sky were the tones it emitted, audible by shortwave radio. The sound was a rapid-fire series of signals that, according to an NBC radio announcer, was "the sound that forevermore separates the old from the new." It was a "chirping in the key of A-flat that the Associated Press called the 'deep beep-beep.' " Each beep lasted three-tenths of a second, with three-tenths of a second of silence afterward, the rhythm repeating endlessly over one part of the Earth and then another and another.

Most Americans didn't know what to make of it. Even some scientists didn't, not at first. Said Paul Dickson in a book about the Soviet satellite subtitled *The Shock of the Century*, "The CIA, Defense Intelligence Agency, Army, Air Force and other Western intelligence worked around the clock to see who would be the first to decipher the beeps."

It is not certain which agency deciphered them first. But it did not take long for all to realize the rapid-fire toots of telemetry, an automated communications process that collected data from the invisible realms of the solar system and transmitted them to monitoring devices on Earth. But where was the information coming from? What did it reveal? For what purposes would it be used? No one in the Western world seemed to know.

"The opening of the Space Age!" the newspapers called it. But looking back at 1957 more than half a century later, it scarcely seems possible. It was still a time of manual typewriters, black-and-white television sets, transistor radios, Mickey Spillane's versions of cops and killers, Archie and Jughead comic books, scratchy record players that played tinny, monaural 45s, and pegged pants for the boys and bobby socks for the girls and fedoras for the businessmen. And yet, despite what seem like props from another era, the space age, which will never end, had begun.

So much poorer would my adolescent years have been without Little Richard. I did not understand what he meant by slippin' and slidin', or by rippin' it up; the heebie-jeebies were similarly unknown to me; and I certainly couldn't figure out why Uncle John thought long tall Sally had everything he needed. But no matter. I knew how I felt when I heard him sing and would later recognize him as one of the greats, a rock 'n' roll pioneer with a beat like no other and a sound that could be mistaken for no other, his voice at once raspy and wailing.

Surprisingly enough, he also was an ordained minister, but he did not have much time for that in '57. His true calling seemed to be creating the unrestrained excitement of his music, the raucous pounding of his keyboard, with occasional breaks to prance around the stage like a pixie who had been attached to electrodes. As for his singing, it was like the blues, if only the blues had been happy.

On the cusp of my teens at the time, I looked forward to each record by Little Richard as if it were a birthday present, although he usually would give me two in a year, maybe even three. Like my other favorite singers—with Elvis, Chuck, and Fats heading the list—Richard's output was prolific, a new song every four or five months. As one dropped off the charts, another popped on.

I remember in particular the song "Keep A-Knockin'," music and lyrics by Richard Penniman, shipping date in August. It made my arms tingle, fingers snap, toes tap. It was not only true art; it was one of the singer's biggest hits. It was also one of the last songs he released before the Soviets launched Sputnik.

That was the day the music stopped.

Richard, born Richard Penniman, was playing a two-week tour of—coincidentally—Australia, and one night, flying from Melbourne to Sydney, he looked out his window and swore he saw the engines on fire—or at least overheated; it's not clear—but all was well because he also saw angels beneath the engines, holding them up. Never before had his senses been so jarred.

Then, on the night of his fifth concert in Sydney, as he performed before forty thousand people in an outdoor arena, he said that he saw Sputnik, having just become airborne, whizzing by overhead. But it did not appear to him as it did to others, assuming others even saw it. "It looked as though the big ball of fire came directly over the stadium about two or three hundred feet above our heads. It shook my mind. It really shook my mind. I got up from the piano and said, 'This is it. I am through. I am leaving show business to go back to God.'"

That was the purpose of the fireball, he believed. It was a message from the Almighty, and the fact that, apparently, no one else had seen anything fitting Richard's description was proof that the message was for him alone. He music was, as some had charged, demonic. In the future, he would sing gospel music, the Lord's songs. Never before had he been so shaken. But never had he been so sure.

As for the problem posed by his contract, Richard decided to ignore it. A greater cause was involved here than mere legalities. "There were ten days of the tour left to run," Richard later explained. "Our tickets home were bought on the basis of a two-week tour, but I demanded passage back to the States for the total entourage ten days early. The incredible thing is that the plane we were originally scheduled to return on crashed into the Pacific Ocean. That's when I felt that God really had inspired me to do the things I did at the time."

They included finding a pulpit to share, perhaps even one of his own. They included signing a contract with a gospel recording company. They did not include rock 'n' roll, which he not only wouldn't sing but wouldn't even listen to anymore.

Little Richard was gone. Long live Reverend Penniman!

What would it take, I might have wondered back in '57, for him to make the return trip from altar to stage?

"As far as the satellite itself is concerned," said President Dwight David Eisenhower, his typical ineloquent self, in one of his few public utterances about Sputnik, "that does not raise my apprehensions, not one iota. I see nothing at this moment, at this stage of development, that is significant in that development as far as security is concerned."

It was nice to hear. But if it was true, why had the president done what he did before cooing to the nation?

> Eisenhower's first response to Sputnik was to call a meeting with the appropriate officials from the Defense Department to review American missile development and find out how the Russians had won the race to space. The backbiting and blame fixing had already begun, the day after Sputnik, when two Army officers said that the Army had a rocket, Redstone, that could have placed a satellite in orbit many months ago, but the Eisenhower Administration had given the satellite program to the Navy (Project Vanguard) and the Navy had filed.

It was not just the Department of Defense from which Eisenhower sought information in the immediate aftermath of the Soviet launch. "White House advisers admitted that the first full week following Sputnik's launch was one 'prolonged nightmare,' with groups from Congress, the Pentagon, and Capitol Hill dashing in and out of the president's office."

Apparently, though, Americans could do nothing other than let Sputnik complete its mission. And a headline in the *Washington Post* in the satellite's earliest days thickened the plot. "Sputnik Could Be Spy-in-the-Sky," the paper proclaimed, and spies, after all, abounded in the fifties. Senator McCarthy was certain of it and had been doing all he could to root them out, punish them, and make America safe again. It had been more than four years since the Rosenbergs, the husband-and-wife infiltration team, had been electrocuted, but perhaps they had done some of their damage beforehand, relaying information that the Soviets would make use of in the future. Maybe they had even helped send Sputnik skyward.

But newspapers were not the only medium that reacted more dramatically than necessary. The dean of broadcast journalism, CBS's Edward R. Murrow, thought that "the key men in Washington had not the imagination to understand what it would mean for the Soviet Union to launch its satellite first."

Edward Teller, a physicist known by many as "the father of the hydrogen bomb," declared that the United States had "lost a battle more important and greater than Pearl Harbor."

The highly respected legislator Mike Mansfield, who would one day be the longest-serving majority leader in the history of the U.S. Senate, said, "What is at stake is nothing less than our survival." Some even expressed their views from the pulpit that the survival of the planet was at stake. "Don't be surprised, my friends," warned a Washington minister, "if He comes today."

"The news," as recalled by Richard Goodwin, later to be a speechwriter for Presidents Kennedy and Johnson, "was a bombshell."

But should it have been? This, perhaps, was the most vexing question of all.

If the U.S. government and the public had taken the Soviets seriously, they would have noticed that the Soviets had announced quite clearly years earlier their intention to place a satellite in orbit and had even placed in American hands the means to track the satellite when it went up. Between 1951 and October 1957, there were more than twenty occasions on which a Russian or someone talking to the Russians issued a public statement that they were headed into space. No fewer than twenty-five articles in the *New York Times* during this period discussed, in whole or in part, Russian plans. The first *Times* mention came on October 4, 1951—six years to the day before Sputnik—when Soviet rocket engineer Mikhail Tikhonravov announced that Soviet technology was at least on a par with that of the United States and could well result in the launching of satellites in the not too distant future.

Other reports from this period provided more specific information. They told of Sergei P. Korolev's announcement to Communist Party leaders that the Soviets could put an artificial satellite into orbit before the Americans. It would be launched by an R-7 rocket, in which he and his fellow scientists had the utmost confidence.

But would the R-7 be operational in time? By 1956, Korolev had begun to fear that the American Vanguard rocket would be ready to power a satellite skyward before the Soviets could accomplish the feat. He ordered his men to speed up their efforts, work longer hours. And so they did: sped up, worked longer, and, as a result, worked carelessly. Paul Dickson explains how haste made waste:

The first R-7 exploded on the launchpad in the spring of 1957, followed by five more failures. On May 15, 1957, for example, an R-7 rocket was launched from the Baikonur complex . . . Its ballistic trajectory was aimed toward the Pacific Ocean, but one of the strap-on boosters detached ninety-eight seconds into the mission and the rocket had to be destroyed. When the IGY[1] began in July, the Soviets still had no working R-7. Just over a week later, another R-7 disintegrated—this time a mere thirty-three seconds into the mission.

But the Soviets would not give up. They kept trying and trying again and, in defiance of the maxim, found it was the *seventh* time that turned out to

---

1. The letters stand for the International Geophysical Year—a period that actually lasted a year and a half, from July 1, 1957, to December 31, 1958—and was supposed to encourage cooperation among the world's scientists, a sharing of both goals and technology.

be the charm. In August, an R-7 proved itself capable not only of avoiding self-immolation, but in all probability, of transporting a satellite into low Earth orbit.

One of the last *Times* reports on Soviet progress before Sputnik became a reality also seemed one of most dire yet published. On September 8, 1957, the paper quoted an American missile expert as saying, "The Soviet is likely to beat the United States in placing a satellite in orbit around the world." Almost a month later, that is exactly what happened.

The great Soviet polymath Konstantin Tsiolovsky was one of the founding fathers of rocketry, yet did not take it seriously. "I thought of the rocket as everybody else did—just as a means of diversion and petty everyday uses. I do not remember exactly what prompted me to make calculations of its motions. Probably the first idea came from my reading of Jules Verne, and it directed my thoughts along certain channels, then came a desire, and after that, the work of the mind."

So this notion of putting a satellite into orbit started out not as the labor of the Soviets' greatest minds, but as the playfulness of men who had the greatest imaginations in other countries and applied them in earlier generations. More than likely, the first seeds of the idea were sown by the American author Edward Everett Hale in a novella called *The Brick Moon*. So impressed was President Ulysses S. Grant by the notion of a man-made satellite that he is supposed to have said—although probably didn't—that Hale's idea was "the biggest thing since Creation, save for the invention of bourbon whiskey and the Havana cigar."

Not only had Hale serialized *The Brick Moon* in the *Atlantic Monthly* during Grant's presidency, which lasted from 1869 to 1877, but Verne had produced his classic novel *From the Earth to the Moon*. By the time 1957 came along, the future had been under way for decades.

And Verne was not the only one responsible, not the only literary master who inspired the Soviet space program; it was a distinction he shared with several others, most notably the Englishman H. G. Wells, among whose novels are *The Time Machine*, *The Shape of Things to Come*, and *The War of the Worlds*. Wells was a British law student who had given up his studies and moved instead to journalism and adventure novels. As for Verne, a French author who could write virtually anything, he previously had concentrated on plays, biographies, satires, social commentary, and short stories.

It was the Soviets, though, who removed the fiction from science fiction in 1957.

It might have been that Sputnik, the remarkable achievement of our World War II allies, since become our Cold War foes, seemed all the more remarkable because of how '57 began in America. A quick perusal of the nation's newspapers on January 1 could easily have been mistaken for the preface to a year that would be neither alarming nor distinguished. It was, as is said in the journalism business, a slow news day. It seemed as if it might be the start of a mundane year.

Millions of men and women had gathered the night before in New York's Times Square to count down the final seconds of 1956. An annual rite, an annual story—the front pages of newspapers were filled with photographs of hundreds of thousands of people, so tightly packed together that movement seemed impossible, even breathing an effort.

In political news, President Eisenhower surprised no one by urging Congress to make moderate progress in race relations, but only that—moderate. In fact, when a lukewarm Civil Rights Act became law later in the year, it was bulldozed through the administration "by the Attorney General Herbert Brownell, without much presidential understanding or encouragement."

But that would change in the autumn of the year, as **Orval Faubus,** the liar who served as governor of Arkansas, forced the president into *im*moderacy—of the worst kind, as far as Eisenhower was concerned. Believing himself to have no other choice, he dispatched federal troops to Little Rock to impose integration in the schools no matter that it had been three years since the Supreme Court forbade the practice.

U.S. Secretary of State John Foster Dulles had been meeting with United Nations Secretary General Dag Hammarskjold to discuss the situation in the Middle East. Even back then, there was a situation in the Middle East, always a situation in that part of the world.

On this holiday when the New York Stock Exchange was closed, the Dow Jones Industrial Average stood at 496.03. Nothing much would happen to it in the next twelve months, certainly nothing encouraging. It would rise and sink gradually and finish at 439.27.

The sports pages were full of surmise. Who would win today's big bowl games? It was Iowa versus Oregon State in the Rose, Colorado versus Clemson in the Orange, Tennessee versus Baylor in the Sugar, and Texas Christian versus Syracuse in the Cotton, a game that would be notable for the final college appearance of the latter school's great running back, perhaps the greatest running back in the history of the gridiron, Jim Brown.

Brown was a "colored man," to use the term so often used back then. But it had been a decade since Jackie Robinson integrated baseball, and Floyd Patterson, also a black man, was the heavyweight boxing champion of the world. So Brown's race was not even mentioned in most of the accounts about him, certainly not if a photograph was attached. Other accounts, however, could not resist labeling him as being of Negroid descent.

In movie theaters, *Friendly Persuasion*, starring Gary Cooper as a Quaker trying to figure out whether to fight in the Civil War, was probably the most popular movie of the day. Nineteen fifty-seven also was the year that American Independent Productions released one of the great drive-in movies of all time, *I Was a Teenage Werewolf*. Surprisingly, more was said about the film than one initially might think. One analysis of it went so far as to compare it to Theodore Dreiser's most wrenching novel, *An American Tragedy*, although this seems a reach beyond reason.

White mink capes were on sale in Manhattan for $149 and white mink wraps for $119. Natural ranch mink coats, which had sold for $3,300 in 1956, started the new year at a mere $2,000.

There seemed little else to say as the new year crawled groggily out of bed and struggled for balance. For some of the year balance was maintained, but by no means for all of it. In no way could Americans prepare themselves for the staggering events they would face before Guy Lombardo and his Royal Canadians next struck up "Auld Lang Syne" as the clock arrived at midnight on December 31, 1957.

And so it was that, as the Waterford crystal ball—actually a giant geodesic sphere, twelve feet in diameter, a glittering satellite of its own—began its descent down One Times Square on December 31, 1956, no one realized that what lay ahead was not to be, as it appeared, a procession of slow news days.

Well before reports about Sputnik filled American newspapers, they would be filled, for varying periods of time and at varying lengths, by Elvis and the Edsel; Walter O'Malley and his fellow baseball fan Fidel Castro; Mafioso Frank Costello and his fellow bibliophile, Cuban dictator Fulgencio Batista; and by Jimmy Hoffa and Ayn Rand and Billy Graham and Bugsy Siegel and Jack Kerouac—just to name a few.

But this account of '57 does not begin with any of the names just mentioned. It begins with a man whom history has chosen to forget and, despite his former prominence, with good reason. He turned out to be a cipher, born to the rank, and a man who would have remained a cipher for the rest of his days had it not been for a terrible accident at his workplace. The man was seriously injured. He was also recast, in the process acquiring the most sinister nickname of the decade.

He tried so hard to deserve it.

PART ONE

Albert "Murder, Inc." Anastasia

1

The Mad Bomber of New York

People first heard of him in November, but only a few, and even fewer cared. After all, his first attempt at destruction was such a modest one, not to mention a failure so great as to be nearly comical. Yet even if he had succeeded, hardly anyone was working at the hour; it is doubtful that he would have caused injuries, serious or otherwise. Further, so homespun was his weapon that it probably wouldn't have done any damage to the building, either. Actually, more than a decade would pass before he could claim either a victim or the appellation by which he lives on, although in a manner that barely escapes anonymity. His nickname, then, was deceptive, an exaggeration of the man's deeds and the impact they had on mid-twentieth-century Manhattan.

But if it tells us little of the man, it reveals much about the newspapers of the era and attempts by the tabloids to increase circulation at the expense of truth, context, and perception. That problem continues to plague journalism to the present, even many of the so-called mainstream outlets. Which is to say that the man, although nearly forgotten now, made a significant, if inadvertent, contribution toward the way news has been presented every year since '57.

If his deeds were not momentous, though, his story is a remarkable one, full of unanswered questions and so powerful a determination to right an undeniable wrong that it amounted to a career.

On the night he so ignominiously began his life in crime, he approached his target carefully; one imagines timidity in his gait, his shoulders hunched forward, eyes flitting about nervously. He moved through the small, dark hours of the morning toward one of the many Consolidated Edison buildings in New York. One of his hands was empty. In the other was a toolbox he had filled, but not with tools.

Then, as now, Con Ed provided gas, electricity, and steam to New York City's five boroughs and adjoining Westchester County. It was, literally, a powerhouse, indispensable to the very existence of these places. But that was of no concern to the man with the toolbox. He believed the company had sinned against him, that it had tortured him before firing him, and nothing else mattered.

He set the tool kit on the structure's windowsill and opened the lid. He pulled a flashlight out of a pocket in his pants, shining its beam on "a length of iron pipe about 4¹/₂ inches long and neatly capped on each end." He had stuffed it with what he believed to be the ingredients of a bomb, including "a flashlight bulb, a battery, a steel spring—and curiously an atypical Parke-Davis throat lozenge."

The man flicked off the flashlight and carefully placed the box on the sill, making sure it was balanced, that it would not fall off. The lid was still open. Satisfied that all was in order, he then turned and retraced his path softly through the night, back to his car. Even at this hour it would take him an hour, perhaps more, to get home. It seems fair to assume that he felt the excitement of someone who had done something naughty for the first time.

He shouldn't have. The mechanism was a dud. The next day, police were called, and several members of the bomb squad took the tool kit, the pipe still inside, to a remote section of the city, where they did everything they could think of except say the rosary to get the contraption to explode. But it wouldn't, not even a budge or a quiver. As the bomb squad members closed in on it, they realized the device didn't even look menacing; it was missing too many ingredients for a detonation, and those it wasn't missing were too sloppily assembled to fire. The bomber had a lot to learn before he could cause an explosion.

But there was more to the story of the night than that. The bomb-in-a-box might have been constructed so ineptly that it did not even deserve its name, but the man's handwriting was impeccable. He had wrapped a note around the pipe, the first of literally hundreds he would write in years to come, and printed his message in neat, block letters.

CON ED CROOKS, THIS IS FOR YOU.

A moment's thought will reveal the man's lack of foresight. If the weapon *had* erupted, the note would have been destroyed. The purpose of the explosion would have remained unknown, as would the man's passion to seek revenge on the power giant that had wronged him. In other words, the man was as well served in one way with his dud as he would have been in another had his bomb been a successful one.

For the first thirty-eight years of his life, he was a nondescript fellow named George Peter Metesky, with no nom de guerre. The very notion, in fact, would have seemed laughable; he was too timid, too easily swallowed up by any group in which he found himself, to merit an ominous nickname. The two people who meant the most to him were the unmarried sisters with whom he shared a residence in Waterbury, Connecticut, and even so, he spent little time with them, had few interests in common. In the neighborhood, their abode was known as the "crazy house," largely because the sisters were mistakenly but "roundly thought of as stern and severe. The private and impenetrable nature of the family would serve only to heighten local suspicions."

Metesky had friends, but only a few, among his fellow Con Ed workers. He also associated with people in minor business transactions, such as buying groceries or filling his gas tank or shopping for bomb components.

But these were only acquaintances, not friends. All of them, though, seemed to find Metesky pleasant enough—that is, if they thought of him at all.

One person who thought of him was a neighbor, a man who witnessed something remarkable one night. After working in his spare time for several months, Metesky invented an electric snow shovel. "It worked great, too," said the neighbor, witnessing a trial run. "It'd pick up the snow and throw it to the left." Metesky also built a power lawn mower, attaching a small engine to his manual version, and a report on the device appeared in an issue of *Popular Science* magazine. Even more impressive, he later received a patent for a piston-driven circuit breaker used for solenoid pumps that were used, in turn, to transport fluids through a sealed suction chamber.

He had a knack, then, did George Metesky, a natural gift with machinery. So far, it was just bombs that stumped him, the damnable bombs, but, of course, they had become the most important contraption of all to him. He tried his best to master them, following the directions he found in various manuals, as well as applying his own inherent skills to the project. But it took a long time before he created his first explosion, and he never achieved the kind of results for which he had hoped.

In time, however, he managed to achieve results for which he had not hoped, results of image rather than substance. As Manhattan's hyperbolic tabloids fought their circulation wars, trying to call attention to themselves by sensationalizing one story after another, they would, in a few years, transform mere Metesky into the "Mad Bomber of New York." Befitting such a sobriquet, he conducted what the rags referred to as a "reign of terror," and with his sisters primly going about their chores above him, ignorant of what their sibling was trying to do in the basement, the nebbish from Waterbury gradually became a fearsome presence in the news.

When he finally was caught in 1957, the reign of terror ended at last, he lapped up the unaccustomed recognition. The cameras shot him; he looked directly into their lenses. The police escorted him past jumbles of popping flashbulbs; he slowed his pace. It was not a display of ego, not in the conventional sense; he simply thought that people deserved a chance to get a good look at a man of his resolve, his notoriety. At last he *was* somebody. Finally, Con Ed's unjust treatment of him mattered.

But not for long. As policemen, journalists, and newspaper readers began to study Metesky, both his person and his photographs, his star flamed out like most of his fuses. Simply put, he just did not look the part. His face showed no menace, not even any character, nothing interesting except a nose that listed slightly to the left. He was, after all, born for the background, the kind of fellow who sat on a park bench, oddly overdressed, chatting easily with the birds to whom he was tossing the seeds he had bought for their dinner.

To say the least, the public had expected something different, a fellow who looked more like a Mafia hit man—an Albert Anastasia, a Bugsy Siegel—than a pigeon feeder. As far as the tabloid audience was concerned, the "Benign Bomber" might have been a more appropriate nickname for Metesky.

He wore wire-rimmed glasses, sometimes a trilby, and usually one of his small collection of old, cheap suits of pilled wool—coat, pants, and vest.

Once arrested, he would end up spending as much time with psychiatrists and their brethren as he did with the police. They jointly concluded that he was not an inherently bad fellow, but rather a sick one—in fact, a paranoid schizophrenic, which, in simplest terms, means that he struggled to understand what is real and what is not, and often confused the two. As for New York Democrats, foes of the current administration in Washington, he was a godsend. With his round face, bald head, and congenial manner, he became known as "the Eisenhower of psychotics." Another phrase for the tabloids.

Regardless of the precise nature of his dysfunction, George Metesky could no more be cured of it than medical science could rid him of the physical disorders that he blamed on Con Ed, the disorders that had persuaded him to stuff pipes with gunpowder in the first place. Suffering first from pneumonia, he later became enfeebled by tuberculosis. Several physicians examined him, but they could do nothing. They sent him back to the shrinks for more care and testing, and once they had finished, they returned him to the police, who in turn shuffled him off to the Matteawan Hospital for the Criminally Insane in Beacon, New York. Sixteen years later, authorities were convinced that he didn't need to be there anymore. It was a decision they probably could have made much earlier.

It was 1973 by now, and Metesky officially had been judged a threat to society no longer. Even more remarkably, his tuberculosis went into the longest period of remission that most of his doctors had ever seen. So he was allowed to return home to Waterbury, where he lived for the next two decades, his days on Earth ending on May 23, 1994, when Metesky was ninety years old. His cause of death is nowhere to be found, but probably was not tuberculosis, despite his having spent half a lifetime as a carrier. He outlived both of his sisters, and the house in Waterbury, in which he remained the sole resident, grew more and more lonely as the years piled up on him.

Summarizing the frustrations that led him to his Mad Bomber days, he said, "I wrote nine hundred letters to the mayor, the police commissioner, to the newspapers, and I never even got a penny postcard back. Then I went to the newspapers to try to buy space, but all of them turned me down. I was compelled to bring my story to the public."

Despite having above average intelligence, Metesky had given up on formal education after a single year of high school. And it on him. "Feeling superior to his fellow students and even teachers, he dropped out of [Waterbury's] Crosby High in 1918, later explaining, 'I just had no interest in the subjects they were teaching.'"

But after that, his feelings of superiority took a beating. Despite his skills as an electrician as well as a mechanic, he could find no employment worthy of him, instead being forced into such menial positions as a movie usher, soda dispenser, and apprentice machinist at a foundry. As one of his coworkers in the latter position remarked, "Well, he was a strange one. He came to work all dressed up in a suit and collar and necktie. He tried to learn the machine business dressed like that. And he hated to get his hands dirty. After a while he left the job and I lost track of him."

So, it seems, did most of the people he once knew. He distinguished himself in this period of his life only by his military service, joining the marines after the Great War and winning a Good Conduct Medal for his performance in Mexico and the Dominican Republic. Two years later he was honorably discharged with the official classification of "excellent." A later hitch in the military earned him the same praise, as well as training in munitions, although one suspects he did not retain much of the latter.

Then, at the age of twenty-eight, Metesky turned up on the Con Ed payroll. He was working at the company's Hell Gate plant in lower Manhattan, cleaning off generators in the boiler room, when one day his world changed forever. For a reason no one ever was able to determine, or admit, a boiler next to him backfired and turned malicious, shooting out a powerful stream of scalding gases and poisonous soot. It knocked Metesky to the floor and continued to pelt him with such force that he could not get up again, his agony such that he could barely even squirm.

> The boiler room filled with an acidic odor that suggested a metallic decay or perhaps even the merging of discordant chemicals. George Metesky staggered backward . . . As the searing combination of gases filled his lungs, he gasped and began to cough violently and uncontrollably . . . and soon the harsh and burning sensations in his chest were accompanied by a gurgling bark, suggesting the presence of blood. Metesky instantly recoiled as the carmine film sprayed the floor and his trousers like a macabre work of art.

His coworkers ran to his aid, sliding him a few feet to safety. But they were afraid to touch him more than that; his skin seemed to be on fire no matter where they made contact. They called the police, and, shortly afterward, an ambulance arrived to take him to the nearest hospital, where he received the best possible treatment. But he already had been seriously injured, and his burns were not the worst of it. George Metesky would never be the same man again.

He later claimed that the accident had led not only to his illnesses, the pneumonia and tuberculosis, but to a general feeling of lassitude that began to plague him daily, stripping him of energy, sometimes even the will to live, for long periods of time. Con Ed lawyers, however, would have none of Metesky's accusations, his whining. Its lawyers not only denied responsibility, but they further denied him worker's compensation for the injuries related to the boiler malfunction, charging that he had waited too long to file a claim.

Metesky was dumbfounded. He had not been physically able to file any sooner, he replied, could barely even hold a pencil with his skin feeling so tender. But the lawyers pelted his arguments with the furiously fine print of their trade. They gave the victim twenty-six weeks of disability benefits and then, their former employee now having been classified as permanently disabled, sent him out into the world without a vocation. He had not even received severance pay. He qualified for federal disability payments, but they didn't amount to much. His rage, which had begun building as soon as he felt the vigor for it, now knew no bounds; the injustice he felt had no time limit.

When he returned to Waterbury, it was in such a weakened condition that he had to spend much of his time in bed. For the rest of his life, he would tire easily; his bed and his workbench, and the pen with which he eventually was able to write his letters, were the main implements of his existence.

Years later, after most of his bombs had been set off, he would describe his feelings in a missive that was redacted by police officials before they allowed it to be published in New York papers. "When a motorist injures a dog," Metesky wrote, "he must report it—not so with an injured workman—he rates less than a dog—I tried to get my story to the press . . . I typed tens of thousands of words (about 800,000)—nobody cared . . . I determined to make these dastardly acts known—I have had plenty of time to think—I decided on bombs."

In 1941, Metesky left two more of them, again primitively assembled, outside Con Ed plants. Neither of these instruments of malice ended up achieving anything malicious, either. But as he had done previously, he left a block-lettered note with the third one, attaching the initials "F. P." at the bottom as a signature. He explained that he would attempt no more destruction for several years, but that New Yorkers should not relax their vigils permanently.

I WILL MAKE NO MORE BOMB UNITS FOR THE DURATION OF THE WAR—MY PATRIOTIC FEELINGS HAVE MADE ME DECIDE THIS—LATER I WILL BRING THE CON EDISON TO JUSTICE—THEY WILL PAY FOR THEIR DASTARDLY DEEDS.

For Metesky, "later" turned out to be ten years, a lengthy period that no one has been able to explain satisfactorily. Not even biographer Michael Greenburg, who has studied the bomber's life more thoroughly than anyone else. "For all practical purposes," Greenburg writes, "through World War II and for several years beyond, George Metesky dropped from sight." However, Greenburg has found evidence that "during this reclusive period after the war, Metesky resumed his bomb-making endeavors. He would later admit to planting up to twenty-four units that would remain unexploded and undiscovered—several at locations in and around the office of Con Ed in the late 1940s."

In 1951, with the United States nestled uncomfortably between the second World War and the Korean conflict, the Mad Bomber set off his first bomb that actually performed. Although it had been placed outside the famed Oyster Bar and Restaurant in New York's Grand Central Terminal, and both the restaurant and the corridor outside it were crowded at the time, no one noticed either the package or the man who had deposited it. And no one was injured when it exploded with more of a poof than a bang.

Nor was anyone harmed when, less than a month later, Metesky deposited another clumsily stuffed pipe of vile intent into a phone booth outside the main branch of the New York Public Library. In a statement, police said they were untroubled. They believed the bombs, still so amateurishly put together, must have been the work of "boys or pranksters." Journalists were similarly blasé, the *New York Times* devoting only three tiny paragraphs on the bottom of page twenty-four to the incident at the library. One can imagine how livid Metesky must have been.

Later in the year, he set off explosives at the Paramount Theater and the Fourteenth Street subway station, although still without harming anyone. That was when the tabloids began their Mad Bomber chant, and the *New York Herald Tribune* received the following message:

> HAVE YOU NOTICED THE BOMBS IN YOUR CITY—IF YOU ARE WORRIED, I AM SORRY—AND ALSO IF ANYONE IS INJURED. BUT IT CANNOT BE HELPED—FOR JUSTICE WILL BE SERVED. I AM NOT WELL, AND FOR THIS I WILL MAKE CON EDISON SORRY—YES, THEY WILL REGRET THEIR DAS-TARDLY DEEDS—I WILL BRING THEM BEFORE THE BAR OF JUSTICE— PUBLIC OPINION WILL CONDEMN THEM—FOR BEWARE, I WILL PLACE MORE UNITS UNDER THEATER SEATS IN THE NEAR FUTURE.

Eventually, the one-sided correspondence between the bomber and the press became two-sided, as the *New York Journal-American* devoted much of its front page to a missive for the criminal.

AN OPEN LETTER
TO THE MAD BOMBER
(Prepared in Co-operation with the Police Dept.)
Give yourself up.
For your own welfare and for that of the community, the time has come for you to reveal your identity.
The N.Y. Journal-American guarantees that you will be protected from any illegal action and that you will get a fair trial.
This newspaper also is willing to help you in two other ways.
It will publish all the essential parts of your story as you may choose to make it public.
It will give you the full chance to air whatever grievances you may have as the motive for your acts.

And the letter continued, at one point providing the phone number of the *Journal-American*'s city editor and asking him to call. The number began ringing the moment the paper hit the streets. As far as anyone knows, none of the callers was George Metesky, or anyone who knew anything about him, and Metesky never made public his reaction to the *Journal-American*'s plea.

In addition to seats at movie houses such as the Paramount, the Mad Bomber's favorite hiding places for his "units" included toilet bowls and coin-operated storage lockers. His favorite tourist sites, other than those previously mentioned, were Radio City Music Hall, Pennsylvania Station, the Port Authority Bus Terminal, and 30 Rockefeller Plaza, then known as the RCA Building. It was as if he were riding around Manhattan atop one of those open-air sightseeing buses, dropping off his specially made parcels at the most popular attractions—a deliveryman making deliveries that had not been requested and were certainly not desired.

The so-called reign of terror, which began late in 1940, then was suspended for that shadowy decade, continued up to the early days of '57. It resulted in the placement of thirty bombs, twenty-two of which exploded. Fifteen people were injured, none killed. His most potent weapon was the one that let loose after Metesky paid a return visit to the Paramount. The date was December 2, 1956.

> A thirty-six-year-old postal clerk named Abraham Blumenthal . . . was immediately thrown from his twelfth row seat. Fierce pain began to radiate from his left leg, where shards of jagged metal had inflicted their damage. . . . Seated about eight feet from the explosion itself, a young mother, Doris Russo, and her sister Joyce, were pummeled with scabrous debris, which settled deep in the face and scalp of each.

Blumenthal and Russo were among those hospitalized, both being kept for several days. After a while they healed completely.

The reputation of New York's police department, also victimized by the bomber, was not healing. All of this time, all of these incendiaries, virtually placed on exhibit in the most public of midtown venues—how hard could it be to find the guy who was placing them there? Surely, after having committed so many crimes, George Metesky had left behind at least a few clues. Surely somewhere the agents of law enforcement could find at least one of them. Couldn't they?

And with 1957 approaching, the police were themselves reaching a peak of exasperation. They were not clueless; one of their problems, in fact, was that they were overwhelmed with clues, tips that turned out to be as phony as the late Carlo Ponzi's investment schemes. Following up on fake leads took much more time than pursuing those that seemed viable, although the latter were few and, as it turned out, provided nothing in the way of useful information.

One day, a large section of Grand Central Terminal had to be evacuated so that fifteen hundred lockers, fully half of the storage spaces in the entire building, could be searched. With only a single master key available, it took thirty-five policemen three hours to find out that none of the lockers contained a bomb.

On another occasion, one that staggers the imagination, a note was left at Grand Central warning that a bomb had been hidden in the Empire State Building and would go off at any moment. The groan from NYPD headquarters must have been audible across the Hudson. Nonetheless, dozens upon dozens of New York's finest were duty-bound to descend on the city's tallest building and search the entire thing, all 102 floors of it! They could not find an explosive mechanism on any of them. Not even a pipe lying around *without* gunpowder in it, nor a note accusing Con Edison of heartlessness. At this point the cops were so wearied by the case, added to their other duties, that they might have come across an atomic bomb in an Empire State elevator and not recognized it. If nothing else, Metesky was succeeding in what might have become one of his secondary goals; he was leaving the New York police force in a state of acute exhaustion. Perhaps they would take out their frustration on Con Ed. After all, it wasn't the Mad Bomber who ultimately had driven them to so bedraggled a state; it was the power giant with its dime-store boilers and cold-blooded minions.

About this time, NYPD police captain John Cronin decided to try a different approach. He called in James Brussel, assistant commissioner of the New York State Commission for Mental Hygiene. A criminologist and psychiatrist as well as a police official, Brussel had developed a reputation for unusual methods of criminal detection. Today we would call him a profiler. Back then he was just controversial.[1]

But Cronin didn't care. He was running out of options. He was willing to try almost anything, and by now Brussel had risen to the top of his list of long shots.

The latter's background was impressive. A graduate of the University of Pennsylvania Medical School, he had served as a psychiatrist aboard the *Queen Mary* and later supervised the army's neuropsychiatric center in El Paso, Texas. Later still, he would provide invaluable service, or so he claimed in a memoir, in the Boston Strangler case. According to a New York newspaper columnist, Brussel was "Bow-tied, Mustachioed and Natty." In a police station, he stood out like a rose in a chive garden.

Cronin asked him to produce a biography of sorts of the Mad Bomber. To the average cop on the beat, it made no sense. Brussel was a fraud, they thought, like one of those phony palm readers who wrapped their heads in bath towels, called them turbans, and stared into crystal balls. He had been received icily before, however, and paid no attention to scoffers. So it would be once again.

Brussel went to work on the files of the case, a whole boxful of them, as if studying for a final exam. After a few days, he announced his results. It

---

1. The FBI had taken up the practice of profiling as early as 1908, establishing a behavioral analysis unit (BAU). Almost a century later, the public had become so captivated by the notion that CBS premiered *Criminal Minds*, a weekly series that chronicles the adventures of a fictitious BAU. The program could hardly have been more popular. As this book is being published, it has been on the air for fifteen years, a hit during all of them with reruns binging on cable.

was an exceptional quantity of information for one to have assimilated so quickly. The quality was in many instances exceptional, too.

The perp, Brussel had concluded, was a single man between forty and fifty. He was overweight, a high school graduate who had no family life, no interest in women. Nor in men; he was asexual. He probably lived with a sibling. Because many of the letters he wrote to the police and newspapers bore a White Plains, New York, postmark, he lived either there or somewhere else close to Manhattan. (In fact, the distance from Waterbury to midtown is sixty-six miles over today's roads.) Brussel even went so far as to tell police that their man might be wearing a three-piece suit at the time of his capture.

There was more: According to an abridged version of Brussel's profile published by some of the New York newspapers, the man was also an "[e]xpert in civil or military ordnance. Religious. Might flare up violently at work when criticized. Possible motive: discharge or reprimand. Feels superior to critics. Resentment keeps growing. Present or former Consolidated Edison workers. Probably case of progressive paranoia."

In addition, Brussel proclaimed, the bomber probably had access to a lathe. He had made a lot of weapons, and all of the pipes had to be threaded at one end.

Captain Cronin felt vindicated. It was, all in all, an extraordinary performance by James Brussel.

Time was running out on the Mad Bomber.

January 21, 1957, was the day it expired. Armed with guns and a search warrant, four police detectives forced their way into Metesky's Connecticut home, sending his baffled sisters fluttering for safety. The cops claimed they were investigating an automobile accident but gave no further information. Metesky seemed to take them at their word; he remained calm, preserving his timid exterior, not asking why they thought that a man who had spent the entire day indoors could possibly know anything about colliding cars.

He took the police on a tour not only of the first floor of his house and the bedrooms on the second, but of his garage, where he kept an old, black Daimler sedan and a neatly organized workbench. Several items were neatly arranged on the floor beneath it. The largest, with its cord wrapped around it, was a lathe. The policemen looked at one another knowingly. It was now that Metesky, having concluded there really *was* no automobile mishap, asked his visitors whether he might need the services of an attorney.

"Sensing a possible confession, [detective Michael] Lynch persevered, 'Never mind an attorney, George. Why are we here?'

"Metesky's eyes narrowed and his breathing became quick and uneven. 'Maybe you suspect that I'm the Mad Bomber,' he offered."

Lynch confirmed the fact. Finally, after thousands upon thousands of wasted man-hours, he stood face-to-face with the man responsible for them.

A few minutes later, Lynch asked what the initials "F. P." stood for. "Fair Play," came Metesky's reply, and according to biographer Greenburg, "his demeanor instantly became one of purpose and self-assurance." Nonetheless, the man's fate was now assured. One of the cops slapped a pair of handcuffs onto his wrists, and he was led off to justice.

His lawyer, if he had even called one, had not yet arrived.

With more important things on their minds, the police did not ask their captive about the throat lozenges, which had been placed in his early bombs but apparently none of his more effective ones. It turned out that Metesky had used the lozenges as "timing devices." He had determined that "their rate of dissolution was constant," which is to say, that they always "melted" in the same amount of time, thus enabling him to calculate precisely when they would have disintegrated completely and the "two points of contact," one on either side of the lozenge, would meet and detonate his device.

But after a while, the Mad Bomber gave up on his candied throat medicine. He had discovered that the lozenges did not really melt at a consistent pace—that depended on the temperature and what Metesky believed to be the imprecise methods of lozenge manufacture. In fact, he blamed the lozenges for almost injuring him once when a bomb blew up earlier than he had expected. What had once seemed ingenious to him had proven to be erroneous. For the rest of his life, he wouldn't buy a Parke-Davis product if it were all that stood between him and a flare-up of TB.

The Mad Bomber's indictment perhaps would be the longest one issued by a New York grand jury in the entirety of 1957. He was charged with forty-seven offenses, including attempted murder, causing damage to a building by setting off a bomb, maliciously endangering life, and, as happened on every one of the more than twenty occasions when he transported one of his stuffed pipes, carrying a hidden weapon.

But to some Manhattanites, the indictment was a kind of character reference. These were men and women who also believed they were being abused by uncaring employers and the dangerous conditions of their workplaces. To them, Metesky was a man, that rarest of individuals, who had had the courage to stand up against "the entrenched and evil corporate Goliath." He became a "cult-hero," a David undaunted by Goliath. Said a member of a radical group called the Diggers, George Metesky "epitomizes the futility of joining or fighting the system. We're all Meteskys. We're a generation of schizophrenic mutants."

By the time the original Metesky passed away, he was back where he had started, and not just geographically. Not only did no one know his name anymore, but few people even remembered his deeds. "The story of the century," as some newspapers called it early in the investigation, was not even a memory for tomorrow.

Nor should it have been. Fifteen people injured, none seriously, and no one killed—*this* was the work of someone known as the Mad Bomber of New York? Supposedly, thirty bombs had been placed prominently in Manhattan, and yet only twenty-two went off—*this* was a reign of terror?

Ultimately, as stated at the beginning of this chapter, George Metesky's story had more to say about the shamefully irresponsible excesses of the press than about the hazards of explosives. Of course, tabloid journalism had been around for more than half a century by now, but the reports on Metesky were continuing evidence of a more sinister twist, a step along the road to even more irresponsible use of ink. A story didn't necessarily have to be sensational to sell a paper; as long as the headlines and language were overripe, as long as the stories were placed prominently and given enough space, the content didn't matter nearly as much as it should have.

Imagine a headline like this:

Mad Bomber Strikes in Heart of Manhattan,
Conducts Reign of Terror,
Two Injured, Admitted to Hospital

Not much of a story in a place like New York, where the population at the time was almost eight million and two people admitted to some hospital or other every two seconds. But with the language inflated, along with the size of the type and its darkness and thickness, the facts are also enlarged, well beyond their true impact.

And Metesky coverage also solidified another journalistic trend. A decade or so earlier, a story probably would not have been considered tabloid material without illicit sex—a big-breasted, thick-lipped blonde featured prominently, perhaps accused of having had adultery with a politician, a priest, or a general in the Salvation Army. But not anymore. By now the definition of tabloid had broadened to include the bizarre deeds of nobodies, the quiet men and women just down the block. As a result, New Yorkers were more frightened than they needed to be and newspaper sales higher than they should have been. Think of George Peter Metesky as a campfire. The Manhattan press had covered him as if he were an inferno. People began to see flames everywhere they looked.

Other crimes committed the year of the bomber's capture, however, had a much more enduring effect. Some of the most nefarious, rather than being the efforts of a lone vigilante, were backed by an organization of a million and a half men, the largest of its kind. Ostensibly having been formed to make sure that working men like Metesky were treated fairly by corporate America, the establishment had morphed into something entirely different by 1957. Its leaders defrauded their membership as much as representing its interests, and they had dedicated themselves to far more ominous priorities than the group's charter ever envisioned.

2

The Committee

After serving his time in notoriety's harsh spotlight, Dave Beck must have been relieved to sink into the kind of obscurity that George Metesky had known for most of his life. Especially because, unlike Metesky, Beck's final years were lucrative beyond his grandest hopes.

His father was a carpet cleaner who barely had been able to support the family. As a result, Dave had to quit school when he was sixteen, providing support of his own by driving a laundry truck. But by 1957, with more than sixty years behind him, his rise to prominence was complete; bald and roly-poly, possessed of a full-faced although menacing laughter, he presided over the International Brotherhood of Teamsters, the most powerful union in the country. And surely the most corrupt. The Teamsters had long been a fiefdom of organized crime. But under Beck, and all the more so under the sinister figure who waited in the wings, the pace of illegal activities had been increasing. Something, legislators finally concluded, had to be done.

On February 26, Beck was scheduled to testify before the United States Select Committee on Illegal Activities in Labor and Management. As is the custom, the committee became known after its chairman, the Democratic senator from Arkansas, John Little McClellan.

No better choice can be imagined, for McClellan was not only a dominating presence in Washington, but one of its strongest voices for ethical behavior. Sixty-one years old as the hearings began, he carried himself with a determined stride and carried out his business with a "thundering voice, imposing stage presence, and commanding personality."

The lingering horrors from his earlier years were visible only to himself and known but to a few close friends. The first of those years were spent in the village of Malvern, Arkansas, population less than ten thousand, and it was what happened there, along with a later series of tragedies, almost

29

inconceivable in the telling and unimaginable in the living, that gave such tensile strength to the senator's later life. An ordinary man would have been broken. In public, at least, McClellan didn't even bend.

> John McClellan did not have a happy childhood. Isaac [his father], a tough taskmaster, constantly pushed his son to study and work hard. Although he expressed appreciation to his stepmother, Anna McClellan, for her part in raising him, John stated, "Life with you and Papa . . . was never what I desired. It was just unfortunate for all of us, but I never blamed anyone particularly."

His boyhood might have been difficult, but as an adult McClellan was magnanimous in discussing it. Perhaps his most frequent refrain was that he was pleased to have been "raised by people who believed that the Baptist doctrine was the true and only, absolute doctrine." Says his biographer, Sherry Laymon, "His Christian upbringing compelled him to do the right thing and to honor his word in his dealings with others. Those principles guided his actions from his youth forward on the baseball field, in the courtroom, and in the halls of Congress."

And it was surely his Christian upbringing that enabled him to survive what must have been the worst series of tribulations to rain down on a human being since Jesus decided to make an example of Job. In a period of but a few years, McClellan suffered through "the breakup of his first marriage, the death from spinal meningitis of his second wife, and the successive deaths of one son in the war, of another son in a car crash, and of the remaining son in a plane crash." The list is preposterous in the depth of its sorrows, in the sheer, raving, excessiveness of it. And it does not even include previous misery, the passing of his birth mother a few months after he was born, an event for which McClellan could not help but feel guilt.

That a man could endure such a bombardment of ordeals is amazing enough. That he could move beyond mere tenacity and become John Little McClellan, the senior senator from Arkansas, a rare example of conscience in the United States Congress, stretches credulity to the breaking point. This legislator, who started studying law in his father's office when he was twelve and was admitted to the Arkansas bar five years later, this Job-like figure who was forced to marry twice and was widowed twice and then childless and alone for the last twenty years of his life, is one of America's great unknown heroes.

He was unlikely to be sympathetic to a character such as Dave Beck.

Beck did not like driving a laundry truck. And he did not like working the same shift every day for the same meager paycheck every week—and the longer he held the job, the more his unhappiness increased. Finally, unable to bear the tedium any longer, he stepped out of character and organized a strike. Neither he nor his coworkers held out much hope for it, and many were afraid to attach their names to a petition. But when the disputes were settled and negotiations finally were over, the laundrymen found themselves recipients of a pay raise, higher rates for overtime, improved working conditions, and a modest pension.

They were amazed. So was Beck. Neither they nor he ever believed that a fellow such as him, gregarious enough in most company but never having displayed leadership skills—not, that is, until he felt pushed to the brink— could achieve such results. But suddenly a man to whom they had paid little attention in the past had shown himself to be a lionheart for the laboring man, and, taking to the role skillfully, Beck was inspired to gather his new batch of followers into a local branch of the Teamsters. It, and other branches, would remain faithful to Beck even when it became foolish, even counterproductive, to do so.

Two decades later, in 1937, he was heading the Western Conference of Teamsters, presiding over soaring memberships of the locals in his hometown of Seattle and throughout the Northwest. He continued to win pay raises for his men, continued to increase their benefits, and continued knowing instinctively how to deal with management on equal terms. There was little doubt that he would succeed Frank Fitzsimmons as president of the national union. And it happened in 1952. Unfortunately for the new president, the beginning of his sovereignty was also the start of its decline.

Beck barely had taken the reins from Fitzsimmons than he felt, more strongly than ever, the lure of misconduct. He had a reputation for being one of the guys, just another fellow who carried his sandwich to work in a lunch pail and dropped in for a shot and a beer at day's end; he never did either, as far as anyone knows, but he acted as if he were that kind of fellow, refusing to put on airs, treating his coworkers with a cordial respect.

But that was not the real Dave Beck. The real man, in truth, was possessed of grandiose ambition, and it did not take long for him to demonstrate it. He "had begun to distance himself from the rank-and-file, to act more like a suddenly wealthy businessman than a union leader. The money that came his way from payoffs and extortion went not to benefit the union, but rather to reward himself with a manner of living he thought befitted his position. He spent lavishly on homes and all the accoutrements of the rich. To many, then, he seemed to have lost touch."

Of course, if he were behind bars, he would lose touch even more, and that was where John McClellan came in, bringing with him, according to one journalist, "the astringent, disapproving demeanor of a stern man of the cloth."

Among others, McClellan chose John Fitzgerald Kennedy, a Democrat from Massachusetts, to join him on the Senate committee investigating the

Teamsters. Beck didn't know much about Kennedy, but he would soon acquire extensive information about his younger brother, the committee counsel and a man just beginning to make a name for himself as a foe of organized crime. The image of the future president's sibling that comes to mind at this point in his life is that of an underfed pit bull, snarling with sincere righteousness as his teeth begin shredding the coattails of a law-breaker. Justice with a crunch: that was Robert F. Kennedy. Brother John, already thinking of a run for the presidency, was equally opposed to Beck and the various sins of the Teamsters, but he would need the workingman's vote in 1960; thus, he was more restrained in displays of opposition to the Teamsters' chief than was his brother.

However, the younger Kennedy, known to friends as Bobby, had no political aspirations and thus felt no restraints; he just wanted to make life miserable for cheaters, swindlers, and double-dealers, for embezzlers and purveyors of illegal goods. He wanted to shatter the world that was organized crime, to disorganize it into oblivion.

Beck was scheduled to testify before the committee on February 26. As the date loomed, he grew more and more nervous. He spent most of the month abroad, not only trying to keep his woes at bay, but avoiding various subpoenas that he knew awaited him at home. And one journalist, perhaps with tongue in cheek, surmised that Beck was boning up on his union studies, hoping to impress members of the McClellan committee with his knowledge of Teamster intricacies and, thereby, his irreplaceability to the union's cause. If so, he needed to have studied a lot more than he did. As would be apparent the first day Beck opened his mouth before the senators, he was more inadvertently funny than diligently informed.

The most likely reason for Beck's February abroad was Robert Kennedy. He knew that Kennedy was investigating him with a tenacity that would soon enable Kennedy to unearth the Teamster boss's darkest secret. Which is exactly what happened. Having already discovered that $322,000 was missing from various Teamster accounts, Kennedy made a trip to Seattle to search for the money. It could not have been easier to find. Blatantly displayed, the cash had been used "to construct [Beck's] private home and swimming pool and pay off personal debts." Kennedy had already put together a long list of malfeasances Beck committed; now he had the cherry to go on top.

The union head finally presented himself to the committee in early March. But he already had tried a preemptive strike, having admitted to journalists that he had arranged a loan of $300,000 for himself from Teamster funds. So he didn't steal the money, Beck insisted; he borrowed it. But under further questioning, he was forced to admit that his loan was interest-free. Then he admitted that he had not yet paid back the money, either in full or in part. And as the journalistic inquisition continued, Beck confessed that he had been given no timetable for repayment. In other words, the loan was not a loan at all, but a gift: to Dave Beck, with best wishes, from Dave Beck.

After confessing to the press, he found himself limited in what he could say to the committee. In fact, he was practically mute. He could not afford to give the senators more ammunition to use against him, and could think of little to offer that would *not* contribute to prosecutorial onslaught. He needed a strategy, a means of dealing with the senators that would not make what was bad even worse.

McClellan surprised no one by calling on the committee counsel to begin the questioning, and as Beck had feared, Kennedy's bite was worse than his bark. Although hardly a constitutional scholar, Beck was at least familiar with his Fifth Amendment right against self-incrimination and more than likely set a record for invoking it in a single interrogation. One hundred seventeen times Bobby Kennedy asked a question. One hundred seventeen times Beck's reply was the same. He sat sphynx-like, stating in apparent calm, "I decline to answer on the grounds that it might open up avenues of questions that might tend to incriminate me."

As the morning slogged on, every person in the hearing room had memorized Beck's paraphrase of the Fifth Amendment. No matter; he kept reciting away, even as it seemed to become an effort, the sweat beginning to trickle down his cheeks and his breathing at times becoming audible. Members of the committee were frustrated, infuriated, and eventually bored at Beck's repetitions. They cracked their knuckles, squirmed in their seats, cleared their throats, whether or not they needed to.

Finally, they had had enough. " 'Do you,' asked Chairman McClellan at one point, 'regard your privileges under the Fifth Amendment as transcending your duty and obligations to the laboring men of this country who belong to your union?'

"Beck's face reddened, his head shot forward, his lips moved as he shaped an outraged reply. Just in time, Arthur Condon, his attorney, drove a knuckle into Beck's back. Three times Beck started to answer; three times Condon's knuckles dug into his spine. Every time Beck felt them, he dropped back in his chair and automatically began his recitation. "I decline to answer . . . ' "

The irony of the Fifth Amendment, of course, is its inherent contradiction; a person who employs it to protect himself from guilt is believed to be doing just the opposite, admitting the truth of the accusation against him. Surely this is not always true. The person testifying has not always committed the crime or inflicted the damage—but what *is* always true is perception's acceptance as reality. Beck's answers to Robert Kennedy's questions could not have incriminated him more, which seemed to have been obvious to everyone in the hearing room except Dave Beck and his associates.

In fact, when the first day's testimony was over, Beck made certain the press captured his obtuseness. He slid his chair back from the table and stretched like a cat who has just enjoyed a nap in the sun. Then he rose and bounced confidently down the aisle, through the courtroom doors, and, smiling from earlobe to earlobe, said to the waiting horde of news-papermen, "I'll be able to come out of this clean and white, one hundred percent!" Reporters jotted down the comment, and so outrageous was it that they stumbled over themselves in asking follow-up questions. But Beck had nothing more to say, not then. He departed from the courthouse, insensible to the impression he had made.

However, at least in part because of that impression, his days at the top of the Teamsters were numbered. After Kennedy had at him, other committee members took their turns, and although none was as ferocious as the future attorney general, the cumulative effect was devastating. After a week or so of grilling, it had become obvious to all, Beck included, that he could not win another term as the Teamsters' majordomo. Nor would he embarrass himself by trying. When he finally was dismissed by the committee, he announced his resignation from the union's presidency.

In the months ahead, Beck dropped onto lower and lower rungs of Team-ster influence. By 1959 his position was such that he could achieve nothing more ignominious than a conviction for labor racketeering in the state of Washington. The charge was that he had pilfered a modest $1,900, the money coming from the sale of a union-owned Cadillac. It was a long way from the theft of $300,000 and a mansion on Puget Sound, a long way as well from the attention spans of East Coast newspaper editors. Once fasci-nated by every false move Beck had made, the editors had lost interest in a man who so rapidly had become such a small-timer, and his $1,900 theft was covered in only a few papers, and in a minimum of space.

Later in 1959, Beck was convicted on charges of federal income tax eva-sion and served thirty months of a three-year sentence. Upon release, and now a widower, he lived frugally in the basement of a house he previously had built for his mother and sister. Because the Teamsters had rewarded Beck for stealing their money by voting him a pension of $50,000 a year, and because he was paying no rent while living at home, he was able to save most of his severance. He began investing it in parking lots. Due to the machinations of a few of his friends, men who had made fortunes by building and managing the lots, then skimming the profits, Beck was able to make a fortune himself; he, in fact, became a millionaire, in today's terms a multimillionaire. It was a status he would not have been able to attain with the Teamsters.

Even more redemption was ahead. In 1965 Beck was pardoned by Washington governor Albert Rosellini for his Cadillac infraction, and ten years later, he received similar absolution from President Gerald Ford for having cheated the IRS, although Ford could have chosen any one of a dozen other improprieties for which to hand over the pardon.

The lesson for Beck was that although crime might not pay immediately, like all good investments it would provide in time.

The former Teamsters' boss died in 1993 at the age of ninety-nine, still moderately robust, a labor leader emeritus, a man whose final years, almost two and a half decades of them, were spent living the deep-brewed joys of undeserved vindication.

Back in 1957, James Riddle Hoffa replaced Beck as head of the Teamsters, and it was like substituting Machine Gun Kelly for the Artful Dodger. Hoffa thought on a much more ambitious scale than Beck, which is to say, he was even more self-serving and ruthless than his predecessor. Although the connection between organized crime and American labor, especially the Teamsters, had roots that dug deeply into the earliest days of the century, Hoffa wasted no time in surpassing Beck by strengthening the alliance. Before long, he had converted the International Brotherhood of Teamsters into a wholly owned subsidiary of the Mafia. In fact, when one talked about organized labor in those days, one often was talking about organized crime; many of their goals, as well as their methods, and even some of their personnel, were the same.

Hoffa's very presence was enough to intimidate those who might have opposed him. He looked like a retired prizefighter, one who somehow had earned his trophies without his face being irreparably damaged in the process, his features having healed with most of their original symmetry. On the cover of Dan Moldea's book, *The Hoffa Wars*, is a large photo of the title character. He seems to be seated, with his left hand folded into a fist and his right hand cupping it. He looks as if he has reached the end of his patience with a clumsy subordinate and is about to deliver an uppercut. His smile is slight, not designed to cover the malignance beneath.

As a child, Hoffa became an adult quickly. Born in Brazil, Indiana, in 1913, he and his brother became "the men of the family" when their father died from a life spent in the black, airless chambers of nearby coal mines. In his last few weeks, he had lost so much of his breath that he was almost mute, barely even able to cough. Jimmy was seven years old when his father gave up the struggle, and he vowed that no such death would ever befall him.

At fourteen he quit school to work as a stock boy and later found employment on the loading dock for the Kroger grocery store chain. His first jobs paid, respectively, twelve dollars a week and thirty-two cents an hour. He handed over most of his paycheck to his mother, who toiled daily in a Brazil laundry. She tried her best not to curse the fates that had led her there, to keep a stiff upper lip for her boys. But they knew she had been ill-used by circumstance, and they would do everything they could to make sure that, from now on, she was spared as much hardship as possible.

It was the Kroger job, more than anything else, that put the finishing touches on the young man Hoffa would become. His duties for the grocery chain were arduous and unremitting. True, even in his early teens he boasted "thick legs, heavy shoulders, and calloused hands," but the strain on them was nearly unbearable. The main problem was strawberries. He and those with whom he worked not only had to load and unload crates of them from one refrigerated truck to another, but they had to do it quickly, so that the fruit did not begin to soften in the transfer. And carefully; the fruit, after all, is a fragile one. They got no breaks, no rest periods of any sort, only the sickening sweet smell of the air.

Finally, the young men decided they had had enough, had put up with enough abuse; their bodies were aging far beyond their years. With the help of a few loading dock buddies, Hoffa drew up a catalog of complaints and handed it to the night manager, who promised to get it into the hands of the right people the next day.

To Hoffa's surprise, the "Strawberry Boys," as other Kroger flunkies had begun to call them, were summoned to meet with store officials. They had no idea what to expect. Would they be fired, have their hours increased, their wages reduced? Would their demands be the end of their employment? Just the opposite. Without bitterness, or even much in the way of negotiation, they were offered a raise of thirteen cents an hour, more than a third of their previous pay. In addition, a kind of relay system was devised so that hirelings could take more breaks, albeit short ones, without the spoilage of their cargo.

And so Jimmy Hoffa, like Dave Beck before him, dumbfounded even himself by becoming a successful labor leader against what seemed great odds. He never figured out why the Kroger officials gave in to him and his boys so easily; perhaps they feared some kind of reprisal if they refused. But they had capitulated. That was the important point, and as long as they had, Hoffa would take advantage of the situation and begin to build a career.

In 1936, at the age of twenty-three, Hoffa married Josephine Poszywak, an eighteen-year-old who becomes the fourth laundry worker in the past few pages of this chapter. The newlyweds lived modestly not only at the start, but even many years later, when Hoffa, by then a figure of national renown, had begun looting the Teamsters' pension fund, dipping into it as if it were a bowl of mints on his desk. By that time, Hoffa and his brother had long since seen to it that their mother no longer had to soil herself with the dirty clothes of others. She could not have been prouder of her offspring.

Like Beck, Hoffa soon reached a position at which he could display his wealth for all to envy. But he didn't really care about the bounty he was accumulating, nor the baubles and bangles he could have purchased with it, what we today would call the bling. After all, he had grown up without it; he was used to its absence.

What Jimmy Hoffa cared about was the little man, and he thought of himself as the biggest little man of them all. For him, power was the true currency, not money, and by that measure he soon became one of the richest men in the country.

Once again like Beck, Hoffa played a leading role in organizing union locals under the Teamster umbrella. But Detroit, where Hoffa worked, was a much more turbulent place than Seattle, and Hoffa had to learn a different set of lessons from his predecessor, to rely more on force, intimidation, and reprisal. On one occasion, his brother took a bullet for his union activities, and a national Teamsters' executive with whom Hoffa had worked closely was murdered by a strikebreaker. Things like that did not happen in Seattle, but in the country's automotive capital, as Hoffa later recalled, "Our cars were bombed out. Three different times, someone broke into the [union] office and destroyed our furniture. Cars would crowd us off the streets. Then it got worse. [The managements of trucking and warehousing firms] hired thugs who were out to get us . . . There was only way one to survive—fight back."

He continued: "The police were no help. The police would beat your brains in for even talking union. The cops harassed us every day. If you went on strike, you had your head broken." Life wasn't always that violent for Hoffa, of course, but more often than not, he lived it outside the law. According to journalist Stephen Fox, who wrote a history of organized crime in twentieth-century America, Hoffa was hauled off to prison eighteen times in one period of twenty-four hours for picketing: "arrested, released, back to the line, arrested . . . Police also brought him in sixteen other times in ten years for extortion, assault and battery." In committing all of his crimes, he carried the escutcheon of the Teamsters proudly before him.

Jimmy Hoffa had never driven a truck, laundry or otherwise, and the Teamsters, almost without exception, were men of the road. But his lack of experience did not slow his ascent to union leadership; he rose to eminence with his foot on the gas all the way. An executive with the combined Teamster locals in Detroit—although a word like "executive" hardly seems to fit a man as rough-and-tumble in his nature as Hoffa—he soon became the head of the entire Michigan branch. He was closing in on Beck.

As World War II broke out, he was summoned for military duty but successfully made the case for a deferment. He could do much more for the American fighting man, Hoffa argued to his local draft board, in his present position than in a trench somewhere in Europe. And he could. And Beck assigned him to precisely those duties.

It was Hoffa who made sure that the trucks ran on time, and that the right trucks were carrying the right merchandise to the right stores for sale, and the right materiel to the right ports or depots or air strips to be loaded onto the right vehicles for transport abroad. In addition, it was Hoffa who saw to it—and it was no less a huge responsibility—that the civilians doing war work in American factories were provided with food, clothing, and other necessities of life. Hoffa was in charge of it all—although he had a great deal of help—and his performance was as exemplary as the tasks were daunting. For all that justly can be said against him, it must be acknowledged that Jimmy Hoffa knew how to do his job—and his job, especially during the war years, was really a score of jobs, all of which he had to juggle, all of those balls to keep in the air, without dropping a single one; day in, he had to do it, day out. And, just as important, Hoffa was called on to perform his virtually acrobatic feats at what might have been the most important time in his country's history.

Never did a ball hit the ground.

At the Teamsters' Convention in Los Angeles in 1952, Beck rewarded him by selecting him as his national vice president. It was inevitable that he do so, but not the best idea Beck ever had. Once more, at a critical moment in his career, he was oblivious.

Hoffa had no sooner assumed his new office than he began a series of behind-the-scenes maneuvers aimed at forcing Beck to step aside for him. Beck and his men fought back, and dissension began to run through the Teamsters' rank and file like a river overflowing its banks. As things turned out, though, Hoffa would not need any help from his fellow, dissatisfied union members to force Beck into the remunerative retirement that awaited; it would be the McClellan Committee that excised him from power.

But Hoffa eventually would have disposed of his boss even without congressional assistance. As the man who served as Hoffa's so-called strongest arm recalled in a book written for him, "The differences between the two were marked."

Hoffa behaved as many Teamsters thought a Teamster leader should behave. He was never far away from the picket line and was often out front. He was a tough and agile bargainer who won from employers as much for his members, or even more, than Beck had for his. He was always available to hear their grievances. If he took payoffs, well, who didn't, and besides he seemed to use the money less for his own personal aggrandizement than as the means to amass the necessary power for himself and for his union. Everything about Hoffa was Teamster.

Yes, everything was Teamster. In the worst sense of the word.

Before the McClellan Committee was through with Beck, Hoffa was ready to step into the void, and when his ascension became official, he wasted no time in fomenting "conflicts of interest among employers and union leaders . . . and denial of democratic process to members." To the preceding should be added Hoffa's ability to turn graft into something of an art form, and to practice it so frequently that it might have been one of the union's bylaws.

Yet even before Hoffa had followed in Beck's footsteps, before he had perfected the flagrant behavior of the highwayman, he already had pocketed more illegal cash from both inside and outside the union than all of his pockets put together could hold. He did not just rifle through the pension fund, but insisted on kickbacks for contracts granted, bribes for other services and favors performed, and all manner of villainy, some of it undertaken for his underworld associates. As a result, he could afford to be one of the Motor City's leading philanthropists. He donated large sums to local charities, making sure the newspapers always had the story, and in 1956 received his unjust deserts. It was then that Detroit, Michigan, declared April 20 to be James R. Hoffa Day, the honor bestowed because of "his dynamic leadership, courageous labors, and valuable sense of civic duty."

Among those attending a dinner for the public embrace of Hoffa were "the Catholic bishop of Chicago, a prominent rabbi from Philadelphia . . . and, of course, Dave Beck. Ford, General Motors, Sears, Montgomery Ward, and other Detroit- and Chicago-based corporations bought blocks of the $100-a-plate tickets." Executives of smaller companies also paid their respects, as did leading law enforcement officials and politicians.

It was a lengthy evening of accolades and encomiums, allowing time for ovations both sitting and standing. But finally, as the festivities drew to a close, Hoffa took the podium not only to express his gratitude to those who had come to pay homage to him, but to bring down the house with an unexpected announcement. He was donating all proceeds of the night's affair, which turned out to be some $250,000, to build the James R. Hoffa Children's Home of Jerusalem. Ground would be broken, he stated accurately, four months later in Israel.

Virtually as one, the diners rose and clapped their hands for their benefactor until their palms reddened. He bowed his head in humility. However unintended, it was gilded black comedy at its most extreme.

Hoffa's charitable efforts had no effect on the McClellan Committee. He had become a bête noire of the senators even before his first day of testimony. On February 22, 1957, as plans were being drawn up for the facility in Jerusalem, Hoffa made headlines of a different sort in America, when transcripts were released of a wiretapped conversation between him and the New York thug Johnny Diogardi, otherwise known as Johnny Dio. It seems that, as Beck's vice president, Hoffa previously had been responsible for several nonexistent Teamster branches called "paper locals." The organizations were imaginary, but the money that financed them was real, and it went straight to Hoffa, Dio, and other slithering creatures of the night. But the phony groups had even more ways to enrich those who had created them. For instance, whenever there was a union election, 100 percent of the fake locals' membership would cast its votes for Hoffa's side. It was an astonishing display of solidarity. It did not seem to strike anyone as unusual.

The wiretaps went on to reveal that these sham branches were not enough for Hoffa. He and Dio, drunk on success and the acclaim of subordinates, wanted more. They drew up plans for a vast expansion of the paper locals, including one that would purport to represent thirty thousand New York cabdrivers. It was a scheme of breathtaking audacity, and one wonders at the sanity of those who thought a scam of such magnitude could go undetected. It didn't. Thanks to the wiretaps, the fake locals were detected before they could do nearly as much damage as their creators had intended.

Members of the McClellan Committee were flabbergasted by Hoffa's effrontery. No less were they struck by the vow he took, under oath, that he was without ties to organized crime. In fact, by this time those ties were so well known that Hoffa discussed them openly. Not to law enforcement officials, of course, and certainly not to his senatorial inquisitors. But Hoffa often chatted about his network of shady playmates in conversation with those playmates—for instance, Frank Ragano, a mob lawyer who also served as Hoffa's attorney. He "was candid with Ragano about the teamsters' [sic] compacts with mobsters. In frank conversations, Hoffa rationalized that he and earlier IBT leaders had been compelled to use Mafia muscle in the 1930s and '40s to counterbalance brutal strikebreakers hired by companies fighting the union. Mob support was the keystone of Hoffa's success. . . . Hoffa said that mobster influence had helped the union grow and obtain unparalleled wages, fringe benefits, and working conditions for its blue-collar workers."

It was true, and many knew it. But the only ones who could prove it—Teamster officials who were leading better lives than ever before under Hoffa's thumb, as well as the boss's various mobster allies—were making too much money to talk.

Hoffa first appeared before McClellan and his mates on August 20, 1957. Again, it was counsel Kennedy who began the interrogation and got right to the point, asking the witness how many times he had been arrested since joining the Teamsters.

"Well, I don't know, Bob," was the reply, the words by themselves containing enough of a smirk so that Hoffa could utter them with a straight face and still convey his disrespect, "I haven't counted them up."

Kennedy *had* counted them up, he told his witness, and the number was seventeen, almost all of them the result of violence on Teamster picket lines. These were hardly major offenses, and Hoffa had not played a significant role in every one of them, but Kennedy was just laying the groundwork.

Still, Hoffa fumed at the question, and all the more at further and more damning questions. Just as much, he fumed at what he perceived to be RFK's brash and hectoring manner. "[T]hat spoiled brat . . . that crumb bum" he would later say of his antagonist, "Someday I'm gonna break both his arms."

Kennedy could be even more antagonistic. It is reported that one day during the hearings, he and Hoffa happened to choose the same restaurant for lunch. As the latter was being seated, "a voice rang out . . . It was Bobby. He stalked up behind Jimmy, strong-armed the Detroit muscleman, and spun him around. Hoffa grabbed Bobby's suit coat and slammed him against a wall. . . . The battle spilled over to the afternoon session of the committee, where the men argued over whether Hoffa had threatened to break Bobby's back."

At another afternoon session, a few days later, RFK's older brother took over the questioning and asked about a small loan the union head had made. The recipient was the top man at a Teamsters' local, Eugene "Jimmy" James. The amount was $2,500. But when James repaid the loan, the sum had mysteriously risen.

" 'There were no services performed,' said John Kennedy, 'and yet the money, the $2,500, went up to $6,000 in—what, two years or three years?'

" 'I can't answer that, sir,' Hoffa said."

" 'When the original loan was only $2,500, why would it go to $6,000?'

" 'I can't answer that, except for the fact I can't answer that.' "

Hoffa tried to portray himself as the victim of the Kennedy brothers, a poor fox set upon by rich boys at the hounds. But the vacuity of his responses notwithstanding, the union head was not an ordinary crook; besides the power he had accumulated both by his performance during the war and the mere fact of his office, he was also a notable figure who could not be pushed too far, even by members of the United States Senate.

Writing in what might have been the nation's most popular magazine at the time, the *Saturday Evening Post*, journalist Homer Bigart said, "As Teamster boss . . . Hoffa has a stranglehold on the American economy any time he wants to squeeze. Teamsters drive the trucks that distribute the vital necessities of life—food, clothing, fuel, and merchandise—more than 80 percent of all freight moved in this country. A word from Hoffa can shut off supplies from stores and factories. Not even the dead escape him: A Teamster drives the hearse."

But for the time being, lost in the echoing, marbled halls of Congress, Hoffa was out of his league. Perhaps the most damaging testimony he gave was not testimony at all, but his recorded voice on the wiretaps with Dio and the contortions his body went through as he listened. Hoffa's lawyer was livid that the tapes were being aired in so public a forum, but as he knew would be the case, his objections were overruled, and he had no choice but to join his client in listening. Of course, the tapes already had been played in public, but their encore, this time in front of an august assembly of U.S. senators and the cream of the Washington press corps, all of them having gathered in one of the Capitol's most elegant forums, made the content seem all the more damning. When the tape was finished, Bobby Kennedy started in again.

It was humiliation added to embarrassment. Hoffa twitched and increased the velocity of his blinks as he stumbled time and again, trying to explain away what he and Dio had talked about on the phone. And as the days went by, he began to sound almost punch-drunk in his replies to Robert Kennedy's questions. "To the best of my recollection, I just on my memory, I cannot remember," he said to one query. RFK, looking incredulous, mocked Hoffa by repeating his words. " 'To the best of my recollection, I just on my memory, I cannot remember'—that is your answer?"

Even committee members chuckled at that one, as they did later when Hoffa, drawing a blank on yet another question, attributed it to his "disremembrance."

At that neologism, spectators laughed like the audience at *The Ed Sullivan Show*, and McClellan, although he might have liked to join in, punctuated the mirth with his gavel and said, "Let's have order."

Most of the time, though, Hoffa "faced Kennedy and the senators with a belligerence equal to their own and, for a time, created a stalemate." He did so in a style that was uniquely his own. Because Beck already had appropriated the gambit of invoking the Fifth Amendment when a truthful answer would have served him poorly, Hoffa decided he had to come up with his own brand of evasion, something original. And so his version of avoiding self-incrimination, as seen above, was to retreat to a faulty memory. Disremembrance.

He is said to have relied on such a response more than a hundred times. New York Republican senator Irving Ives, normally a mild-mannered legislator, could not keep his seething to himself. Inventing a neologism of his own, he told Hoffa that he had "the most convenient *forgettery* of anybody

I have ever seen. . . . By golly, you have not taken the fifth, but are doing a marvelous job crawling around it."

Because of Hoffa's alleged "forgettery" about dealings with Dio and another unsavory character named Bernard Spindel, the Teamster boss was indicted on five counts of perjury. These joined other indictments already outstanding in New York for spying on union associates and perjuring himself before a grand jury. Hoffa had to rely on Ragano and other lawyers to keep track of his indictments; even employing the best of his attorneys' recollections, he had trouble making a guess at the tally. Even RFK had not kept count.

A different tally, though, was easily calculated. By the time Hoffa's part in the hearings had ended, he was "charged with thirty-four additional improper activities. Committee charges now totaled an all-time record for McClellan's men of eight-two, ranging from labor racketeering to collaborating with organized crime figures. The most serious charges were . . . Hoffa's ownership of the Test Fleet corporation [nominally owned by Hoffa's wife, who ended up $125,000 to the good as a result] . . . and the bogus Sun Valley land deal." The former was a truck leasing operation that certain companies were forced to employ, the latter a scam whereby the Teamsters sold lots to executives of the union, who found the prices steadily increasing as the costs of utilities, road paving, and other "amenities." were factored in. Said a local Teamster official, "There were a lot of really mad people when they knew they'd been taken. But Jimmy justified his position and didn't apologize to anyone. I loved the guy, but I do hold that against him."

The chairman of the committee, who had led a life of unwavering probity and ineffable heartache, simply did not understand a man such as Hoffa. "This has become a sordid story. McClellan said to the labor chief. Lord Almighty, you are the man at the head of it. You have the responsibility. But apparently instead of taking any action you are undertaking to do everything you can to perpetuate the situation."

Somewhere deep inside, Hoffa must have snickered at such naivete.

In fact, even greater malfeasances may be added to Hoffa's previous accounts, as he also profited from prostitution, gambling, and countless variations of the protection racket. Even more ominously, he probably arranged, or at least gave his blessing to, a murder here and there. He almost certainly was involved in a plot, perhaps more than one, to kill Fidel Castro, and just as certainly, although perhaps more casually, speculated with others about a means to assassinate Robert Kennedy's older brother when he became the nation's chief executive. "The United States is being run like a police state," Hoffa declared at one point, "and [John] Kennedy is turning the U.S. into a country like the one ruled by Adolf Hitler."

In 1967, after three years of appeals for his most recent convictions, one of which was the attempted bribery of a grand juror in Chattanooga, Tennessee, Hoffa and his lawyers finally gave up. The man who was now the

Teamsters' former head surrendered to federal officials and took up residence at the high-security penitentiary in Lewisburg, Pennsylvania, where he was supposed to spend the next thirteen years of his life.

He did not even reach the halfway point. In December 1971, President Richard Nixon commuted Hoffa's sentence to the time he had already served, which was less than five years. Few Teamsters were happy about their old boss's freedom, but those of the union's higher rank, who had shared in many of their old boss's spoils, saw fit to award him a lump sum pension of $1.7 million. Today we would call it a golden parachute, and the sum would be worth more than $15 million.

However, although Nixon's commutation gave Hoffa back his freedom, it might have cost him his life, although unwittingly. He was a free man again but no longer a powerful one and, more than anything, Hoffa longed for power and, among other things, its ability to protect him from harm. For the most part, he defined power as regaining the Teamsters' leadership.

But it was not going to happen, not in these fading hours of his life. One of the conditions of his early release from Lewisburg was that he abstain from all union-related activities. Hoffa agreed, yet expecting him to keep his word was like expecting an alligator to become a vegetarian; it simply was not in his nature.

What he had to do, even with a pal such as Nixon in the White House, was be careful about the union activities in which he *did* participate; he had to be subtle, sly, making certain that he worked with only a few trusted allies, and in utmost secrecy. If members of the rank and file, already upset about the huge pension Hoffa had received, and more upset about having lost all or at least most of their own pensions, found out that the man who stole from them was once again making decisions affecting their lives, an uprising in the union might have torn it apart.

The problem for Hoffa was that subtle and sly were not adjectives that fit him. Besides his public shaming by the McClellan Committee, despite his years in jail, he was still arrogant, still had his swagger, still seemed to act as if the Teamsters were his personal property and as susceptible as ever to his will. It was a misunderstanding doomed to end poorly.

One murder of which James Riddle Hoffa was *not* guilty was his own, about which no one knows anything conclusively, and, at this late date, no one is likely to turn up any evidence.[2]

Shortly after 2:45 p.m. on July 30, 1975, having just eaten lunch at the Red Fox Restaurant in suburban Detroit, Hoffa disappeared from the face of the earth, never to be seen again. He was sixty-two years old and still

---

2. However, a 2019 movie called *The Irishman* is based on the claim of a gangster named Frank Sheeran that he murdered Hoffa. Evidence, although not certainty, is that this might be true.

scheming. The chances of his having reached sixty-three are, to say the least, remote. If he did, and continued to exist, he would be 106 at present.

Seven years to the day after Hoffa vanished, he was declared legally dead.

The how and where of his disappearance are the greatest riddle of them all.

The McClellan Committee hearings are, at best, a historical footnote now, but they deserve to be much more: material for chapters, books, multivolume sets. Not only were the hearings among the most important events of 1957, they were one of the most explicit and necessary awakenings that Americans ever have had about the excesses of Big Labor, peeling away layer after layer of seeming respectability. Never since have the Teamsters exercised such a corrupting influence on American industry; never since has a union official, any union official, been so widely known for such ignominious reasons. How many of you reading these words can name the current president of the Teamsters?[1]

---

1. James P. Hoffa Jr., a fellow much better behaved than his father.

3

From Apalachin to Havana

Just as Jimmy Hoffa had been no run-of-the-mill captain of labor, the men with whom he did his least upstanding business, either directly or through intermediaries, were no run-of-the-mill hoodlums. They were the royalty of their dark kingdoms, and Hoffa was their equal in the fine points of obtaining and abusing power. He was at ease with men such as these; many of them, after all, had started their working lives as something like Strawberry Boys themselves. But when Hoffa was at the pinnacle of his influence, the stakes weren't a few extra pennies an hour and longer breaks between fruit-toting shifts; then they were millions of dollars if all went well, or possibly murder or jail terms if plans were not executed to perfection.

Still, these were Hoffa's people; like him, they were graduates of back-alley education, men of the world, the underworld. They were, or became, his pals.

But Hoffa was happy not to have been anywhere around them on November 14, 1957.

In the tiny upstate New York village of Apalachin (population 277 at the time and pronounced Apple-achin' by the locals), about one hundred Mafia leaders from the United States, Italy, and Cuba met for fellowship and serious deliberations about business. It had become an annual event, held as far off the beaten path as possible. But exigencies always seemed to make each year's get-together something special, sometimes even alarming. This year it was, in large part, the McClellan Committee, which would continue to meet until the spring of 1960 and would remain in the press all of that time. True, most of the bad publicity had gone to Beck and Hoffa, and also true, with the two of them no longer testifying, the hearings were no longer in the headlines. But the dons of the underworld feared that the McClellan gang might be setting a precedent, and that they, too, might be summoned to appear before a congressional lynch mob one day. For men who lived their lives on a razor's edge of recklessness, they could be epitomes of caution when the situation called for it.

Prominent among the dons were Frank Costello and Meyer Lansky, Lucky Luciano and Al Capone, Carlo Gambino and Sam Giancana, Bugsy Siegel and Bugs Moran, Vito Genovese and Frank Nitti, Joe Profaci and Russell Bufalino and Albert Anastasia and so many other men who were captains of small city empires, but captains nonetheless. For so long, they had run their crooked businesses and remained anonymous. How much more time, they might have wondered in the still of the night, did they have?

The cops knew about them, of course—local, state, and sometimes even federal. Journalists knew about them, especially the increasing numbers of reporters on newspaper crime beats. But top police officials had been paid off, and the hacks had been warned that if they published an exposé, someone else would be publishing their obits in the coming days' editions.

So they had nothing to worry about, they tried to reassure themselves, nothing substantive. Not yet.

It was a cold day in Apalachin, gray-skied and windy, as most of the U.S. contingent of the underworld made its way to outskirts of the tiny community from as far away as California, Texas, and Florida. One of them, in particular, didn't want to be there—and he turned out to be prescient.

Chicago boss Salvatore "Sam," sometimes "Sam the Cigar" Giancana, had offered his city for the convocation. He ran hotels in the Windy City, and could make meeting rooms available with the best security money could buy; he ran motels and could spread out his colleagues at night, all over the city and suburbs, so they could sleep well, without fear of being apprehended en masse; he ran rental car agencies and could provide transportation no matter where the conferees were staying, no matter where they were going. And he ran prostitution rings, so no one had to be lonely after the day's business had been transacted. He ran *Chicago*, for Christ's sake! Nobody was going to interfere with Sam the Cigar's business, not in his kind of town.

But other Mafia heads didn't think a city would be safe. Cities were too big, too crowded, hard to control. Thugs did not like crowds; it was one of the fundamentals of keeping transactions confidential. Someone always was on the make in a place such as Chicago, always someone who could be paid off for some incriminating information, or for a theft, a mugging, maybe even a hit.

But the $100,000 mansion owned by Joseph "Joe the Barber" Barbara and buried in the backwoods of Tioga County, a place that was impossible to see from the road, a place with no pedestrians anywhere in the vicinity, with even hunters out of season now—that *did* seem safe. Who would imagine so much chicanery and firepower ensconced in so remote a location? It was perfect. The princes of organized crime had met there the previous year and nothing had happened. They could see no reason not to return.

And, so, for one of the few times in Sam Giancana's career, he had been overruled. He was furious, and it was not just a matter of ego. As his personal plane began to descend into the tiny airport near Apalachin, he was looking out the window, sensing that something wasn't right, squinting as if he should be spotting something but wasn't. Maybe his fellow Mafiosi were right, he forced himself to decide; maybe he was just feeling the after-effects of the McClellan Committee.

"Sam the Cigar" and his fellow potentates were picked up at the airport and driven as close to the Barber's house as their limousines could get, then tramped through the woods the rest of the way. This made Sam even *more* unhappy. The Barber pays a hundred grand for a place on some of the cheapest real estate in the entire country, and he doesn't even put in side-walks! What kind of a guy *was* this?

When Giancana and the others were safely behind Barbara's walls, the woods began to stir, slowly, stealthily. Agents from the federal bureau of Alcohol, Tobacco and Firearms, who had hidden themselves behind tree trunks and rock outcroppings, dressed in the muddy gray of the rocks and the brown of dead leaves, and who were stationed far enough from Barbara's manse so that it was barely in sight, now closed in. They were like an ocean wave in slow motion. Afraid that the dons had someone watching the woods with binoculars, the lawmen were hunched over as they moved, sometimes even getting down on hands and knees. They barely so much as cracked a twig.

In addition to the McClellan Committee, another order of business on the '57 underworld agenda transcended the ordinary. Of course, increasing the take from various gambling enterprises had to be discussed, as did loan-sharking, the occasional need to eliminate a competitor, and safer, more efficient means to traffic in liquor and narcotics. They always had to be discussed. But so did an item that, some years earlier, would have been entirely unexpected.

More than any other subset of organized crime, the Sicilians were thought to be men of honor, a word that, in the Mafia lexicon, was synonymous with loyalty. Men of honor were dedicated, trustworthy, would rather have their fingers sawed off with a rusty blade, one joint at a time, than snitch to the cops. But there had been rumors of late, troubling rumors that, even without the inducement of finger removal, a few Sicilians had been feeding information to the other side. The Teamsters were solid; at this point, the union was securely under Hoffa's thumb. But the Sicilians, of all people—*they* were leaking! It couldn't be, could it?

They were known to their *paisans* in the mob, in addition to their home-land, as the Cosa Nostra (literally "our thing" or "this thing of ours"), and many of them were just boys, eager but inexperienced; they would have much to learn even if they weren't dropping the dime on cohorts: "How to keep younger, ambitious gunmen in line" was a concern of the elders. "What rackets to parcel out to what members in what territories" was another. So, they might have more business to take care of this year than usual. And some of it could be unpleasant. No one wanted a confrontation with the Cosa Nostra, no matter what the members' ages.

As it turned out, they would have *less* business to take care of this year, not more. For no sooner had the conference's attendees emptied their brief-cases and lit up their fine Havanas; no sooner had they sunk into Barbara's extra-padded sofas and easy chairs and begun to blow smoke rings; no sooner had they begun to work their way through the civilities of small talk—no sooner had all of this taken place than a horde of heavily armed New York State police officers, under the guidance of the ATF, burst onto the porch, pounding on the front door and crashing through it without waiting for an invitation. The meeting had been raided before it even began. This wasn't supposed to happen in America.

The cops arrested fifty-eight gangsters . . . Among the luminaries were four current and two future heads of New York City's five Mafia families. Perhaps fifty other Mafiosi escaped into the woods and back roads around the home. Among those who fled, but later were placed at or near the Apalachin meeting, were the boss of San Francisco (James Lanza), the missing fifth head of a New York family (Tommy Lucchese), and three other members of the national Mafia Commission . . . These five pushed the total to sixty-three embarrassed gangsters.

It was the biggest single haul of hoodlums ever made in the United States. As for those who got away, most did not get away for long, and investigative reporter Dan Moldea suspects that before they were captured, they provided a burst of unintended humor: Keystone Kops, only this time in color, with the Dolby sound of reality.

The sight of all those gangsters—in silk pinstripe suits, wide-brimmed hats, tailor-made shirts, expensive hand-painted ties, and pointy shoes—running like hell for the pine woods around Barbara's home was a memorable specta-cle for those who watched it. As the mobsters sprinted through the trees they were caught by members of the police dragnet who were waiting with open arms and loaded guns. Some of the fleeing hoodlums ran down a road which led to a washed-out bridge and were caught there. One had to be gingerly picked out of a barbed wire fence.

According to the McClellan Committee, "50 [of those apprehended] had arrest records; 35 had records of convictions, and 23 had spent time in prisons or jails as a result of these convictions; 18 of these men had been either arrested or questioned at one time in connection with murder cases." In language not so neutral, the committee went on to discuss the size of the gathering. It was "symptomatic of the growing power of the American underworld. This growth is reflected in expanded economic enterprises, the continuing operation of vast illicit enterprises, and the infiltration of top hoodlums into labor, management, and management associations."

The growth was also reflected in the infamy that the Mafia was attracting. Not that it was more of a threat to society than it used to be; it was just that journalists love to tell tales about criminals, and their readers, the overwhelming majority of whom were safe in their living rooms, loved to read accounts of menace that posed no menace to them. It was like immersing themselves in crime fiction, that kind of vicarious thrill, the kind provided by the latest Rex Stout or Dashiell Hammett, James M. Cain or Simenon. The difference was that the characters with whom Americans were acquainting themselves in the press sprang from real life, so much so that, on rare occasions, their pictures even appeared on the front pages of the daily papers, usually wearing handcuffs and surrounded by cops.

Even the word "Mafia" was now a part of the national vocabulary, as threatening in its own way as the word "Sputnik" had become so recently. Both were words with sinister connotations. Distant, the pair of them, but sinister.

"Well, I hope you're satisfied," said a disgusted Sam Giancana to [Buffalo chieftan Stefano] Magaddino a few days after the Apalachin raid, the two of them speaking on a bugged telephone. "Sixty-three of our top guys made by the cops."

"I gotta admit you were right, Sam," Magaddino said. "It never would have happened in your place."

"You're fucking right it wouldn't," said the boss of Chicago, who within a few years reportedly would be sharing a mistress with the president of the United States.

The police learned of the gangster conclave because they did their jobs and did them well: employing solid investigative techniques, putting in long hours on the phone, and diligently studying the minimal information they could gather. They checked and double-checked with some of their sources and staked out others; from local restaurateurs they had learned about dinner reservations that had been made for large parties in mid-November, and from motel operators they had found out that, as early as

August, Tioga County had virtually no vacancies from November 13 to 15. On the twelfth, they were watching the highways into Apalachin for an excess of big, black cars. They were watching the skies for an influx of private planes. It is not likely that officials needed any help from the Cosa Nostra.

But the raid was not as efficacious as those who conducted it had hoped. When police thundered into Barbara's residence, they found nothing more than a houseful of old men sitting around tables, some of them having receded almost out of sight into the padding of the Barber's tasteless, overly upholstered furniture. No weapons were visible, no documents contained incriminating information. Papers and maps and the equivalent of today's spreadsheets were laid out on carpets and tabletops, but they contained nothing except financial information, facts and figures decipherable only to the men who had brought them to Apalachin. In other words, as far as appearances were concerned, the most ruthless men in the country could have been salt-of-the-earthers, businessmen engaged in legitimate vocational affairs.

The only difference was that most of them "carried wads of money, between $2,000 and $3,000, an extraordinary amount of pocket money" for legitimate businessmen, but nothing was illegal about it. "[W]ithout evidence of a crime and finding no unlicensed weapons, the police had no choice but to release everyone, without photographing them, without fingerprinting."

This, then, was the reward that law enforcement officials had received for so much hard work and lengthy vigilance, for such precision of planning and execution. It was like catching the biggest trout in the stream and then having to throw it back. The authorities knew who most of these men were and what they did to make those wads of theirs, but they had known that long before. Sam Giancana might have complained that sixty-three of his business associates had been "made," but, in all likelihood the majority were already made, which is to say, known to either local police or federal agencies. At most it meant only that a few well-to-do hoodlums who previously had been anonymous now would have their own manila files. But they would be stuffed into cheap metal cabinets with no damning information in them, perhaps never to be pulled out again.

Further, none of Joe the Barber's guests was committing any crime in Apalachin. And none planned to do so—although they would discuss crime almost exclusively. As for the crimes they had ordered or committed in other locales, *where was the proof*? The good guys might have known their jobs; the bad guys, on the other hand, were masters of evasion.

Further still, Tioga County did not have a vagrancy statute. Its absence prohibited "obviously well-heeled bums from being held while police investigated them." Meaning that the Mafiosi were free to go, to transact their business elsewhere. Their limousines were summoned back to the Barbara estate, the single-file procession of long, black cars lengthy enough to suit a funeral procession for a head of state. The attendees at the conference that never was were returned to their homes or to the airport where their planes awaited.

And, so, the Apalachin raid, hastily put together yet dazzlingly efficient and highly praised in newspapers, resulted in a grand total of no arrests and only a little more knowledge about the scope of Mafia activities than had been assembled previously. The manila folders still were depressingly slender.

But as had been the case with the performances of Dave Beck and Jimmy Hoffa before the McClellan Committee, punishment came simply in the publicity. The underworld was no longer as far "under" as it had been before, which was a victory of sorts for law enforcement. With the good guys showing a remarkable degree of efficiency, if not the results for which they had hoped, the bad guys would have to be more cautious.

Oddly, the country's most respected band of law enforcers, the FBI, was apparently in the dark about the raid. None of its agents took part in it; none spoke to the press about it afterward. When future Attorney General Robert Kennedy, still serving the McClellan Committee but under whose aegis the FBI would one day operate, was told of the Apalachin sortie, and was further informed that J. Edgar Hoover and his men were not participants, not even aware of the raid in advance, he was startled. "The FBI didn't know anything about these people, really, who were the major gangsters in the United States," Kennedy said, surely biting his tongue in understatement. "And that was rather a shock to me."

Actually, the FBI *did* know something about the Mafia, but not much, and its ignorance raised sinister questions. Among Hoover's closest associates, men in the inner sanctum of agency influence, were some who later would claim that their boss wanted FBI knowledge of the Mafia kept to a minimum, nothing too incriminating, nothing that was not available to most other legal agencies.

If this is true, what is the explanation? That Hoover didn't realize how serious a threat the Mafia really were, and he had enough to worry about already? Possibly. Or was it that he *did* know how serious the criminals were, and for that reason did not want to be one of their victims someday? Also a possibility.

Or, taking a large step into speculation, was it because Hoover had associates in the Mafia, people with whom he occasionally did business, or maybe just traded information? No evidence supports such a charge; however, learning what we have come to learn about Hoover since his death, we have no reason to dismiss the surmise, either.

But after newspapers published their accounts of what had happened in Apalachin—front-page coverage everywhere, radio announcers broadcasting with the "Extra!" "Extra!" enthusiasm of newsboys—the FBI was forced into taking action. Or at least into going through some of the motions. Hoover increased the size of his organized crime task force, and its members started making scattered arrests here and there, now and then. Most of those apprehended were mid-level Mafia functionaries at best, and, if incarcerated, they did not remain behind bars for long; high-level lawyers saw to that. But at least the FBI was doing more than it had done before. Whether it really wanted to or not, the agency had put organized crime on alert. Low-level alert.

So far, it had been a bad year for lawbreakers in the United States. Metesky got caught; and Beck lost his job; and Hoffa lost face and probably his life; and the Apalachin raid, despite its shortcomings, proved to be a public relations campaign for an organization that depended on shadows and obscurity.

And things were about to get worse. One of the two most esteemed underworld dons survived an attempt on his life, although it seems a miracle that he did. A second mafioso did not survive, and he was so violent and deranged a figure that his termination sent chills through the precincts of organized crime—if the Mad Hatter can take a fatal bullet, when will it be my turn? And almost finally, one of organized crime's most dashing bon vivants was murdered at his leisure, despite having arranged for the Mafia to make uncountable millions in the years ahead. Never before had so many prominent criminals met their Maker, or come close to meeting him, in so short a period of time.

So many bullets were flying through the air in those days, almost indiscriminately, it seemed, and almost ceaselessly. One of those bullets was of particularly reckless intent; had it achieved its purpose, the Mafia would have been thrown into a frenzy of disarray, a civil war of sorts. It was hard to believe that anyone could have ordered such a hit. Hard to believe that its target was Frank Costello.

Francesco Castiglia came to the United States in 1895 at the age of four and soon afterward Americanized himself to Frankie. Adopting Costello as a last name, he also adopted such childhood pastimes as assault and robbery. He was thirteen when he first broke the law. At the age of seventeen, he became acquainted with a jail cell and would serve four terms behind bars in the next ten years for bottom-feeder criminal activities. When he was released after the last of them, he did not, as some people did upon release from confinement, vow to go straight; instead, Costello vowed to take up a different kind of illegal enterprise, something with a better yield, little chance of violence, and less chance of getting caught.

For reasons unknown, about this time Costello took another vow: never again to carry a gun. Thus, he became unique among his fellow hoodlums. Also unique were the degrees of intelligence and business acuity with which he was blessed, despite his not having spent a day in school. The guy was a natural. All he had to do was avoid that bullet with his name on it, and his future seemed assured.

Over the two decades after Costello walked out of jail for the first and last time, he rose so high in the ranks of the Mafia that, when he was semi-retired, still serving as a consultant to his former underworld associates, he was known as the "Prime Minister" of organized crime. He was also an ambassador to the law-abiding world. Far more than the rough-hewn Hoffa, Costello was able to cultivate friendships with judges, politicians, tycoons, socialites, philanthropists—he fraternized with all of them, and they were pleased to be seen in his company, slipping into the aura of dignified, flawlessly attired, and graceful peril that he projected. Costello's was the ultimate dream of the immigrant: to ease his way into America's true power structure.

To make sure he stayed there, the Prime Minister also mingled with the forces of law and order. But it was not so much his mingling as his money that solidified the relationships; his monthly expenditure on bribes amounted to more than most people made in a year.

He liked to think of himself as a gentleman, a businessman; and the older he got, the more legitimate his businesses became. Eventually he was investing in real estate, oil, and the automotive industry among other enterprises—laundering cash that had started out filthy and making sure that it remained clean ever after.

His renown only spread. Journalists sought him out; he gave them his time, and they gave him the patina of respectability. And they helped to make him a celebrity, a virtual tourist attraction, often visible at the most famous nightspots in New York.

> Over at Toots Shor's saloon on West Fifty-first Street, Costello was part of the crowd of celebrities, movie stars, writers, Nobel Prize winners, and sports fig-ures who made it into a place where, as one writer observed, a salesman from Iowa could rub elbows with the likes of Joe DiMaggio and bump into Frank Sinatra while going to the restroom. Costello himself is said to have tipped his glass to Supreme Court Justice Earl Warren, who did the same in return. (Maybe, just maybe, that last gesture passing between the two men meant something since it was the Warren Court which, despite ruling against Costello numerous times in other matters, finally decided in his favor in the deporta-tion case [allowing him to remaining in the country despite his more-than-dubious background.])

During Prohibition, the young Costello supervised the sale of alcoholic beverages to high-end speakeasies and private parties on Park Avenue and Long Island. Then he turned his attention to various gambling enterprises, eventually becoming one of the major forces behind the Mafia's single most profitable American enterprise—Las Vegas, Nevada, the oasis in the sand upon which organized crime began construction in the forties. It would be decades yet before the expression "If you build it, they will come" became part of the national lexicon from the movie *Field of Dreams*, but it quickly would apply to Las Vegas. It did not take long for the city to become the most glamorous urban locale in the United States, despite being situated in the most barren surroundings.

All in all, Costello was putting together an impressive curriculum vitae, especially when one considered that, during a prison stay as a child he took an IQ test and scored 97!

Costello was a man of habit, of routine, slipping into it as easily as the suits that were so exquisitely tailored for him and the shoes of finest leather that were shined for him daily. He and a bookkeeper who was one of his criminal associates "liked to start off their day in the Waldorf [Astoria Hotel] with a shave and manicure in the mirrored opulence of the barbershop . . . and the barbershop became an informal headquarters."

Soon other associates, among them his friend and the other most esteemed underworld figure, Meyer Lansky, joined Costello to neaten up in the morning. Because the seats at the Waldorf were leather, they provided the mobsters with comfort. Because they were angled to face the front door, they provided a good view of the street, so they could see—and draw their weapons in time for—the approach of rival gangsters with guns.

In addition to being a man of routine, Costello was a man of principle, at least as he defined the term. He had friends who made their money from narcotics and prostitution, and he did not hold their vocational choices against them. He, however, preferred the "clean" rackets, the numerous opportunities provided by gambling, from punch cards to horse racing, from casino games to lotteries to numbers.

And Costello continued to play his own kind of numbers game with fate. In addition to eschewing a weapon, he declined the use of a standard, Mafia-issued, bulletproof limousine, instead choosing to make his way around Manhattan on foot or in a taxi, as might an ordinary man of commerce.

He did not, however, appear like an ordinary, unarmed New Yorker. His features drooped; his eyes, cheeks, and nose seeming to have melted down a little. And "with black hair brushed straight back from his forehead, brown eyes, and creases around his thin lips," he appeared dubious about all he saw. "His nose was sharp and gave him a Cyrano de Bergerac look."

The look of his residence was notable, too. "His apartment was a seven-room penthouse on the eighteenth floor [of 115 Central Park West] . . . The living room was enormous, with antique gold hangings with scalloped valences, lamp tables of beautiful mahogany, antique lamps, and a wood-burning fireplace with a Howard Chandler Christy oil painting above it."

Perhaps his most notable feature was the result of an accident that infuriated Costello so much he gave serious thought to ending a surgeon's life. He had had an operation to remove a tumor—benign, apparently—from his vocal cords, but the procedure did not turn out as it was supposed to; as a result, his voice developed a "husky and rasping" quality. It was, of course, appropriate; no matter how dandified he might be in his manner, a tough guy always should be able to call up his natural self, someone with whom lesser mortals, and that was just about everyone, would not dare to trifle. Costello had his voice to remind others who he was. But he did not need special effects. If he knew you well enough to speak to you, you knew the kind of man he was.

The former Francesco Castiglia was the éminence grise of organized crime, in large part because he organized it to run more efficiently than ever before. He was as much a CEO as a prime minister. By the time 1957 came along, he had managed to trod the Earth for sixty-six years—a remarkable display of longevity for a man in his field. In fact, according to statistics of the time, sixty-six years was precisely the life span for an insurance adjuster, an elementary school principal, or a carpenter. Frankie Costello had beaten the odds. But it seemed, on the night of May second, that he would beat them no longer.

Costello and his friend Phil Kennedy, the owner of a Manhattan modeling agency, were having a late dinner at a restaurant in the theater district. As the evening wore on, and as always happened, they were joined by others who wanted to be seen in the Mafioso's company, including the publisher and owner of the *National Enquirer*. But at ten thirty or so, the night still young and more hangers-on sure to begin hovering, Costello said a reluctant good night. He had to go home to take an eleven o'clock phone call from the famed Washington, D.C., attorney Edward Bennett Williams, who would one day own the Redskins and Baltimore Orioles. He told his companions he looked forward to seeing them again soon.

Kennedy decided to leave, too, and accompanied Costello outside, hailing a cab for him. Because the two men lived within a few blocks of each other, they shared the ride home. But someone would have accompanied Costello regardless, usually more than one person; he was not left alone on the sidewalks of New York whether it was night or day; rain, snow, or clear. He was too valuable to be left unattended.

Costello was the first stop. As the cab pulled up to the curb in front of his apartment, he dropped some bills into Kennedy's lap and slipped out of the backseat, striding into his apartment lobby. He pushed the "up" button on the elevator and listened to it rattle toward him.

It was then that he heard another sound, this one off to his side, like the explosion of a firecracker. But it wasn't. It was too short for that. And could have been deadly. A "washed-up boxer named Vincent Gigante" had "rushed through the door" of the apartment building behind Costello; he "held in his right hand a .38-caliber revolver" and "fired a single shot."

"This is for you, Frank," Gigante said, and dashed back outside, into a Cadillac that was waiting for him, having pulled up as the cab departed. It became a famous line in the world of organized crime, although as irony more than anything else. "This is for you, Frank," words that could be uttered lightheartedly because . . .

> By flinching and turning at the right moment, Costello avoided the potentially lethal trajectory of the bullet, which punctured the front of his fedora and exited out the back. The single bullet skimmed the skin on Costello's skull above the right ear and then struck the lobby wall. Miraculously, aside from a slight head wound, Costello was not seriously hurt. But Kennedy, alerted by the shot, ran back into the lobby and found Costello nursing his wound with a bloodstained handkerchief.
>
> "Someone tried to get to me!" Costello cried out as he sat on a leather couch in the lobby.

Kennedy called an ambulance, and Costello was rushed to the emergency room of nearby Roosevelt Hospital, where he learned that the bullet had not only missed a vital zone, it had done little more than graze his hair, giving him a second part; he was bloody, but not excessively so, and not seriously injured. His head was cleaned and bandaged, but before he could leave the hospital, the police arrived. Costello, eager to return to his apartment, and despite the doctors' orders to spend the night for observation, invoked yet another underworld equivalent of the Fifth Amendment. "I didn't see nothing," he told the cops and anyone else who would ask later. And he probably didn't; the shooter was standing in darkness and had fired at his target's profile as Costello was facing the elevators.

The next day, the injured man was visited at home by more policemen, these from the organized crime detail, and so probably acquaintances of Costello. "I don't know who could have done it," he told them, repeating the answer several times. Then, as if trying to top himself, he came out with "I don't have an enemy in the world." He meant it as a declaration of innocence, but it played better as a punch line.

Costello knew who was behind the hit. He was certain of it, perhaps even expected it. But like all Mafia business, he saw it as a matter of personal concern, not public. He would keep the name of the man who ordered the transgression to himself. And he would mete out justice himself.

In 1957, Vito Genovese was known, with some hyperbole, as the "Boss of all Bosses." A fierce, frenzied, wealthy, gun-toting lout, Genovese headed several Mafia families; unlike Costello, he did not waste his time on "clean" trade. In fact, along with his partner, Charles "Lucky" Luciano, Genovese was responsible for expanding organized crime's heroin distribution from America to most of the rest of the world. Decades later, Microsoft and Apple could have learned from the Mafia's business plan. Genovese and Luciano were as efficient in their "dirty" work as Costello was in his "clean."

That Genovese put out the contract on Costello might have been obvious to the victim and certain of his high-ranking colleagues, but the police never considered him a suspect; after all, Costello and Genovese were not competitors, at least not directly. Which perhaps gives a clue to motive: Genovese and Luciano, having become masters of their specialty, might have wanted to add Costello's business to their empire. "Dirty" *and* "clean"—they would have it all! Megalomania, after all, is not a disease that goes into remission; rather, it is an ailment constantly feeding on itself.

But there are more questions, the biggest of all being why Genovese had assigned the hit to a gunman either so nervous or optically challenged that he barely hit his prey from a distance of a few feet. Was it supposed to be a warning rather than a murder? What if the clown got lucky and *did* kill Costello? Even the don couldn't figure that one out. Some people speculated that no one really wanted to fire on a man such as the Prime Minister, much less kill him, so the assignment kept getting passed down the line of command until it reached rock bottom. The rock was turned over and up lumbered Gigante, ready for action. He dusted himself off, loaded his pistol, and, one imagines, tried to stop shaking. His name does not arise again in the history of underworld vengeance.

But *did* he load his pistol? *Fully* load it? Another mystery neither Costello nor anyone else could figure out was why he only fired one shot. Was Gigante foolish enough to have taken on his mission with only a single bullet at the ready? For a gunman of such limited ability, that could have been fatally lethargic thinking. But if the .38 *held* more bullets, why didn't he keep squeezing the trigger? Did he think he had scored a bull's-eye? Or was it that Gigante's first and only shot had so thoroughly sapped his courage that he went from washed-up boxer to washed-up assassin in a matter of seconds? He could, after all, accurately report that he had hit his target.

Ultimately, though, the Prime Minister saw no reason to waste time on what hadn't happened. It was not the way of so practical a man. He hadn't been killed, thank the Holy Trinity, and quickly returned to his normal round of activities, not the kind of more cautious lifestyle that might be expected of someone who had just come within an inch of losing his life. He resumed his morning shave and manicure, cabs to and from dinners and meetings with his partners in clean crime, and evenings at the theater or Carnegie Hall, the typical life of a successful New York man about town.

Police officials, however, assigned two beat cops to keep an eye on him for a few days. They were well hidden, but Costello, with a sixth sense for these things, knew they were there. Actually, he didn't need a sixth sense, for he also knew the way cops operated.

So, on the first day of the vigil, the chap with the bandaged head, ever the gentleman, decided to have a word with the blue suits tailing him. And, as was his way, it was a cordial word. He opened his apartment door and, even though the cops were around the corner of the hallway and out of sight, he turned in their direction and wished them a good morning. Unnerved, they did not respond. Then he invited them in for breakfast with his wife and him. Probably even more unnerved, they might have stared at each other wide-eyed, wondering what to make of such an invitation. Surely they shouldn't be accepting hospitality from one of the most elite criminals in the United States, should they?

But Costello already knew they were watching him, reporting on his every move; the tail was no secret. Therefore, they decided, they had no reason to starve while standing idly about. The two law officers took off their hats, wiped their feet on the welcome mat, and entered the casa Costello for a morning meal.

One of the cops, Costello learned, was a countryman named Ralph Salerno. According to journalist Selwyn Raab, "the unruffled Costello bantered with him. 'What's an Italian boy like you doing with all these Irish cops?' Costello is said to have asked. 'They pay you peanuts. Come along with us. We pay bananas and they come in big bunches.'"

The cop, so far as anyone knows, stayed with the force, and he and his partner remained in the Costello apartment until their subject left, whereupon they, too, departed, the two officers of the law looking for all the world like the gangster's personal escorts.

Frank Costello died of a heart attack a decade and a half after the attempted murder. As the end approached, he had begun to collaborate with author Peter Maas, "who earned fame with previous crime books like *The Valachi Papers* and *Serpico*. Maas knew from his earlier works the institutional history of the Mafia and saw the unprecedented power of Costello and his unique in American history. Both men met and talked for hours with an eye toward a blockbuster." And their book surely would have been that.

But Costello's heart gave out before the men's dreams could be realized. He was eighty-two years old when he passed, and his courtly behavior toward all of his teammates, except the Genoveses, remained intact to the end. It would have given him pleasure, but not surprised him, to know that his obsequies were attended by New York's crème de la crème, most of whom seemed genuinely moved by his passing. The prevailing sentiment was that there would never be another like him. So far, there hasn't.

If Costello was a gentleman—let us imagine him as the guest of honor at a formal dinner, white-tied and tailed, in a private room in one of New York's finest dining spots. Albert Anastasia, then, may be pictured as a butcher in the back, meat cleaver in hand, bloody apron across his girth, rendering large animals into raw but humanly edible portions.

The preceding portrayal notwithstanding, Anastasia is a lovely name, once belonging to the last of the Russian grand duchesses, and for that reason, later belonging to Ingrid Bergman, who played her in a 1956 movie. In 2018, an elegant Broadway version of the film opened on Broadway. Nothing about Albert was elegant; curly-haired and stone-faced, he was perhaps the most savage human being ever employed in the nation's most savage trade. Even his fellow gangsters proceeded carefully in his company. They thought him deranged; he was "the Mad Hatter," the "Lord High Executioner"—but never called either to his face. Anastasia would put a bullet through a man's forehead as casually as others might flick an ash from a cigarette. And once he discharged the bullet, he sometimes remained to watch its effect, his pleasure at knowing he had ended a man's life only increasing "by his psychopathic enjoyment of watching suffering victims die." Slowly . . . Albert always wanted his victims to die slowly.

No one knows what his IQ was, but it is likely that Costello dwarfed him. Anastasia was paid labor, little more. He could no more have run the Mafia than men such as Costello and Meyer Lansky could murder with "psychopathic enjoyment" of the sight. But, as the two dons knew, they could not make the Mafia operate as efficiently as it did without men such as Albert and his equally conscienceless boss, Luciano, providing backup. The most necessary evils, the men might have been, of an occupation that itself was necessarily evil.

A native of Calabria, Italy, close enough to the Sicilian border for his sons to be considered Cosa Nostra, Umberto Luciano and his family immigrated from their native land when Albert was seventeen. There were five Anastasia boys. One became a priest and returned to Italy. Three became punks of an ordinary sort. The fifth became the Lord High Executioner. Within two years of having been extended a welcome at Ellis Island, and not yet having reached his twenties, Albert had committed his first murder, killing a fellow longshoreman in a quarrel whose subject is no longer remembered.

Sentenced to death, he was shuttled off to Sing Sing, not far from the United States Military Academy at West Point, to await his demise. Due to a technicality, however, Anastasia had to be given a second trial, and by then four of the witnesses who had testified against him the first time had disappeared. None of their bodies ever was found.

The result of the retrial, and its paucity of evidence, was that Anastasia was ordered to spend two years behind bars for illegal possession of a firearm. It was a misdemeanor, not even a felony, and the law could inflict no greater penalty under the circumstances. What a great country, this America, the young man must have thought! Who needed streets paved with gold when you could serve two years in prison for murdering someone and then seeing to the murders of anyone who could implicate you?

Five years after his release, and by now one of the heads of the International Longshoreman's Association, Anastasia again was convicted of taking a life and again released because witnesses either vanished or decided it would not be in their best interests to appear in court.

Before long, Albert joined Lucky as one of two men in charge of all underworld enforcement and was made the boss of a subdivision of the Mafia that became known as Murder, Incorporated. What it meant was that Anastasia now had achieved managerial status and no longer had to make the kill himself all the time. Nor did he have to squeeze a neck to the breaking point, a task he sometimes had performed in the past. Of course, his new position was a mixed blessing, as Anastasia always had enjoyed being a hands-on kind of guy.

Instead, he was ordered to order others to take lives on behalf of the mob. He convinced himself that his life would be easier this way, but he was not consoled. The problem was that the executive's life was not altogether satisfying for a psychopath. Albert did manage to save a few choice liquidations for himself, however, and had to admit that he enjoyed being more selective about his prey. He farmed out small-time hits to his subordinates; his victims were now exclusively men of rank.

Murder, Inc.! The newspapers loved it. So cold was the notion of death as an American industry, a bureaucracy of violence—so gripping was it, a big black headline just waiting to happen. As a name to inspire fear, the Mad Bomber of New York had nothing on Albert's boys, which even became the subject of a book published in 1951 called *Murder, Inc.* The coauthor, Burton B. Turkus, was a former assistant district attorney who had somehow managed to survive his authorship, perhaps because Anastasia was pleased at having made inroads into the literary world.

Turkus described Albert aptly as "the one who got away" from punishment, claiming that "this hard-mouthed, curly haired hoodlum has been close to some thirty assassinations with gun and ice pick and strangling rope, either in person or by direction. . . . The killings claimed by the torpedoes of the troop he commanded ran well into the three figures." Yet he probably served less time for more brutality than any other figure in the world of organized crime.

But even before his exploits had been memorialized between hard covers (and in 1960 there would even be a movie about Murder, Inc., with a gruff, gray-haired actor named Howard Smith playing the role of Anastasia), it might have been that the Mad Hatter felt not only pride but pressure; after all, he had begun to arouse envy among some of his fellow assassins, and a gunman has no more dangerous enemy than another gunman who is jealous of him. Having heard a rumor that Vincent "The Executioner" Mangano and his brother Philip had put out a contract on him, Anastasia struck preemptively. On the same day, Philip was murdered and Vincent disappeared, never to be seen again.

As 1957 approached, Albert Anastasia's luck was beginning to turn, as it almost always did for people in his line of work. He was getting into too many arguments, expressing too much dissatisfaction with his lot, and to the wrong people.

The mob's single greatest source of income in those days, with Las Vegas still in the growth stages, was Havana, the Cuban capital, which had reached its maturity years earlier and since become the world's first Mafia-run city. But Anastasia was dissatisfied "with the division of spoils in Havana. [He] didn't think he was getting his fair share and had apparently let his discontent be known. It was causing a ripple of concern among members of the Havana Mob." And, as those members well knew, Anastasia was not a man who would stop at mere ripples.

Three weeks after the sky had begun to beep, and just as Sputnik's battery was about to give up so that it would be silent again, Meyer Lansky, ever the diplomat, summoned "his number one boy," Santo Trafficante. He told him to meet with Anastasia, try to talk some sense into his head. He was stirring up too much dissension in the ranks, both Lansky and Costello believed, and that was not good for business.

The problem was, trying to talk sense to Albert Anastasia was like trying to reason with an inanimate object. Few even had bothered to try. But Lansky thought he had the solution: Offer Anastasia a bribe, he told Trafficante, a bigger cut of the Havana proceeds than he previously had been receiving. Specifically, Santo was to offer Albert the entire proceeds from the casinos and showrooms of the Havana Hilton. It was, by any reckoning, a substantial inducement.

Any reckoning, that is, except Anastasia's. He refused the peace offering angrily. He might not be the shiniest card in the deck, but he knew what he was worth, or thought he did, and would hold out for the proper amount.

It was not a wise decision. As the expression goes, he had just signed his own death warrant.

Trafficante reported back to Lansky. Their offer only had made the Mad Hatter madder. Lansky shook his head ruefully and reported back to Costello. Trafficante already had packed his bags, and, after having delivered the bad news to his boss, departed to catch a flight to Florida on his way back to Havana. It was a trip he made frequently; he was the mob's eyes and ears in the Cuban capital, where there was much to see and hear at this time.

As for Anastasia, needing to cool off after having been so grievously undervalued, he decided to treat himself to the official Mafia means of relaxation. He "walked to the nearby Park Sheraton Hotel for a haircut and shave. He had been sitting in the barber's chair for ten minutes, relaxing with a hot towel over his face to soften his rough beard, when two masked men—allegedly a pair of swells named Larry and Joseph Gallo—walked into the barbershop and opened fire with automatic handguns."

Anastasia was dead immediately. With the towel over their victim's face, the Gallos hardly needed their masks.

Even though most Mafiosi realized that a loose cannon such as Anastasia could easily go too far one day, and that he might have to be silenced before he brought the whole organization tumbling down, the Park Sheraton hit was one of seismic proportions. If the underworld's most diabolical killer could himself be exterminated, what did that mean for the rest of his associates in crime should they happen to step out of line? And who was to decide when someone had taken that step?

At any rate, there was no proof that Costello, Lansky, or anyone else in the world had demanded the end of the man who put the "murder" in Murder, Inc. As for those who could have provided testimony, they were like Costello after Gigante's errant shot: they "didn't see nothing."

Anastasia's death, and the feeble attempt to inflict a similar fate on the Prime Minister, both of which took place before the Apalachin Conference, were yet more reasons for this year's get-together—perhaps the most important reasons of all. Something was amiss in the precincts of organized crime, and too much was at stake not to fix the problem as quickly as possible. As strange as it sounds, the Mafia was getting too violent.

But the Apalachin confab was broken up before it even started. Nobody knew it at the time, of course, but with six weeks left in 1957, the worst year it had ever known had ended. There would be no more feuds festering, no more insurrections. To recap: Dave Beck—embezzlement of union funds. Jimmy Hoffa—links with Mafia confirmed. Frank Costello—could easily have crossed the great divide. Albert Anastasia—*did* cross the great divide. The Apalachin Conference—raided before anything could be accomplished.

Thank God for Havana.

It is a digression, but an irresistible one, to point out that another thug of sorts also died in 1957, on the same day as Anastasia, and this man's passing received far more attention from both journalists and readers than did Murder, Inc.'s master of the trade.

This man was a criminal who did not use a gun. Instead, he used his mouth, and with it uttered some of the most toxic lies ever made public, taken seriously, in American history. He did not kill people; he destroyed their good names. He called them communists, subversives, a threat to everything our nation stood for. He claimed he had firsthand knowledge of card-carrying agents of the Soviet Union employed by the State Department, people who were making policy under the guidance of their Kremlin masters. He swore it. He had a list. But he was lying. "He had no list," writes historian Jill Lepore. "He had nothing but imaginary pink underwear."[1]

Actually, a few of his victims *did* pass away, committing suicide after their reputations had been battered to the point at which they could no longer find either friends or employment, or any meaning in life. The most famous such victim probably was the actor Philip Loeb, known to millions as the oft-irked husband Jake of Molly on the early television hit *The Goldbergs*. For no substantial reason, he was listed as a communist in the McCarthy-inspired publication "Red Channels" and was dismissed from the show by its sponsor, General Foods. He was paid a handsome severance, more than $377,000 in today's money, but he was in debt at the time; the money did not last, and he could not add to it. No one else would hire him, not even for the smallest part, and he needed to be hired—not only because of the money he owed, but because he loved his work and was the sole support of a mentally ill son. In September 1955, he was finally broken. By then, television, radio, and theatrical executives refused even to talk to him; he secreted himself in a Manhattan hotel room and one day, before the month was out, swallowed a bottle of sleeping pills.

As for those more fortunate than Loeb and able to find employment, they often were reduced to menial positions, poverty-level work. For some tasks, they could no longer use their real names; paychecks came only under the cover provided by aliases.

In addition, this criminal who never was commonly regarded as such, never at risk of incarceration, this man who somehow held the title of United States Senator from Wisconsin, boosted the Cold War paranoia. His intention, he said, was to weaken the growing power of communism under the red, white, and blue. In reality, he aided the hammer and sickle by making communism seem much more prevalent in the United States than it really was. Otherwise, why would a man of his eminence talk about it so much, accuse so many of being adherents?

Because he did, and because so many Americans were easily frightened in the postwar era, when he ran for reelection in 1952, he won 52 percent of Wisconsin's vote. He had received democracy's seal of approval for another term of continued combat with the red menace. It was combat

1. The reference is to communists sometimes being known as pinkos.

that weakened democracy's very foundations. It was counterproductivity in action.

One of the weapons in the man's arsenal was manipulation of the press. There was, for instance, his two-stories-for-the-price-of-one gambit, neither of them worth the newsprint. He would summon reporters to his office in the morning, telling them he would have a major announcement later in the day. The story would make the afternoon papers. Then, in the afternoon, he would make a minor announcement, dressed up in bluster and often fallacious. The story would run the next morning. He was impossible to avoid, a master of piling up column inches.

When Joseph Raymond McCarthy died, after ailing for a long period, "officials [at Maryland's Bethesda Naval Hospital] listed the cause of death as 'acute hepatic failure' . . . They would not elaborate further." *Time* magazine, however, would. It "reported unequivocally that Joe died of cirrhosis of the liver." In other words, he died of alcoholism, after years of increasingly drunken behavior and alcohol-addled accusations in public.

By this time, even journalists who initially had supported him were able to do so no longer. Publications throughout the United States and Europe, usually gracious to the deceased, "discussed the passing of a ruthless demagogue who had threatened American civil liberties, savaged government employees, and damaged the nation's image abroad."

A few papers, though, including New Hampshire's comically right-wing rag, the *Manchester Union-Leader*, presented a different view. In capital letters, to underscore what likely would have been the senator's version of truth, and the decibel level with which he would have expressed it had he been able, the journal editorialized, "McCarthy was murdered by the communists because he was exposing them when he began to arouse the United States to the extent of the communist conspiracy in our government, in our schools, in our newspapers, and in all branches of American life."

Was there any truth in the *Union-Leader's* screed? Yes, of a sort; throw a handful of sand into the air, and, if you look carefully, you'll see a few granules glitter in the sun. But they are not gold. Some of the people McCarthy accused of being communists actually *were* communists, but in virtually all of these cases the State Department knew about them and already had begun investigating. In a few other cases, offenders had been removed from governmental positions before McCarthy even heard of them. And in a few others, the offenders were spared vituperation by having died.

And many whom McCarthy had accurately identified as communists or commie sympathizers did not hold positions of influence. They could not threaten the security of the United States even if they had so desired. For all of the geopolitical influence they had, they might have been members of the Flat Earth Society. Most in this category held onto their vocations, and America was none the worse for it. The milk, after all, tastes just as sweet when brought to the door by a fellow advocating the overthrow of capitalism.

In retrospect, it is apparent that all too many of the names McCarthy smeared were simply everyday Americans, going about their jobs without doing harm to anyone, regardless of their ideologies, until their positions were taken from them by employers fearful of incurring McCarthy's wrath. And when he did, the harm that these everyday Americans did to no one was instead done to them.

There was more than one way for a man to organize his crime.

The state of Nevada had legalized gambling as early as 1931. But more than a decade had passed, and its largest city, little more than a village compared to cities on the two coasts, had not become the tourist attraction for which elected officials and would-be moguls had hoped. The first few motels along what eventually would be known as the Strip had been built, and Clark Gable would drop in from time to time to relax between films; in 1942, he was staying at El Rancho Vegas when he learned that his wife, the actress Carole Lombard, had been killed in a plane crash as she was returning to Los Angeles after a war bond rally.

The following year, Betty Grable and bandleader Harry James were married at the Little Church of the West, an adjunct of Las Vegas's Hotel Last Frontier. But, with few exceptions, that brings the city's celebrity roster close to an end.

The town had a few other lodgings, as well as the inevitable bed-by-the-hour roadhouses and some low-rent casinos; other than that, though, Las Vegas had little to offer. Bars, yes, but one could find a place to drink anywhere. The same with restaurants and swimming pools; these attractions were no reasons to drive into the desert, especially because the restaurants weren't much more than diners, the pools small and often overly chlorinated. Other than gambling, the city in the sand had none of the attractions of Los Angeles, with which it was hoping to compete someday, even though it was 270 miles away.

But by the mid-forties, a postwar building boom was under way in Las Vegas, with the Mafia having decided to move in and make the city its first-ever urban renewal project. In charge was Benjamin "Bugsy" Siegel; a more unlikely choice cannot be imagined. One of organized crime's most infamous denizens, he ranked with Albert Anastasia for inflicting heartless violence. For rugged good looks, though, Siegel was in a category of his own. "The most fascinating young man," he was to screenwriter Anita Loos, "tall, dark, and rather Italian in appearance." Warren Beatty would play him in a 1991 movie.

Once, in either a confessional frame of mind or perhaps a spurt of braggadocio, he told Lansky that he had murdered at least a hundred people in his life. It was like breathing, he said, just something he did; a tug on the index finger, and another fellow human being breathed no more. But, unlike Anastasia, Siegel could pass for sane, not to mention affable, when the occasion called for it. He "dressed up well," as today's expression has it.

So he ended up putting away his gun for a while when, for some reason, the Mafia chose him to supervise construction of Las Vegas's first superhotel, a towering structure, modern to a fault and the first to have its own casinos on the premises. Siegel's mistress at the time was a gun moll whose life is sadly but accurately summed up in the title of her biography by Andy Edmonds, *Bugsy's Baby: The Secret Life of Mob Queen Virginia Hill*. Because of her long legs and red hair, she was known as "The Flamingo." It was in her honor that Nevada's grandest new structure was named.

It was budgeted for a generous $1.2 million, but Bugsy was a bigger thinker than that. He enjoyed doing such things with money as losing it by the tens of thousands of dollars at craps tables and stuffing it by the hundreds into the cleavage of virtually any woman whose chest appeared near his hand. And, for the ultimate in fiduciary enjoyment, he determined to build a hotel like none that the western United States—perhaps even the Western Hemisphere—had ever seen before. His success was extraordinary. So were his costs. The final price tag for The Flamingo was $6 million, five times the allotted amount. Never before had anyone played so fast and loose with so much Mafia money. From back East, where the accountants kept the ledgers, came rumblings of serious discontent.

But,' ultimately, there seemed no reason for them. Despite Bugsy's profligacy, the hotel was out of the red more quickly than had been anticipated, even at its swollen cost, a remarkable feat. And almost every time someone pulled the handle of a slot machine, something that happened thousands of times a day at The Flamingo, the sovereigns of the underworld grew even richer—in large part because "Benny Siegel was alive with new ideas. Midweek bingo games were instituted to entice locals . . . and Benny was in the hotel every night . . . meeting, greeting, and charming, charming, charming."

The triumph that was The Flamingo proved to be the inspiration for a burst of more construction in the desert; one day's foundation was being laid in the previous day's sand dune. By the early fifties, Bugsy's palace was surrounded by other hotels and motels, nightclubs and strip joints and restaurants, barbershops and nail salons, massage parlors and tobacconists, office buildings and, off at the fringes, homes that were better described as mansions, with ever more cement continuing to smother the dry earth.

Whether Bugsy ever intended to live in one of these dwellings is not certain. But he never was given the chance. On a damp night in the summer of 1947, about six months after The Flamingo had opened and as Bugsy was still bathing in the reports he was sent of nightly profits, he sat comfortably in the living room of his own Flamingo, Miss Hill, who, in addition to her residence in Las Vegas, also owned a house in Beverly Hills. A business associate of Siegel also sat in the Hill living room but on the other side of a long coffee table. It was a fortunate placement, for Bugsy lounged in an easy chair that was squarely in the crosshairs of a .30 caliber M1 carbine. The man who aimed it stood unseen in darkness on the front lawn.

His target barely moved; he might have been nodding off. For the man with the carbine, the hoodlum could not have been an easier target. The man opened fire and shattered the night. He didn't stop until he had squeezed the trigger more times than investigators could later count, blasting through the front window as if it hadn't been there. He might have set a Mafia record for most bullets ever expended on a single target. Among other damage inflicted, they would "smash in Benny's left eye, crush the bridge of his nose, and shatter a vertebra at the back of his neck. His right eye was blown out completely, and was later found fifteen feet away from his body."

Siegel's business partner had dived off his sofa as the shooting began, scrambling for safety and emerging terrified but unhurt in the kitchen. It is not certain whether Miss Hill was home at the time, nor if she was, what she was doing or how she reacted.

It was a typical Mafia hit in that no one ever could prove the who or why. The why might have been that Bugsy was stealing from the mob, pocketing some of The Flamingo's profits, believing they were owed to him because of the hotel's runaway success. Or it might have been that he was showing off just a little too much to suit his more conservative padrones in crime. Or, another guess, the Mafia bean counters, who seldom had any input when it came to operational decisions, simply could not forgive the cost overruns on The Flamingo; the men with the account books might have persuaded the men with the guns that an example had to be set for future contractors, who were unlikely to be as fortunate in profligacy as Siegel had been with The Flamingo.

To this day, the murder of Benjamin "Bugsy" Siegel remains officially unsolved.

Still, his fate had been the most unfortunate of ironies. He had started something more lucrative than anyone could have imagined. By the mid-fifties, it was not just The Flamingo that was enriching underworld coffers; it was the entire city that surrounded it, a solid gold oasis, the first-ever Mafia theme park. It was as well an investment that outdid anything Wall

Street could have offered, glittering under the exotic desert sun, a mirage made blindingly real.

But it could not yet compare to Las Vegas South, basking so profitably in the Caribbean.

Fulgencio Batista, of Spanish, African, Chinese, and Taino descent, the latter being a now-extinct tribe of Caribbean Indians whom Columbus met on his first voyage to the New World, was "El Mulatto Lindo." It means "the pretty person of both black and white ancestry." The nickname's connotation of effeminacy, however, could not have been more inappropriate.

In 1957, Batista was well into his second term as the president of Cuba, although dictator is the more fitting term, and tyrant even better suits him. The hardships he imposed on the island's peasants were back breaking and spirit crushing. They went from birth to death in unending poverty and toil, with no chance of bettering either themselves or their children. Hope was a curse, a feeling that the islanders did not dare to consider.

From morning to night, most of the Cuban population worked the land, farmed it under a sun set to medium bake, almost beyond mortal endurance. They pulled loose the island's most valuable export, the sugar cane used in distilling rum; then they bundled it, crushed it, boiled it, and filtered it until it was ready to make fortunes for the few, beverages for the many, and for themselves, the men and women of the fields, barely a living wage. Some farms had mechanical harvesting devices, but they were limited in what they could do; more than half of the island's cane had to be harvested by hand. Those who did the harvesting were religious. They did not pray for salvation, though, for that would have required hope. No, they prayed for rain. A downpour would not only cool them off, but loosen the roots of the cane, making it easier to tug the crop from the earth.

Other Cubans slaved in oil refineries, where the stink could be worse than the demands of the labor, although the labor would have been bad enough if performed in a rose garden. The oilmen spent their days handling fifty-gallon drums: filling them, rolling them, pushing them up splintered wooden ramps into the backs of trucks or train cars. Their skin became slick, slimy, resistant to soap; so much oil was in the air that men could taste it. They took it home with them. Their clothes, their families, their shanties—all were the products of petroleum.

And then there were the master Cuban tobacconists. Such a glamorous product they made. Such unremitting drudgery they suffered. They worked in unventilated rooms, creating the cigars for which the tiny nation was known worldwide. After enough years on the job, some men were able to produce cigars without even looking, and so quickly that it seemed as though their fingers were performing magic tricks, making stuffed, ripe cylinders out of flat sheets of tobacco. Meanwhile the smell and tints of the world's best leaves—formed into fillers, wrappers, and binders—had become ingrained in their flesh, their hands long since having turned a darker shade than the rest of their bodies. And their fingers smelled as if their tips could be struck with a match and inhaled, satisfying the most discerning of aficionados. It could have been worse. They preferred the scent of tobacco to that of oil.

The Cubans did what Batista ordered them to do, but the man was a sycophant as well as a despot and did what Trafficante and Lansky ordered *him* to do. In fact, Batista was as enthusiastic about following instructions from his gangster supervisors as he was about taking their bribes, for to show them obeisance was to bathe himself in the reflection of the Mafia's regal status on the island.

The contrast between Cuba for the Cubans and Cuba for Americans and other wealthy tourists was stark, barbarous. It seemed that the island was, in fact, two islands. One of them was described by a visitor as "a mistress of pleasure, the lush and opulent goddess of delights." This Cuba was a hedonist's pleasure like no other on Earth.

According to the American intellectual Susan Sontag, Batista presided over "a country known mainly for dance, music, prostitutes, cigars, abortions, resort life, and pornographic movies."

And playwright Arthur Miller, accompanied in Havana by his tourist attraction of a wife, Marilyn Monroe, described the city as "a Mafia playground, a bordello for Americans and other foreigners."

Yet they came, as did many others, and rode waves of illicit excitement from one dawn to the next. Among the more famous people to be seen in Havana in those days, in addition to the preceding, were Marlon Brando and Frank Sinatra with his on-again, off-again spouse, Ava Gardner. Ernest Hemingway was a more frequent sight because he had a home ten miles east of Havana; Finca La Vigia, he called it, meaning "lookout house." And movie star George Raft was the most easily spotted. Raft had played a gangster in so many films that eventually he was granted honorary Mafia membership and allowed to be a part-time errand boy for hoodlums who needed help with their chores. Often, he was put to work as a greeter at one of the hotels, standing outside in a white dinner jacket, shaking hands with his right as cigarette after cigarette burned down in the left.

Among Havana's leading entertainers in these glory days were Nat King Cole, Eartha Kitt, and Dizzy Gillespie and his band, all of whom, being of African American descent, made a lot more money and performed a lot more often in Havana than they could have done in the United States. The Caribbean had no discrimination.

Flights to Cuba were cheap, in some cases $50 for a round trip from Miami. Depending on where you lived in America, the island capital could be a less expensive destination than Las Vegas.

Hotel rooms were also cheap, even at such Xanadus of accommodation as the Nacional, the San Miguel, the Habana Libre—and the hotels themselves were large and elegant, priding themselves on their casinos and floor shows that would dazzle even Busby Berkeley. Spectacles such as these, albeit on a smaller scale, were also a point of pride at Havana's countless nightclubs. Racetracks and sex shows were among the attractions, and huge, neon-lighted signs pointed the way from one form of debauchery to the next, twinkling even through the sunlight at noon, which sometimes awakened those who lived the nightlife.

The streets were a remarkable sight, crowded with old American cars, the kinds of gas-guzzling, tail-finned monstrosities that are so prized by U.S. collectors today: 1949 Cadillac Coupe de Villes, 1947 Bristol 400s, 1946 Plymouth De Luxes, and Chevrolet Fleetmasters of the same year, to name a few.

Later generations of these guilty pleasure automobiles still cruise the streets of a much more austere Havana today. In one sense, the sight is a melancholy one, with mid-twentieth-century vehicles crowding a now infirm twenty-first-century city. But the daily parades of these land yachts are, however inadvertently, a paean to Cuba's past splendors, and it is rare to see anyone in the old cars without a fresh, newly waxed smile, just as it is rare to see one of the cars with so much as a smudge of dirt, a scar of rust. Cubans to this day love their old American autos, treat them like idols on wheels. They are also the only kinds of cars most of them can afford.

Yet as the Mafia withdrew enormous sums of money from Las Vegas South, even if not enough to suit the wishes of the late Albert Anastasia, far more American money poured in. "The country's most precious resources—sugar, oil, forestry, agriculture, financial institutions, and public utilities—were all up for sale. Foreign capital washed over the island." Most of it came from the United States, and a good amount even was legitimate, as it was provided by corporations, lending firms, and in some cases from the federal government, which, to its everlasting shame, supported the Batista regime and its attendant cruelties.*

"It is true," says author T. J. English, who has written astutely about Cuba, "that Havana had one of the highest standards of living in all of Latin America, but this prosperity was not spread evenly through the nation. And as the decade wore on, the gulf between the haves and have-nots continued to widen." With this the United States was not concerned; all that mattered was that the have-nots resisted the propaganda of communist rebels, and under Batista, they had no choice. As for the haves, they already were on board.

---

*Among individual investors in Cuba in 1959 was John Foster Dulles, President Eisenhower's Secretary of State and model of rectitude.

And, of course, deposits large and small in the Cuban economy were left every minute of the day on casino tables by gamblers who had expected precisely the opposite result—a seven, an eleven, blackjack, a flush. It was "a Mafia playground" indeed, and no one had reason to think anything would change; the Havana branch of the American underworld counted on increasing prosperity into the 1960s and beyond; its members, after all, sat on the boards of the island's most important banks, industries, and businesses of all sorts.

What could go wrong?

Although the mob's main man in Cuba was Trafficante, it was with Lansky that Batista developed something of a friendship, based on both of them being self-made men, and both being committed bibliophiles. Lansky read daily, no matter what his duties were, and thrived on the feel of a book in his hands, the tingle of ideas and emotions wafting up from the page. As for el presidente, he "told the story of how, at the age of thirteen, he used his savings to purchase a biography of Abraham Lincoln. Batista became a great collector of books and would eventually compile what was believed to be the island's largest private library." He would never, however, at least as far as anyone knows, practice any of the lessons of Lincoln's life in his own. In fact, he would not even be aware that a civil war was fomenting in his own country until it was too late.

So Lanksy owned organized crime's most extensive private library, Batista the largest on his island. It is perversely amusing to imagine the scene: the gangster and his marionette sitting in one or the other of their studies, sipping brandies and smoking their cigars, debating the merits of a work of classic literature, or perhaps, as was beginning to happen in the United States, considering Ayn Rand's wildly controversial new book *Atlas Shrugged*. Although it was published late in the year, it immediately became '57's most talked-about volume.

> *This Galt, I admit he's a thoughtful fellow, Francesco, but I'm not that impressed.*
> *Why not?*
> *He cannot be governed. Let him stay in his valley, that's what I say.*
> *I don't know, Senor Presidente. I think some of his ideas are the solutions to some of America's most troublesome problems.*
> *Perhaps some. A few.*
> *I probably wouldn't handle them the way he did, but he's onto something, no doubt in my mind.*

Thus, the connections between the mob and the Cuban government were secured, both personally and professionally, financially and literarily. So powerful did this union become, and so offensive, at least to some Americans, that historian Arthur M. Schlesinger Jr. proclaimed, "The corruption of the [Cuban] government, the brutality of the police, the government's indifference to the needs of the people for education, medical care, housing, for social justice and economic justice . . . is an open invitation to revolution."

As far as the man hiding in the Sierra Maestra Mountains was concerned, he believed he had long since been invited. Believed, in fact, that history would commend him as the force responsible for the revolution and regard him as its star performer. But the timing had to be right. That is what he was waiting for, the precise moment to strike. And when it arrived, and he and his men were finished with el jefe and his henchmen, the rest of the century would belong to him.

He was right on all counts.

No one saw it coming.

Fidel Alejandro Castro Ruz's father was that rarest of Cubans, a *wealthy* sugar cane farmer. After a divorce, he fathered seven children out of wedlock with his mistress, Lina Ruz Gonzalez. Fidel was one of them, and like the other six became legitimized when father and paramour married.

The boy's life began promisingly. He was sent to the finest private schools on the island, and his father had the highest hopes for the young fellow. But even the Jesuits, who spared no rod and spoiled no child, seldom giving up on one, admitted they could do little if anything with young Fidel. His manners were defiant; his language, coarse. Even with his father's money, he often dressed as if he were a tenant farmer's pup, proud of his peasantry. His grades were poor, even though his intelligence wasn't, and what his teachers told him had no value to him other than as a soporific.

What the Jesuits didn't know was that if Fidel had been able to study Lenin, Marx, and Engels, the latter two the authors of the *Communist Manifesto*, he would have awakened with a start, and his name would have shone atop the honor roll. But it goes without saying that, under Batista, communists never were part of the curriculum.

Barely into adolescence, Fidel was a rebel without a cause only because he was too young to have figured out one. But he was looking, ever looking, and after a few years causes began coming to him in rapid succession, his fires constantly being stoked by having heard about this injustice or witnessed that one or read about yet another kind of perceived inequity. But he was not yet ready to wear the mantle of full-fledged rebel; his emotions were deeply engaged but his ideas scattered, in need of discipline.

Only when he took to the playing fields as a schoolboy, engaging in a number of sports. did Fidel seem to settle himself, to enjoy the activity and the company of his peers, the camaraderie of competition. Baseball was his favorite sport, not only his most consistent source of pleasure as a child, but his one reliable wellspring of contentment as an older man. He would sit in the stands, fondling a cigar and staring out from under his patrol cap, cheering on his favorite teams, the most skilled players.

He never acknowledged the irony. Fidel Castro did much to popularize baseball in Cuba, from the year he took over the country until the year he died, and the island might have produced more good players per capita than any other nation in the world. But many of its biggest stars over the years dreamed of escaping the reign of their most avid fan, longing to settle in baseball's homeland, being rewarded with the world's largest paychecks as they played before the world's largest crowds. And they dreamed, most importantly, of what happened in the United States when the bottom of the ninth ended, as not only the players but all of those men and women in the stands would leave the stadium and, blessed as they were with freedom, go wherever they wanted to go, do whatever they wanted to do.

It was for this reason that, as an older man, Castro seldom got to see his nation's best players on his diamond. Not all of them, not as they grew into athletic maturity at least, for some had realized their American dream. Either they were allowed to leave Cuba by legal means or they sneaked away under cover of night, thereby inspiring more to follow their example. In 2018, twenty-nine Cubans played baseball in the American and National Leagues. There was a time, long past, when Castro, too, fancied himself on a major league roster. But as much as he enjoyed baseball, it was merely a diversion for him; he was inspired to do more with his life than play games.

In his oral autobiography, for which a lackey named Ignacio Ramonet asked the questions and Castro provided the answers, he recalled his first show of defiance toward those who outranked him. In his early teens, he attended a school not only tedious but offensive because, at least in his opinion, it taught the virtues of American imperialism. And, so, he and some of his friends took action. "We'd made slingshots out of a forked branch of a guava tree and some strips of rubber," Castro told Ramonet. "There was a bakery nearby, and we took all the firewood for the oven and made ourselves a parapet, a fort, and we organized a bombardment that lasted half an hour . . . I thought it was wonderful! The rocks landing on that zinc roof . . . By the time two or three were hitting the roof, there'd be two or three more in the air—we considered ourselves experts at that. You couldn't even hear the yells and screams that we imagined the teacher was making for the noise of the rocks hitting that roof. . . . Oh, we were vengeful little devils."

One wonders what the bombardment of a Cuban bakery with rocks had to do with rage at American imperialism, but a boy who will one day be a vengeful big devil must start somewhere.

Years later, on July 26, 1953, after taking part in rebellions in Colombia and the Dominican Republic, Castro turned his attention to his own country and the despised President Batista, who seemed to Castro the true rebel, a man who had rebelled against the better interests of his people by selling them out to the forces of foreign capitalism. Only he, Castro had decided, could bring the good life to his homeland, and that meant the end of control from abroad.

A mere twenty-seven years old at the time, he led a ragtag gang of anti-imperialists in an assault on the Moncado[2] military barracks near Santiago, close to the point at which, half a century earlier, Theodore Roosevelt would become an American icon by steering the Rough Riders up one of the San Juan Hills in the Spanish-American War.

No such lionization awaited Castro. He and his men quickly were vanquished by government troops. One hundred sixty-five of them accompanied him to the barracks, and some were executed. Most, including Castro, were arrested and jailed. As for Batista, "[h]e showed no great signs of concern. The failed attack had been quelled with a minimum of military casualties. Batista denied that there had been any kind of 'massacre' of captured rebels; those who had survived and were in custody would be tried in a court according to Cuban law."

The real rulers of the island professed similar indifference. "To the mobsters, casino owners, and businessmen who oversaw commercial activity in Havana, the incident was little more than a distant echo. After all, the Moncado attack had taken place in Oriente, on the extreme far end of the island from Havana."

It seemed, as most in Cuba thought, "a minor affair." It was not. Castro put his incarceration to good use, conducting a graduate school of sorts. He taught his fellow prisoners the principles that were motivating him so strongly, the precepts he had taught himself when hiding in the Sierra Maestras, after having finally gotten his hands on copies of Marx, Lenin, and Engels. His men, many of them uneducated in the formal sense, proved to be surprisingly attentive pupils—and more; like their instructor, they became inflamed by what they were learning, by the notion that they could be part of history's large picture, making the future into something different from what it otherwise would be on their island, so much more livable for their families. An island so ripe for overthrow was the Mafia's Cuba.

Momentum was building. Men who already had the courage to fight now had added the philosophical underpinnings to understand precisely *why* they fought; to their resentment, inspired by government-enforced poverty, now was added an intellectual foundation. The combination made for a more effective fighting force than Castro previously had led—and, in fact, for a more effective military corps than Batista commanded. Castro named his newly educated comrades, and the great numbers he would add to them in the future, the July 26th Movement. The rebel had found his cause and would remain true to it for the rest of his life.

---

2. In some instances spelled "Moncada."

Upon being freed from jail, the surviving members of the movement began a campaign of guerrilla warfare against military outposts large and small. But unless necessary, they did not inflict casualties; rather, they sought weapons and ammunition, and they stole as much as they could carry or load onto mules, buckling the poor beasts at the knees. Before long, the rebels were as well armed as the government. The time was almost right.

Nineteen fifty-seven was not the year Castro gained control of Cuba, but the turning point, the year in which his forces reached full strength and, thus, the year Batista finally had to take the rebels seriously. It was also the year, as the dictator would learn, when it already was too late. A band of guerrillas not directly associated with Castro but certainly inspired by him, young men calling themselves the Student Revolutionary Directorate, attempted to break into the presidential palace in Havana and assassinate Batista. It was the most audacious act yet by those who opposed the president, and for the first time he and his American cohorts began to fear for their lives as well as their continued hegemony.

It was also in '57 that Batista, under siege militarily, found himself under siege journalistically. As a result, he began to censor the Cuban press. It must have seemed his only choice but was perhaps the biggest mistake he ever made, and it came at the most inopportune of times.

For a time, Castro's forces effectively cut off communication to and from the island. Unable to learn what was happening in any other way, the *New York Times* sent one of its most prominent correspondents, the liberal Herbert Matthews, to Havana. First, he interviewed Batista and was received warmly at the palace, where the incumbent's carefully rehearsed answers portrayed an imaginary Cuba, a fantasyland in which few of its citizens lived. Matthews listened politely and took notes. Seldom did he nod, though; little did he believe. When he asked Batista whether his country had more wealthy Americans than wealthy Cubans, Batista circled around an answer. He did not confirm that various factions in the United States were acting as string pullers in the Caribbean, but neither did he deny it.

Only when Batista insisted that the Mafia had no influence on the island did he really stumble. If that were true, Matthews wanted to know, who were the men inside all of these suits he saw?

What men?

The men in dark limousines and sunglasses, the ones placing the big bets in the casinos, the ones drinking with the celebrities after their shows, then escorting them back to their lavish hotel suites for post-party partying.

Batista acted as if he never had heard of such a thing. Tourists? Cuba, he insisted, attracted a high caliber of visitors.

Unsatisfied with answers such as these, which were beginning to mount, Matthews cut his interview short and departed for the far less glamorous headquarters of the tyrant's foe.

"Matthews was no neophyte," writes T. J. English; "he'd reported on Italian fascist Benito Mussolini's forays into North Africa and covered the Spanish Civil War for the *Times*. But the journalist obviously was dazzled by Castro. 'Taking him, as one would at first, by physique and personality, this was quite a man—a powerful six-footer, olive-skinned, full-faced, with a straggly beard,' wrote Matthews in the first of his three articles."

Matthews fell quickly under his subject's spell, something a chronicler of events must not do. His assignment was to provide accounts as objective as possible on the turmoil in Havana; rather, his dispatches were so subjective in places that they sounded more like press releases. Their lack of perspective could be appalling. To be fair, this is a judgment more easily reached in hindsight than at the time; in the fifties, virtually anyone who challenged the despot Batista was, ipso facto, granted a grace period. Still, Matthews's judgments marked the beginning of a long period of ignorance in the United States about what really was happening ninety miles offshore.

And those judgments infuriated Batista. But he dared not impose prohibitions on the American press; the coverage would only get less accurate and more negative, and the attention of reporters from around the world soon would be roused. He was feeling the vise beginning to squeeze.

And it did not let up. Soon a crew from CBS News followed Matthews to Cuba. After that, among other journalistic outlets, came a reporter from *Paris Match* as well as others from smaller central American papers. Some of the coverage was as favorable as that of Matthews, some more so, some less. But praise for Batista was hard to come by. Exposed for the kind of leader he really was, he could lead no longer. Or even continue to reside on his native isle, which was the most painful realization for him.

"Early in December 1958," wrote Meyer Lansky biographer Robert Lacey, "Fulgencio Batista sent his children's passports to the American embassy to be stamped with U.S. visas. On December 9, President Eisenhower dispatched a personal emissary to Batista promising unhindered access to, and asylum in, the dictator's Daytona Beach [Florida] home, providing that Batista was willing to leave Cuba rapidly and quietly."

And, so, he was gone. Just like that. After almost two decades, Batista left the country he once had ruled precisely as he was told to: as quickly as possible, without making a peep. The scruffy man in the mountains had forced out the mob's man in the presidential palace.

Shortly afterward in New York, Lansky and Costello closed a door behind them and deliberated lengthily, seriously, and, it must be admitted, fearfully. The future of the Mafia might well be at stake; it would continue to exist without Havana's revenues, of course, of that they had no doubt. But the question was, how lucratively? The two dons decided that the only thing they could do for now was have Trafficante talk to Castro, to get his ear, to win his heart, or at least his compliance. Still in Cuba at the time, Trafficante agreed, and he made an appointment.

But not eagerly. He was plainly nervous at the prospect, not certain that Castro was the kind of man who understood Mafia reasoning, not certain he would react peaceably if he didn't. Nonetheless, the effort had to be made. With investments in three casinos and millions of dollars supporting the heroin trade that flowed in and out of the casinos, the underworld probably had even more to lose under Castro than either the American government or any of the country's corporate investors.

Trafficante tried to look at the bright side. After all, he and the rebel leader had much in common. Both were leaders of other men, defiers of convention, and skilled users of firearms. But Castro's were the guns of a soldier, Trafficante's those of a killer; the Cuban saw nothing in common between them. And he wasted no time in letting the Mafioso know that. The conversation between the two men was more of a monologue, as Castro insisted on the bona fides of the revolution he was leading and spat out the disdain he felt for all that the American criminals represented.

> While most mobsters dashed back to America when Castro seized power, Trafficante, who spoke fluent Spanish, remained in Cuba, confident he could retain his lucrative casinos by bribing the new regime. He soon learned that he was mistaken. Castro's government did not cooperate with gamblers or drug traffickers; it appropriated Trafficante's holdings, imprisoned him, and threatened to execute him. There are two versions of how Trafficante escaped Castro's revolutionary justice: he was kicked out after all his property was confiscated; or he bribed a prison official who released him without the knowledge of higher-ups.

However Trafficante managed to flee, he soon was back in the civilized confines of Manhattan, where he broke the news to Costello. Havana was lost, gone; for the time being, at least, the forces of organized crime had significantly less to organize.

Castro put together a provisional rule to give himself time to lay the groundwork and select the personnel for a more enduring administration. Then, on February 16, 1959, he had himself sworn in as the Cuban prime minister. The July 26th Movement, confined to the island's wilderness little more than two years before, seemed to have gotten off to a triumphant start in the precincts of power.

Before long, still wearing the halo that Matthews and others had lacquered over his head, Castro visited the United States, where his goal was to wage what has been called, with accuracy as well as wit, "a charm offensive." For the most part, it succeeded. He arrived in Washington, said the *New York Times*, in an article not written by Matthews, as a representative "not only out of another world, the world of fierce Latin passion, but out of another century—the century of Sam Adams and Patrick Henry and Tom Paine and Thomas Jefferson." Crowds at the airport shouted "Viva Castro" when he landed, newspaper editors cheered his speech to them, people lined the streets for a glimpse of him.

Castro was charming on television, charming on radio, charming in public addresses. He was not charming, however, in a private meeting with Vice President Richard Nixon, to whom he took an instant dislike. And vice versa.

> Rather than seek out possible areas of accommodation, Nixon confronted Castro with his shortcomings in a vain effort to talk him into changing his behavior. Why don't you hold free elections? Nixon demanded. Castro explained, "The people did not want elections because the elections in the past had produced bad government." Why don't you stop the executions of Batista's people? Because, Castro explained, he was carrying out "the will of the people." And so it went for three hours, as they talked past each other about a free press, fair trials for accused war criminals, and individual rights.

The following day, Nixon's contentious exchange with Castro made headlines all over the country. Having been preceded by Eisenhower's similarly newsworthy refusal to meet with the Cuban at all, the initial glow of Castro's journey began to fade.

The *Times* also had second thoughts, and they seemed significant. Among them was that Castro "did not give the impression this week of great talent for government." Yet in the very next sentence, it kissed off the criticism. "The real question, however, is whether this lack of administrative ability is very pertinent to the present situation." It is a puzzling juxtaposition.

But even the *Times* eventually would have to admit the pertinence of Castro's inability. When he returned to Havana, he made a decision that was the beginning of the end for Cuban hopes of economic growth. He left it to one of his ministers to make the announcement.

"One of the first decisions of the new revolutionary government of Cuba in January 1959 was to shut down the national lottery and the casinos. Both were inappropriate to the ethic of the new, reformed Cuba. If the country's tourist business depended on gambling, announced [government official] Miró Cardona, then the tourist business would just have to suffer."

It was a foolish thing for Cardona to have said and an even more foolish edict to impose. Yet impose it the new government did, and apparently it occurred to no one at the time that if wagering were to be eliminated, the process would work only if it were a gradual one, with a Plan B ready to be substituted for it as a means of continuing the flow of tourist money to Cuba.

But Castro had no Plan B, only an extension of Plan A. He "confiscated sugar estates of more than 1,000 acres [some of them owned by the mob] and banned foreigners from owning Cuban land [some of it owned by the mob]." By this time, the American government had joined the Mafia in being livid at the new Cuba, frustrated beyond words at the amount of money that no longer would be flowing northward.

Actually, it is unfair to say he had no Plan B. The first few years of Castro's regime produced improvements, to some degree. More homes and schools were built, and medical care, of a better quality, was made available to more Cubans than ever before. The country had a different look to it, a new, if modest, efficiency. The new administration started well.

But it did not take long for it to run out of money for further upgrades. Taxes were raised for people who barely had enough money to pay their taxes initially. Soon, the entire economy began to teeter as much, even more, than it had under Batista. The tourist trade was crucial to Cuban prosperity, and the great majority of tourists had been Americans. Now, despite their proximity, U.S. citizens no longer had a reason to visit Cuba, and neither did anyone else. No one wanted to go on tours whose primary attractions were sugar cane fields, oil refineries, and cigar shacks. Better homes and schools and more effective medical care—as admirable, if short-lived as they were—did not draw sightseers.

Although no other islands in the area provided all that Batista's playground once had offered, what they did provide was an unthreatening atmosphere, beautiful beaches, and elegant new resorts. For the most part, the peasantry was cordoned off from the new construction, out of sight of vacationers who wanted their consciences to vacation as well. In time, the Caribbean began to cater to a different trade, welcoming the Club Meds and other heavily programmed playgrounds that relied neither on casinos, big-name entertainers, nor prostitutes. Instead, the attractions included tennis and golf, sailing and yoga, child care, magicians and circus acts, and the opportunity for guests, carefully secured, to fly on trapezes. *La familia* had been exiled; the family, in search of wholesome entertainment, came to inundate the islands.

Further defacing the portrait of Castro as savior was the fact that many of the nation's poverty-riddled farmers—in addition to the aforementioned athletes—began to flee from their homeland. Nothing like it ever had happened before. No boatlift had carried Cubans away from Batista's island—certainly not because he was a more humane leader than Castro, but because Castro had raised such hopes, raised them so high, underpinning them with the ideals of democracy—and then had wasted little time in dashing them. The soul of the Cuban peasant was crushed. Batista was the devil they knew; Castro quickly became the devil they did not know.

Those who sought escape from the island risked not only their leader's wrath if caught but, perhaps even more perilous, ninety miles of choppy, often violent seas between their nation and the United States. Some thought they could navigate them by themselves, or with one or two family members in a boat that was not designed for ocean travel. Others organized caravans of a sort, setting out in a number of crafts under the cover of starless nights, hoping not only that the waves did not swallow them but that their sense of direction did not fail.

As they departed and watched the only home they had ever known disappear behind them, the runaways were both sorrowful and hopeful, frightened and exhilarated, and perhaps, most of all, bewildered. What were they to make of revolution, the very idea of this word that had sparkled before them for so long? Cuban men and women had been poor under capitalism's notion of parity and already could see that under communism they would remain penniless. Capitalism was supposed to give all men a chance, which it didn't; communism was supposed to make all men equal, financially and otherwise. *That* it seemed to be doing, but it was the equality of want, not of opportunity. The only chance poverty-stricken Cubans seemed to have lay not in government at all, but in flight.

Once the successful escapees reached Miami, an unusual alliance began to form. Some of the local Mafiosi joined forces with some of the law-abiding Cuban exiles and began to plot Castro's death; the former would provide the arms, the latter the necessary knowledge of the island's terrain. Jimmy Hoffa, who long had been taking a small cut from the mob's Havana profits, is said to have joined in the planning. Almost surely Meyer Lansky took part as well.

None of it succeeded, however, and when Fidel Castro, once the young, inspiring insurgent, died of undisclosed causes on November 25, 2016, at the age of ninety, his governance long had been a disaster for all. There seemed to be no way to rule Cuba fairly; the island was cursed.

"In the end," Castro said, close to the day that would be his own end, "people have to acknowledge that we have been steadfast, defended our beliefs, our independence, wanted to do justice, and were rebellious." But his regime had been steadfast in *what*? It had defended *what* beliefs? If so many people had paddled away from the island, and so many more seriously considered the notion, how independent could they have been? Was there any reason to believe that Castro defined justice differently from Batista? Perhaps. But the effect on the populace was the same.

The old men and women who remained in Havana throughout Castro's rule looked back wistfully on his early magnetism and promises. But if they were of sufficient years, they looked back even further, on the glorious days of high-wattage corruption that had preceded Fidel. Suffering and strife abounded either way, but the latter was at least a better show.

Those days, however, would never return except as recollections more wistful than accurate. About today's Havana, T. J. English writes:

> The gambling casinos are long gone, but many of the old hotels are still in existence, some ragged and faded, others shining monuments to the past. At the exquisite Hotel Nacional, where Luciano and Lansky once lived and held secret Mob conferences, there is a special room off the lobby called the Salón de la Historia. Its walls are adorned with life-sized murals of gangsters inter-mingled with celebrities and movie stars. At the Hotel Sevilla (formerly the Sevilla Biltmore), framed black-and-white photographs of the mobsters who once operated there line the walls of the Roof Garden. . . . In the streets, vintage American cars from the 1940s and '50s are everywhere.

And so the cars again, the floats in the parades that seem to mock the island's penury, the proud cavalcade of Detroit's glittering past, now lush in the grandeur of the Caribbean sunlight, a lushness hauntingly captured by Francis Ford Coppola in *The Godfather II*. The sun beats down in shades of overripe peach as the late afternoon begins to give way to dusk. It is a bright yet somehow melancholy portrait.

These days the sun beats down on Buick Roadmasters and Lincoln Continentals, Chrysler Imperials and New Yorkers and Cadillac Eldorado Biarritz convertibles. It beats down on Desoto Fireflite Coronados and even, of all things, Edsel Rangers and Corsairs, which were at one time such hearty, four-wheeled jokes to Americans that they have been given a chapter of their own in this book. In 1957, we could not wait to get rid of them. Cuba could not wait to receive them. And a very few of them are still on the roads today.

Not only that, they are driven proudly: on the Carretera Central, the Via Blanca, and especially on the Malecón, the highway next to the sea that carried so many Cubans either to freedom or to death years ago.

The windows are always down on the cars and the radios almost always at the full limit of their decibels. The stations to which they are tuned don't matter much, for the mambo is playing on almost all of them, and driver and passengers alike are shouting out lyrics whether or not they know them. As has long been the case, the mambo is everywhere in Cuba; hundreds of songs fill the roadways and sidewalks and sometimes even carry like distant memories into the lobbies of the ancient hotels, their cacophony adding up to one glorious, never-changing national anthem. If you were born on the island, some people say, it is music you can hear in your soul. It is "conversation with the gods," according to the meaning of "mambo" in the Kongo language.

The melodies, so exuberant, are both improvised and syncopated, with a piano and flute leading the way as "the violin executes rhythmic cords in double-stops." Cowbells clatter, maracas rattle, and congas—the drummer fingering so frantically it seems his fingers will shake loose—provide even more percussion.

As a dance, the mambo is a complicated series of steps, impossible to explain or visualize on the page, but also impossible to mistake if you are looking at it. It is foreplay, as the tango is in Argentina and rock 'n' roll was becoming in the United States.

Standing on the sidewalks are men and women who have set down their shopping bags and purses to watch the cars, even though they have seen them so many times before; they are listening to the music that gushes through their windows—not despite, but because of, its excessive familiarity. For it is theirs, something that belongs to them, something that no leader can tax or take away. Some pedestrians are making mambo moves on the sidewalk, the streets for a few moments hinting at the dance halls that used to be.

If you are an American of a certain age, and want to relive our country's four-wheeled past, you don't have to go to Havana to see the cars. Rather, you can go to the ever more popular antique automobile shows. Or, more fancifully, you can close your eyes and envision the autos as they taxi down the runway, tail fins a-flapping, waiting for final clearance from the control tower. They are still beautiful in their way, comic in their opulence. They are steel and chrome paeans to both an earlier Cuba and an earlier America, and paeans as well to a kind of style that no longer is manufactured today, to flash and fandangle, to the glories of highway excess and impracticality.

Even today, they are the strongest bonds between the antithetical lifestyles of Cuba and the country to the north that gave so many of them sanctuary.

The McClellan Committee on the one hand, the Apalachin Raid and Castro's rise to prominence on the other: Both had similar effects. The power and public presence of the Teamsters were limited after the former, and the same was true of the Mafia in the wake of the latter. And just as no one can name the current leader of the Teamsters, neither—with the possible exception of John Gotti—can anyone name a recent "star" of the underworld. It boasts no more Frank Costellos, no more Meyer Lanskys, no more Mad Hatters. Both organizations continue to operate, sometimes in league with each other, but they are not as forbidding as they used to be, not as great a threat to the nation's welfare. And to the extent that they remain threats, it is on a more restrained, less publicized level. Fewer people are victimized.

Movies continue to glamorize organized crime, but virtually all of them are set in the past. Today's organized criminal activity is less profitable than it used to be, as well as less pervasive. Today's Teamsters provide pension plans that are safe, for the most part, from greedy, sticky-fingered executives.

It is fair to say that both America's largest union and the country's corps of underworld bandits have been in decline for more than half a century now. But both continue to exist, to engage in iniquitous activities to various extents. This is especially true of the Mafia, which was founded on iniquity. But thanks to men as widely disparate in their natures and goals as John Little McClellan and Fidel Ruz Castro, among many others, what was so sinister in 1957—*because* of '57—is less so today.

PART TWO

Chevrolet Bel Air, © Frank Schulenburg/CC BY-SA 4.0

Ford Edsel, GPS 56 from New Zealand

4

Highways to Everywhere

When they were new, America's big gas-slurping automobiles clogged the city streets. They were being manufactured at a record pace in Detroit and, with such innovative notions as trade-ins, dealer financing, and other forms of credit, they were being purchased at a record pace as well.

The problem, though, lay not with overkill in the factories and showrooms, but with "the road system [that] was woefully inadequate. Except in New York, Chicago, and Los Angeles, the major urban areas had few or no high-speed expressways." Traffic jams did not just choke highways but turned smaller, less-direct streets into parking lots, with the blare of auto horns so constant as to be something of a single, continuous sound. And to make matters worse: "Except for the Pennsylvania Turnpike and a few other toll roads in the East, the country had no four-lane highways connecting the cities." If it was rush hour, as Americans ironically had begun to call the daily periods of unmoving traffic, it was because pulse rates were rushing, not automobiles.

Problems with U.S. thoroughfares had existed for a surprisingly long time. In 1919, a soldier named Dwight David Eisenhower traveled by army convoy from the East Coast to the west, often moving so slowly, and on such inadequate thoroughfares, that he longed for the relative ease of storming the Normandy beaches. He had, ever since, had been distressed by the conditions of American land excursions; the roads were too narrow, too indirect, too bumpy, sometimes buckled, sometimes muddy, at other times scarred by potholes that never seemed to be filled. "Bridges cracked and were rebuilt, vehicles became stuck in mud and equipment broke." It sounds like a description from a previous century.

Returning home from World War II, in which he had risen to the rank of general of the army as well as to a heroic status that surpassed a mere title, Eisenhower was still thinking about American highways, still dismayed by them. And dismayed all the more because "he had been impressed by Hitler's system of *Autobehnen*," a remarkably efficient and well-maintained network of roads that was as much an asset to the movement of troops and materiel in battle as it was to civilian motorists in peacetime. If Hitler had had to transport armies over roads like ours, Eisenhower was convinced, the war would have ended in victory for the allies much sooner. Something *had* to be done to get Ike's countrymen from one place to another more efficiently.

Then, in the summer of 1956, he finally got his chance. As his first term as president came to a close and he prepared for his second, Eisenhower believed the time was right to solve what he had long seen as one of the country's greatest domestic problems. With the blessing of both houses of Congress, he was able to sign into law the Dwight D. Eisenhower National System of Interstate and Defense Highways Act of 1956, known by all as simply the Highway Act, or Eisenhower's Highway Act, which he believed to be not only one of the most significant accomplishments of his administration, but "the most ambitious road program by any nation in all history." In fact, according to Ike's biographer Stephen Ambrose, it "was the largest public works program in history, which meant that the government could put millions of men to work." Not even any of FDR's New Deal ventures could compare with it. The Interstate highways would take ten years to complete, according to plan, and construction was to begin, the president ordered, without delay. "No river or ravine, no gorge or gully, no urban or suburban land would stand in the way of the onrushing auto age."

By the following summer, the reconfiguring of American roads was at full speed, with the laying of forty-one thousand miles of new motorways that would, according to Eisenhower, "eliminate unsafe roads, inefficient routes, traffic jams and all of the other things that got in the way of 'speedy, safe transcontinental travel.'"

The critic and polymath Lewis Mumford went even further, although not happily so. After many of the forty-one thousand miles were laid, he would look at winding stretches of them as he approached and say, "Our national flower is the concrete cloverleaf."

Stringent rules were put into effect for the new Interstates. "They were required to have at least four lanes, divided, and to be entirely free of intersections. Lanes were to be at least twelve feet wide and there were to be ten-foot-wide shoulders at both the outer and median edges of the highway. . . . curves would be utilized to enhance the aesthetics, and also the safety of the highways, but these would be broad and sweeping so that adequate sight lines could be maintained."

The scope of the undertaking, or rather undertakings, plural, was positively Brobdingnagian. It was not just that so many highways and bridges had to be built in so many places; repairs needed to be made on thousands of existing roads. Eisenhower believed that the planet had not seen anything like it before: that the pyramids didn't compare with the Highway Act in terms of national commitment; the Roman aqueducts didn't compare; the Great Wall of China was a backyard fence.

Certainly the initial cost estimates did not compare. And once overruns, due to the inevitable fraud and kickback arrangements, and no less inevitable inefficiencies, were taken into account, the price tag for the new roads would rise into the billions of 1950s and '60s dollars. Some of the financing, according to initial calculations, would come from new taxes: on automobiles, trucks, tires, and, primarily, gasoline. What would happen, then—viewed cynically, or was it realistically?—is that the "gas taxes would be spent on new roads that would allow greater traffic, which in turn consume more gasoline, providing more revenue to spend on more roads, leading to more gas consumption and so more tax revenue." The logic, as explained by historian William I. Hitchcock, was perfect. Perfectly circular, that is, and the events it described caused all manner of problems.

But as a backup position, another source of financing was put into place. The new network also would be capitalized by the issuance of bonds supported by the newly created Interstate Highway Trust Fund. Money would come pouring in as if through an open spigot; Eisenhower was certain of it. He believed it would be enough to support the American *autobehnen* for which he longed.

In his book *Open Road: A Celebration of the American Highway*, Phil Patton wrote perceptively about what happened next—in particular, as concerns the circular logic. He realized that the terrible growth it described was, in fact, built into the new legislation.

> The Interstate system was . . . a program that by its nature was open-ended, one that many people doubted would ever be finished. Politics inevitably added miles to the length of the system . . . When a Democratic administration came to power in 1961, it promptly raised the gasoline tax from three to four cents[1] to finance more Interstates, most of them in urban areas where Democratic support was stronger and the howls of motorists caught in traffic jams were louder.

Although it would take a few more years, howls of a different nature eventually would be raised against Eisenhower's vision, the reasons for which were becoming alarmingly clearer to at least some of the nation's citizenry with each day of construction. It seemed that, in some places, the

---

1. As this is being written, the federal tax on gasoline is 18.4 cents a gallon.

process of laying new roads was destroying old neighborhoods and their reassuring sense of the familiar; and, worse, the roads left hundreds of thousands of Americans displaced or, at the least, disoriented. Civic structures were razed, though still in use; small businesses were plowed over and carted away as scraps. Cars were moving with greater ease over longer distances, but at a cost. History was being wiped out.

When the Federal Highway Administration finally got around to presenting a report to Congress on the effects of the road building, it had a tale to tell that was as gloomy in its own ways as it was impressive in others.

The FHA investigated "sixteen cities engaged in highways contests. The list was alphabetical, from "A, (Atlanta, 4 miles displacing neighborhoods); to B (Baltimore, with 5.5 miles of displacement of historic sites); to C (Cleveland, 8.8 miles of parkland, [of] historical and religious interests . . . 'As neighborhoods are sliced in two and cemeteries are relocated, neither the quick nor the dead are safe,' said the *New York Times*."

And according to architecture critic Mary Holtz Kay, "worse was to come. The original 41,000-mile interstate system, by now expanded to 42,500 miles, wasn't half built before the Commerce Department was talking about another '100,000 miles of scenic roads and parkways, and a quarter of the projected mileage through places never before serenaded by the tappets of internal combustion.' All to get back to nature, which was looking less natural."

But at least at the time of its passage, and much longer as far as most Americans were concerned, the Highway Act was one of the most popular pieces of legislation in the twentieth century. For automakers and stockholders, it meant profits beyond their most optimistic expectations. For the companies that serviced the auto industry—such as upholsterers, tire manufacturers, plastic mat makers, even the novelty firms that turn out those little air fresheners in the shape of Christmas trees—it was no less a windfall. For the construction businesses that were chosen to build the highways, the Act was like winning a lottery; for the men the businesses hired to do the jobs, it was like winning lotteries of their own—smaller in amount than those that had rained down on their new employers, but larger than they had ever dared to dream.

Putting it all together, the Act, it was said, "would move enough earth to cover the state of Connecticut knee-deep; it would claim enough land in rights of way to equal the acreage of Delaware; it would pave a surface equivalent to that of West Virginia. The concrete it consumed would build six sidewalks to the moon, and it would use as much lumber as produced by 400 square miles of forest, as much drainpipe as the water and sewer systems of six Chicagos."

And, of course, for American motorists, the majority of whom were not troubled by the destruction of neighborhoods in distant locations, or sites with historic value, which simply meant that they were old, the act provided more freedom, access, and speed than ever before. It was like the opening of a frontier, new destinations suddenly appearing and being reachable with ease. In any contest between the future and the past, the future always will win.

One other individual, someone whose name had not come up in any of the public discussions about the Interstate Highway Act, was to be another beneficiary—for a few years, at least, until he went to jail. He was a man, says someone who knew him well, whose

> ascendancy could not have come at a more opportune moment for him and his union. American's love affair with the automobile had led the administration . . . to make a fateful decision. While the rest of the world was throwing funds and effort into modernizing mass transit to move people, the Eisenhower administration went a different route. Mass transit, and especially the railroads, became foster children. The government went on a massive road building campaign, to link every section of the nation, from the Atlantic to the Pacific, from the Mexican border to the Canadian border, from the large cities to the small towns, with a web of fast interstate highways. One thing that means was that henceforth the nation's goods would move to market by trucks instead of trains. If trucking companies grew rich and powerful, the Teamsters union, which controlled the drivers, grew richer and more powerful. There were thousands of trucking companies, but there was only one Teamsters' Union, and only one James R. Hoffa.

By late in 1957, the new highway plan was fully operational, with jackhammers blasting concrete into large pieces of shrapnel in virtually every state in the union. The new America was taking shape, and let us imagine that we can see it happening from an impossible perspective, from a camera with the kind of close-up lens not yet invented, a camera that has been installed aboard the Soviet satellite circling the Earth, looking at the unprecedented American activity. Let us imagine the pictures it is taking, pictures of a country changing its look faster than any country ever had before—all of those gray strips of highway, elongating each day as they shoot off from each other at all imaginable angles, the pattern making no sense from low Earth orbit and only slightly more from ground level. From our satellite's vantage point, it looks as if pieces of ribbon have been snipped and are tying up the terrain into oddly shaped parcels. In some places, where the ground rises, it seems as if the Earth is bulging beneath the strips, as if trying to break through the new binding.

But the construction is doing more than just changing the face of United States, now and forever; in the process it is changing the country's fundamental nature. Of a highway project in the nation's capital more than a century ago. It was said that it "developed an original spatial vision," a comment dismissed by some as esoteric. It is not. The vision was felt viscerally. It changed perceptions: the nation seemed to be growing, the population feeling a new sense of freedom and accompanying exhileration. The United States, like a flower at the peak of its bloom, was opening up. Ahead to 1957, the Highway Act is creating population shifts, in some cases from rural to urban, in other cases the opposite. It is giving gradual birth to the modern suburb, with new schools and churches, new recreational areas, new vistas. The Act is solidifying a different set of social patterns, a previously unforeseen way of life. People now can drive longer distances to maintain friendships or begin new ones; they can attend social, cultural, and athletic events that would have been out of range for them before; they can indulge themselves in the illusion of wandering freely o'er the land, as if they had laid out the roads themselves rather than the roads having dictated the routes.

And the new roads are altering the lives of men and women as consumers. To give but one example: A new kind of restaurant will soon appear, the fast-food restaurant, where there is no wait for heat-lamped hamburgers and french fries so greasy they could stain a steel beam and beverages that are liquid sugar. Eventually, we Americans will eat so often at McDonald's, Burger King, Wendy's, and the Colonel's that we will take out food there and bring it home; the restaurants will be our treats for the kids, a cheap night off for mom from kitchen duties. And we will eat at a fast-food pace even at home, in our own dining rooms.

More than any other factor, fast-food restaurants will contribute to a nation of people whose waistlines strain at their belts. Obesity will become one of our nation's great health problems. "Fatso" will go from being a term of opprobrium to a medical diagnosis, a serious one at that.

In time, small shopping centers will begin to line some of the new roads, one abutted to the next, like a series of downtowns without any town or center. They will enable us to shop more conveniently than before, providing a variety of stores within easy walking distance of our parking spots. Thus they will provide us with a greater variety of merchandise in a smaller amount of space. They will give contractors the idea for today's daunting malls, enormous structures that eventually will put old-fashioned storefronts out of business. Small-town establishments that once boasted "The Lowest Prices in Town" will be gutted inside and "Available for Lease."

The new roadways will become lined with big box stores, a term that did not exist in 1957. These are emporiums for which there is no room elsewhere in the landscape, buildings so large that it seems airplane hangars could be stored in them, where, if our legs are up to the challenge of walking from one end to the other, we always can buy what we need. We will join throngs of others who always can buy what *they* need, and, on special occasions, we will give to the acquisition of new products the competitive zeal of a contact sport. A Lowe's will carry enough home goods to furnish a county. A Home Depot will need a two-level parking lot. A WalMart will be a city under a single roof. The larger the retail establishment, the smaller the individual consumer.

In the nineteenth century, Walt Whitman wrote to those of poetic sensibility about public thoroughfares not nearly as well built or kept up as those of which I am writing. In his *Song of the Open Road*, he practically ran himself off the road in his enthusiasm. "Oh public road . . . You express me better than I can express myself / You shall be more to me than my poem."

Frank Lloyd Wright, alive and attentive when the new highways were being fastened onto the terrain, was even more enthusiastic. "As new and greater road-systems are added year by year they are more splendidly built," he said. "I foresee that roads will soon be architecture too . . . great architecture."

Wright was surely one of the few to see the concretizing of America through such a prism. Still, for many motorists, the sparkling new bands of pavement seemed to demand sparkling new autos to glide across them, and as people traded in the cars they had been driving before the Highway Act for deluxe, post-Highway Act models, exports to Cuba reached unprecedented heights. So little did Batista and Castro have in common, but both agreed that Cuba should not put an embargo on the big old autos from America. They had become a staple of life on the island, one of its most sustaining imports and most treasured possessions—although sometimes, to save money, the cars had to be owned jointly.

Meanwhile, in the United States and inspired by the Dwight D. Eisenhower System of Interstate and Defense Highway Act, the automobile had reached new heights of popularity and social significance. The fifties were, in fact, the only decade to have its own official car.

5

The Design of an Era

The new highways became speckled with vehicles seldom seen before. "Small cars from overseas are extremely popular as the number of imports [in 1957] doubles from 1956. The hot imports include the German Volkswagen, the Swedish Volvo, the French Renault, the English Austin, and the Italian Fiat."

But these cars were *only* speckles. They were practical, not showy; sensible, not sexy—and in the era of recession-interrupted Eisenhower prosperity, as if the foundation were being laid for the Kennedy glamour to follow, it was the latter that Americans wanted. So it was sexy that Detroit gave them, fueling the era's fantasies, for just as power is a glamorous attribute in a person, so it is in an automobile. The roar of the engine, so distinctive a noise, means strength, dynamism; it cannot help but grab the attention of all within hearing distance, many of them seduced by machines capable of louder roars than ever before.

As for the speed of the car, it was a combination of sex *and* power, with the goal sometimes being to leave the onlooker envious, trying to imagine the feel of such acceleration in an auto of his own, a "g" force that called to mind a fighter jet. Speed in transport always has been prized by Americans, going back to the days of the Pony Express, to steamboat races that literally were explosive, and before that, to stagecoaches, and even earlier, to lone horses and solitary riders, such as the mythic rider Paul Revere. In fact, speed has been prized by all people at all times; think of the movie *Ben Hur* and its famous chariot race in early Rome.

By the time 1957 came along, there was no better way for Americans, especially those new to their driving licenses, to reveal what they wanted to show about themselves, to say what they wanted to say, to make declarations of their goals and personalities, than by their choice of automobiles. America had so many different kinds of cars back then that a driver had no trouble prying himself from the pack, customizing a car that was his and his alone. For it was not just speed that mattered; it was, in addition, individuality.

And it was easily achieved. There might have been more different models in '57 than before or since, available in a mad variety of colors and with an extraordinary combination of accessories. Someone capable of doing the math, for which he would need one of those still experimental computing machines, might have been able to determine that it was possible for every person in the country to own a car that was different, even if in the smallest combination of details, from that of every other American.

But for all of the choices that Detroit offered, one vehicle more than any other spoke to its time and place, a piece of multi-horse-powered sculpture that was the pace car for a generation. "If any single car defines the Fifties, it has to be the crisply face-lifted '57 Chevy—led by the top of the line Bel Air." That was the opinion of the auto editors of *Consumer Guide*, although, admittedly, the judgment carried a touch of bias; the book in which the opinion was offered was a history of Chevrolet from its earliest motor cars in 1911. Publisher: *Consumer Guide Press.*

The bias notwithstanding, though, the editors' judgment turned out to be the right one, passing the ultimate test of time. "Not until years later," the *Consumer Guide* staff concluded, "was the '57 recognized by many as the sharpest Chevy of the decade—best looking of the 1955–57 'classic' era, if not the make's full life span—as well as an engineering marvel."

But more than engineering set the Bel Air apart from both its predecessors and competitors. Consider all of those hues and tints and shades—1957 was probably the most glittering year in the history of the American automobile. As an internal Chevrolet document about the Bel Air explains, "Seventeen exterior colors are available for 1957, seven of these being new. The colors are grouped into sixteen solid color exteriors and fifteen two-tone combinations."

Separating the tones from one another on the Bel Air chassis were gently flowing streaks of chrome, on some parts of the car, in some of its gentle swoops, subtly reminiscent of today's Nike swoosh. In fact, the car was festooned with chrome; so many glittering metallic accents had been added to the roof and body, the bumpers and door handles, that, in combination with the thick whitewall tires that were fashionable back then, the car seemed to glow even when a cloud slid past the sun. Yet, as garish as the preceding might suggest, the Bel Air was, for its time, stylishly restrained.

According to the National Automobile Dealers Association, to purchase one of these colorful, restyled Bel Airs in the two-door sedan model, one would have had to spend $2,338 in 1957. Today, the same vehicle, in pristine condition, suitable for display in the antique car shows or hypnotically solitary viewing in a collector's garage, would cost between $55,000 and

$60,000. In the shows, says auto historian Quentin Willson, "the Bel Air is one of the most widely coveted U.S. collectors' cars."

And the most coveted of Bel Airs was the convertible, which sold 47,562 units in '57, more than any other model from any car company in history. Because of scarcity as much as appearance, today's price for the "ragtop," like the discovery of a master's painting not previously known to exist, is hard to predict; that it would be close to a six-figure sum at auction, however, seems likely.

It is the way of things. Good art is made better, and therefore more expensive, by time. Even good highway art.

These days, though, it is hard to find either art or individuality on the American road, what with one car looking so much like another. So many models feature a long hood and short trunk lid, making the front of the car look out of proportion to the rear, the vehicle appearing to have been backed into a wall at high speed. And so few color choices are offered today that we are forced into a conformity on the road that has not existed since the days of Henry Ford and the Model T. Today's cars are gray, navy blue, black, white, and not much else. The vocabulary of the onboard computers seems to increase, with some sounding more and more like a passenger, from year to year. Other than that, a 2016 model is a 2017 model is a 2018 model.

The '57 Bel Air, referred to by some as a "junior Cadillac," had been redesigned from the previous year's version, and the effect on the eye could not have been more striking—nor can mere statistics give a true sense of its impact on the automotive public. Nonetheless, the car is two and a half inches longer than previous Bel Airs and an inch and a half lower—it is, thus, sleeker, less boxy in appearance, than its ancestors. Fender hoods extend a couple of inches over the headlights, calling to mind the eyelashes of an especially sultry woman. They make the car look longer than it is, and the hood actually *is* longer, as well as flatter, than it previously had been; these dimensions, too, contribute to the Bel Air's new slimness. In fact, the same internal Chevrolet document cited earlier boasts that "[e]very detail is styled for a lower and longer silhouette, to emphasize a perfect transitional vehicle to the jet age." Of course, its "peppy 'small block' V-8 engine" didn't hurt, either.

And *Wired* magazine, in praising the Boeing 707 as one of the ten classic airliners of all time, called the plane "as much a symbol of American postwar progress as the '57 Chevy and Apollo 11."

If you came of age during mid-century and look back on it now, you understand the place that the Bel Air holds in the automotive pantheon without relying on a recitation of facts and figures. You understand that it is the car you see when you hear Chuck Berry's "Roll over Beethoven" booming into the night. Or when you hear Fats Domino's "Whole Lotta Lovin'," or James Burton's tightly plucked but soaring guitar solos on Ricky Nelson's "Waitin' in School." These songs are dashboard speaker music, and the dashboard is the Bel Air's.

Can one picture these scenes with any other car emitting the music? Of course, but not as easily; something is not quite right, not quite in sync; it is as if you are watching an old film in which the audio and video are playing at slightly different speeds. "The '57 Chevy Bel Air sums up America's most prosperous decade better than any other car of the time," declares Quentin Willson. "Along with hula hoops, drive-in movies, and rock 'n' roll, it has become a Fifties icon."

And so it is this liveliest of Chevys that you see when you imagine a car full of teenagers cruising through the parking lot behind the local drive-in restaurant at a maximum of five miles an hour—no speed desired here; this is pure display—so that those already parked have more time to admire your wheels. *And* your percussion, because everyone sitting next to an open window in the Bel Air, front seat and back, is leaning out and whacking his palms on the door. Let us reprise Little Richard's "Keep A-Knockin'" as it enters the restaurant parking lot packed with teens. "Keep-a-knockin' but you can't come in." Slap, slap. "Keep-a-knocking but you can't come in, whooooo!" Slap, slap. "Keep-a-knockin' but you can't come in." Slap, slap. "Come back tomorrow night an' try it agin."

Again, yes, you can imagine hands beating against the exterior of another car, but it just isn't the same. Stand a Bel Air upright on its rear bumper and suddenly you have a jukebox, a Wurlitzer on wheels. You can't say that about any other car.

In the same vein, the Bel Air is the only vehicle that seems especially designed for the young driver to go up and down the aisles of the drive-in theater before settling into a spot with a good view of Michael Landon before he turns from gorgeous to hideous and becomes the title character in *I Was A Teenage Werewolf*. Cars had no bucket seats in those days, no compartment between male driver and female passenger to prevent the young man from slowly sliding over toward his date as he stretches out his right arm and prepares to lay it softly across her shoulders. If she responds by nestling closer to him, the night is placed prominently in his scrapbook of memories. If not, he will lie to his friends and claim she was almost in his lap.

Even before a person reached driving age, he could dream about the Bel Air that he hoped would await him when he turned sixteen. In the novel *The Car Thief* by Theodore Weesner, such a boy is anticipating the birthday that will set him free. "In easy fantasies, imagining he was the owner of the car, he drove around the corners and front of the strange schools during their lunch hours, to let himself be seen . . . He intentionally parked his Chevrolet Bel Air or his Buick Riviera under their eyes. He was able to see himself in these moments as he imagined he was seen by them, as a figure from a movie, a stranger, some newcomer come to town, some new cock of the walk with a new car, with a plume of city hair."

It is no easy accomplishment for a car to be considered the most distinctive in a decade ruled by perceptions of glitter. For one thing, said a couple of men who knew what they were talking about, it was necessary to provide the equivalent of glitter not just for the eyes, but for the satisfaction of other senses as well.

"The automobile business," testified American Motors President George Romney before a 1958 Senate committee," has some of the elements of the millinery industry in it, in that you can make style become the hallmark of modernity." They did. Safe cars appeal only to "squares," William Mitchell, GM's styling director told a *Fortune* reporter in 1956, "and," he added, "there ain't any squares no more." . . . Companies spent millions on research, trying to anticipate or set style trends. The Chevrolet Division of General Motors, for example, hired seven psychologists in 1957 to investigate the effect of Chevy's "sounds and smells." The result of this program? Chevrolet's general manager proudly announced, "We've got the finest door-slam this year we've ever had—a big car sound."

The sound of a car door slamming, it seems, and one's reaction to it, would not be worth a battery of psychologist tests—at least not to those running the great American industry of the fifties. Then again, that is perhaps *why* these men were running the great American industry. Attention to detail, always important, gets no more detailed than this.

However, General Motors's greatest aural triumph of the decade was not even devised for an American. Nor was it a Bel Air, and perhaps, although made by Chevrolet, it is more appropriately considered sui generis than Chevy.

The company was asked to manufacture an automobile specifically to satisfy the tastes of one of the Middle East's most famous potentates. As it turned out he had quite a few unusual tastes, not all of them wholesome. To suit one of them, GM invented a unique feature for this man who, although he did not have a reputation for cruelty, seems either to have enjoyed fantasies of perversion, or to have possessed a sense of humor that had spent too much time in the sun. "In King Farouk's case," writes Douglas T. Miller and Marion Nowak in their history of the fifties, "Detroit turned out a customized special, complete with a horn that imitated the squeals and howls of dogs being mangled under the wheels."

One imagines the king and a car full of his toadies laughing uproariously every time the chauffeur toots. What a story it will be at court tomorrow! Such jealousy will there be among those not in the car, not having been invited to join in the good times, the fantasies of animal torture under the wheel.

But, with all due apologies to the late King Farouk, a maimed canine sound effect is a feature far beneath the dignity of the true members of the road's royalty, the Chevy Bel Airs driven by the young Americans of long ago, the boys and their girlfriends who felt their junior Cadillacs in the marrow. They might not have reproduced the sounds of mangled puppies, but even better, *far* better, they played some of the twentieth century's most important music, songs that had an equal appeal to both sexes and all races, and thus had a powerful appeal on the culture, one that, although never abating, remains insufficiently recognized today.

6

The Vagina in the Grille

If it was a remarkable year for Chevrolet; it was an even more remarkable year for the company's most persistent competitor. Ford not only managed to sell more units than Chevy, but to make more money. It wasn't easy, of course. Not only did it have to contend with the Bel Air's success on one hand—a million and a half of them were manufactured in '57, outselling any individual model from any car company in the world—but, on the other hand, Ford had to contend with the travails of its own product, a new and much ballyhooed entry into the marketplace. It was supposed to be Ford's answer to the Bel Air. It was instead one of the greatest mistakes in the history of American manufacturing. It was to automobiles what New Coke later would be to beverages.

In fact, it might be fair to say that the two vehicles represent the decade's extremes, not just automotively but culturally. The Bel Air was a sign of the decade's ascent to the future, the sixties and beyond; the new Ford, if company executives ever could agree on a name for it, would be just another version of the past, which is to say, an old-fashioned clunker dressed up in accoutrements meant to be modern but more accurately described as risible.

Ford had been planning its new car for a long time, and the goal for it was an ambitious one. It was to appeal both to the beginning motorist and those with experience behind the wheel, and it would be an image maker for the whole company. So far, though, the company had not even come close to Chevrolet's star performer—not in the clay models on its workbenches, not on the drawing boards, not even in the lunchtime daydreams of the company's best engineers, who were perpetually sketching, perpetually wondering if this was possible, or that, whether one design would catch the public eye or another. Or, as they could not help fearing, maybe neither.

100

So even though Ford's bottom line was good news in '57, it was gloominess, not elation, at company headquarters at the beginning of the year as it began to try yet again to catch lightning on four wheels.

"The tragic disappointment surrounding the Edsel was reflected in the search for a suitable name for the car." So writes historian Douglas Brinkley, and he is correct in finding the quest for a name an omen for the car's short-lived future.

Brinkley tells us there was only one stipulation for the new vehicle's moniker, and it was dictated by family politics. The late Henry's Ford's late son was named Edsel, and the two men lived in constant conflict with each other, the sire expecting too much from his child and giving too little in the way of approbation when his child succeeded, as he often did when left to his own devices. Thus the new car was not, under any circumstances, to be named "Edsel." When the name was brought up early in the selection meetings, the response of Benson, Henry's grandson and Edsel's son, was that his father's name would be the car's name under one condition, and one condition only: "Over my dead body!"

The process of seeking out some other name seems to have begun at least a year earlier with a committee meeting at the company's Special Products Division. Its responsibility was not a name per se, but the instructions for selecting one.

1. The name should be short, so it will display well on dealers' signs.
2. It should have two, or at the most three, syllables to give it cadence.
3. It should be clear and distinct, to aid in radio and television.
4. It should start with the letters C, S, J, F or others subject to calligraphic sweep for ornaments and advertising signatures. Heavy-footed letters as M, W, and K would be out—too rooted.
5. It should not, of course, be prone to obscene double-entendres or jokes. It should not translate into anything objectionable.
6. It should be American; foreign expressions are taboo.

With these steps as guidelines, some lower-level Ford executives were assigned to work as poll takers, dispatched to Detroit-Wayne (County) Major airport, downtown train and bus stations, athletic stadiums, and other large gathering places. Their assignment was to ask people at random what they thought would be a good name for a new vehicle.

It was an absurd idea. First of all, the question came at them out of nowhere, without any context; virtually no one in all of Michigan had been wondering about what to call a not-yet-existent auto. Most people could not think of a response. Or they said something that the poll takers would have been ashamed to repeat in mixed company. Or they just looked oddly at the men questioning them and shooed them away, annoyed that they had been stopped for so preposterous a reason.

When this sadly random effort failed to produce the desired result, "the Special Products Division [of Ford] enlisted the help of its advertising agency, which sent a representative to Dearborn [Michigan] with a binder containing six thousand names, in alphabetical order and cross-referenced. 'But my god,' said Richard Krafve, the head of the division, 'we don't want six thousand names. We only want one!' That is, one *good* name. Everybody in the company cringed when Benson Ford began promoting the name 'Drof,' which was Ford spelled backward." Only Nosneb, which was Benson spelled backward, would have been worse, and not by much.

Drof seems to have popped into Benson's mind on one of the many occasions when "[he] went out on the town and drank himself into stupefaction." It was a ritual that usually began after lunch, wherein he would consume different amounts of different liquors on different days. Then, before dinner, sitting in his den at home, he became more precise, pouring exactly "three fingers of Canadian Club into a glass," trying to catch up with his even more alcoholically inclined wife. Edith Ford, who, not being burdened by employment, had no persuasive reason for sobriety, always got a head start on her spouse. It was decided not to ask Benson for any more suggestions.

At any rate, with both Edsel and Drof out of the running, that was two names down and the rest of the English language to go. Until the new car finally had its appellation, it was to be known at company headquarters as the E-Car.

But why *that* letter? E for Edsel? No one could, or ever would, say. Of course, as a kind of memorial to Benson's well-liked father, the "E" as an internal designation seems obvious. Again, though, why? Edsel was, after all, the first name to be eliminated from consideration. But with the prototype called the E-Car, Edsel's name again began to slide to the front of the Ford company's minds.

Security could not have been tighter around design headquarters. Few people had keys to the studio, and if one was lost, all locks to the entire floor would be changed and the keys replaced immediately. Guards stood watch over the studio twenty-four hours a day, seven days a week. And: "A man periodically swept with a telescope the high terrain around the studio, checking for spies." Now, if only the new vehicle would turn out to be worthy of such precautions.

Although the E-Car still lacked a name, work proceeded without delay on its look.

By late summer 1955 the design was established, including some of the features that would make the new car distinctive: a grille which detractors claimed was shaped like a horse collar; horizontal wings in the rear of the car that were at odds with the vertical tail-fins then dominating the market; a unique transmission arrangement in which gears were shifted by a cluster of push buttons at the center of the steering wheel. On August 15 the curtain rose for a showing of the clay model of the new car, and the Product Planning Committee burst into a standing ovation.

The model hardly deserved such a reaction. Maybe the planning committee members were just tired of sitting. Or maybe their feet had fallen asleep, and they thought that standing might awaken them again. But a grille reminiscent of a horse collar? And once the product was manufactured, comparisons would get worse. As for buttons in the middle of the steering wheel to shift gears, it was not just a bad idea but potentially a lethal one. One's first reaction when shifting gears is to reach for a rod on the steering column, not to beep the horn. But the rod wasn't there, and the car would not respond to a mere mention. More dangerously, someone who *did* intend a hearty toot might instead end up shifting from high to reverse, and God only knew how the engine would react to such conflicting orders. Even as a pure gimmick, the buttons were lacking; one of the '57 Cadillac models had "on its dashboard a lipstick, vanity case, and four gold cups."

At this stage, though, despite what many at Ford regarded as progress with vehicle design, the men in charge of E-Car development were still flummoxed; their toy remained nameless. How could a company make something as complicated as an automobile and not be able to formulate something as simple as a name? It was, potentially, a more serious problem than it sounds. Perhaps a name would have inspired design ideas, ideas that would flow into each other and result in the car for which they all longed.

A sociologist with a PhD from Columbia was approached for suggestions, but he thought a better idea would be to pass the assignment along to the great American poet, Marianne Moore. A Pulitzer Prize winner, she also won the National Book Award for her verse, and it was said of her by a fellow poet that "in looking at some apparently small object, one feels the swirl of great events." But we're talking about a car here, folks, and a woman who writes

> a grape tendril
> ties a knot in knots till
> knotted thirty times—so
> the bound twig that's under-
> gone and overgone can't stir

was not the best choice Ford could have made. But it certainly couldn't be worse than sending employees to the airport and train and bus stations. Could it?

Actually, it could. Among the suggestions Miss Moore provided after more than a month of artistic concentration and consultation with her muse were the following: "the Resilient Bullet, the Mongoose Civique, the Andante con Motor [which, with whopping inappropriateness, is a play on the musical term meaning "slowly, but with motion"], the Varsity Stroke—and, most resonant of all, in her final missive, the Utopian Turtletop."

Ms. Moore was thanked for her contributions—she had, in advance, appropriately refused compensation—and sent back to her day job.

On November 8, 1956, the Ford executive committee met to review a list of sixteen possibilities for names. Shortly before, the list had contained four hundred wild guesses and, at least according to one report, had started out at eighteen thousand. Another round of man-on-the-street polling was decided upon, but this time the names, the sixteen finalists, would be provided to the interviewees rather than the other way around. It was a much more sensible approach, and thus produced much more sensible results. Corsair proved the favorite of the choices given, with Ranger and Pacer not far behind. Still . . .

"The Executive Committee listened unimpressed. It was clear they were not greatly excited by any of these proposals, which had taken twelve long and arduous months to research and analyze, and Ernest Breech, chairing the meeting in the absence of Benson's brother, Henry Ford II, said as much. If that was the best selection available, Breech declared, looking around slowly at every member of the committee, he didn't care for a one of them.

" 'Why,' he asked, 'don't we just call it Edsel?' "

No one could think of a reason not to. Benson was long since out of the loop. Everybody else was exhausted. And so, after all this time, all this trouble, all this angst, it was back to square one. But this time it would remain there. Corporate America, in ways known only to itself, had come to a decision, and the E-Car became the Edsel after all.

Unfortunately, the result was that Henry Ford's son, an intelligent, dignified man, and certainly a capable successor to his father as the head of the company despite his father's constant carping, provided the name for the heartiest posthumous laughingstock in automotive history. Possibly, as has been said, even "the biggest business failure of the postwar."

Edsel had been deceased for fourteen years when his shame began.

Benson Ford's dead body would not be available for anybody to step over for another twenty-one years.

In the manner of a debutante making her long-awaited debut, the Edsel came out to America on October 13, 1957—spotlight beams crossing one another in the skies as other lights lit up showrooms from coast to coast, the new Ford thereby appearing not just decorated but bejeweled. The forum for the public introduction was a one-hour television special hosted by Bing Crosby, and it was a coup for Ford that he had agreed to do so. Up to this point in his career, Crosby had seldom appeared on television, much preferring radio and movies, and as the minutes to show time ticked down, the singer with the calmest of sounds began to feel an unaccustomed apprehensiveness.

He was not alone. "Behind-the-scenes tension centered on whether the toupees of Crosby and his principal guest, Frank Sinatra, would stand the test of live television scrutiny—they did—and whether [singer and guest star] Rosemary Clooney's Edsel would start—it didn't." Yet another omen, this one even more portentous than the "tragic disappointment" of the name search that Brinkley had pointed out.

Actually, Edsels had been on the market in selected cities for more than a month before television sanctified their appearance in the popular culture. Starting on September 4, Ford dealerships all over the country had been decorated as if it were New Year's Eve, and, in a sense, the company's sales force hoped it would be exactly that—the beginning of a Happy New Model Year, the sales of which would be worthy of all the spangles and pomp.

And at the start, it seemed as if that might just happen, as a few dealers could not keep enough cars in stock to meet the demand. Only at the start, though, and only a *very* few dealers. "But by November sales were off. And at first there was panic, then despair. By December [with sales now off precipitously] Henry [Ford II] had to go on closed-circuit television to ask worried dealers to hold fast. The same day he was telling his captive audience that the Edsel 'was here to stay,' however [Ford executive, and one of the company's 'Whiz Kids,' Robert S.] McNamara[1] was writing the first of a series of memos calling for the termination of the Edsel at the earliest possible opportunity."

The memos became increasingly frantic. In one of them, McNamara claimed that Ford would not even come close to selling two hundred thousand of the new cars, the projected break-even point, in its first year. He was scoffed at for such pessimism, dismissed as the company's Cassandra. As things turned out, McNamara was a cock-eyed optimist. The new Edsel sold 63,110 models. The total was incomprehensibly, head-shakingly low.

As some have pointed out, the United States was in a recession at the time, a period of breath catching from the hectic buying pace of Eisenhower affluence. As a result, sales of the Edsel probably would have been better even a year later, and almost certainly two years later. But 1957—the 1958 model year—was when the Edsel was born, and with that it would have to live and die. Live for a few weeks and die almost eternally.

---

1. It was the same Robert S. McNamara who, as President Lyndon Johnson's secretary of defense, would go on to lasting ignominy for his conduct of the Vietnam War, which included a ghastly assortment of lies for public consumption.

The recession was a worldwide phenomenon, not as bad in the United States as it was in Europe and Asia, but still a downturn in the domestic economy. It did not last long—eight months seems to be the commonly accepted figure—but they were the wrong eight months, the worst eight months, for the poorly named, and then poorly timed, Edsel.

Although no one at Ford expected the possibility of giving up on the car before Christmas, inauspicious signs added to the bleak sales figures. A journalist for *Consumer Reports* (the magazine respected for its objectivity, not *Consumer Guide*, which produced the special-edition book commissioned by Chevrolet) took a ride in an Edsel model called the Corsair. He did not ride far, however, nor did he ride for long, but his excursion would be the first public explanation of the Edsel's journey to automotive humiliation.

> The amount of shake present in the Corsair body on rough roads went well beyond any acceptable limit. . . . The Corsair's handling qualities—sluggish, over-slow steering, sway and lean on turns, and a general detached-from-the-road feel are, to put it mildly without distinction. . . . The "luxury-loaded" Edsel—as one magazine described it, will certainly please anyone who confuses gadgetry with true luxury.

People throughout the auto industry, not just Ford employees, were stunned; never before had they seen such a negative response to a new product—so negative, in fact, as to be newsworthy, and not just in *Consumer Reports*. Several newspapers and wire services ran copies of the *CR* review, or at least excerpts of it, and even one story of such a derogatory nature is enough to nullify tens of millions of dollars' worth of ads and the nick-of-time discovery of two crooners' toupees.

At least a few of the reasons that the Edsel sometimes rode like a covered wagon on a buffalo trail were outlined in an industry publication called the *Readex Report*. "Quality control over the new Edsel—critical for early, word-of-mouth success—was all but absent. Ford was building Edsels on existing Ford and Mercury manufacturing lines, and gave no emphasis to Edsel-specific training. The focus was on hurrying and making as many Edsels as possible. Some Edsels arrived at dealers with such shoddy build [*sic*] quality that dealers had to sink time and money into making the cars presentable—or even saleable."

It was, to say the least, bewildering. How could a company such as Ford, which invented the mass production of automobiles and had been its most successful practitioner for half a century, possibly make gaffes of such magnitude? Perhaps no one was more bewildered than the historian Geoffrey Perrett, who studied the Edsel's lineage and wrote that, by the time the car reached the market, it "was based on the most elaborate pretesting and market research and was accompanied by the most brain-storming, ulcer-making campaign of the decade."

More than anything else, the Edsel will be remembered for its front bumper, and the chrome ovoid, initially referred to as a horse collar, in the middle of it. Authors Peter Collier and David Horowitz report other descriptions, that the grille "was compared to a man sucking a lemon, to a toilet seat . . . Most of all it was compared to the female sexual organ. (One auto writer said that the car ought to be called the Ethel instead of the Edsel.)"[2]

But perhaps the most commonly articulated problem for the Edsel was simply its name—a dilemma that had not been resolved after all. When "market researchers [sought] to discover the 'immediate associations' that Edsel produced when fired at people in the street, they had come back with answers like 'Schmedsel,' 'Pretzel,' and 'Weasel'—while 40 percent of their respondents had just reacted 'What?' "

In 2000, *New Yorker* reporter Malcolm Gladwell published one of the more culturally significant books of recent years, and if I am correct in my understanding of precisely how *The Tipping Point* works, here is how it might be adapted to explain Ford's unique disaster: The Edsel looked funny and jiggled when driven. It was hardly deserving of praise. But because so flawed an auto had received such waves of promotion that expectations were high, when they were not met, the flaws became a bigger story than they might have been otherwise.

After the Edsel had been in showrooms and on the roads for a few weeks, it began to attract increasing amounts of attention not just because of its defects, but because the amount of attention the defects *already* had attracted had reached the tipping point, which is to say that press coverage of the defects had built up a momentum that went beyond the confines of reasonable criticism and exceeded what even so shoddy a piece of merchandise deserved.

To simplify: The Edsel was inept. Then ineptitude *became* the Edsel, the latter a synonym for the former, and in the process was regarded as a national joke. The car reached this nadir not just because of its inadequacies, but because of the volume of publicity those inadequacies had accumulated. The Edsel became the victim of a perversely negative kind of arithmetic in which one plus one somehow equals three.

If you bought an Edsel, people said at the time, at least you don't have to worry about safety. In one sense, the car was the safest on the market. Nobody would ever steal it.

---

2. With the Edsel in mind, and then some years later coming across the painting by Edvard Munch commonly—yet incorrectly—known as "The Scream," I did not find it difficult to see the mouth of the silently anguished woman in the grille.

After only two model years of E-Cars tumbling off the assembly lines and into the company's storage lots, the *San Diego Union* ran the following headline: "Ford Motor Co. Drops Edsel Line." The subhead: "Poor Sales Blamed."

> Ford Motor Co. today announced that one of its car lines will be discontinued after only 28 months of production. Ford said sales were so poor it could no longer justify the Edsel's existence.

Damage estimates for the debacle ranged from $250,000 to $350,000. That is, in 1957 purchasing terms. Expressed in today's amounts, the spectrum extends from approximately $2,205,200 to $3,087,300. "As John Brooks calculated for a piece in *The New Yorker*, the company could have saved money by giving away 110,810 Mercurys in 1955, instead of trying to build the Edsel." According to Douglas Brinkley, Brooks left a "gentle epitaph" for the car, stating, "Maybe it means a time has come when—as in Elizabethan drama but seldom before in American business—failure can have a certain grandeur that success never knows."

In other words, one generation's blunder can mutate, through the plaintive appeal of nostalgia and the further appeal of the cultural quirk known as reverse chic, into another generation's bold display of pride. That is exactly what happened.

By the time the 1970s had come along, Edsel owners' clubs began to pop up in the United States, some even spreading overseas. Like the *Star Trek* conventions of several years later, the owners held annual assemblies that were promenades of pride. Yes, they carried a degree of self-parody, but self-satisfaction as well; not that many people, after all, could claim that they held title to an Edsel.

Some members of the clubs, and these included people who owned more conventional automobiles, took up collecting Edsel memorabilia as a hobby. They accumulated photographs and toy models of the car, scraps of the infamous grilles, and ads that appeared in newspapers and magazines at the time, backed by cardboard, covered with cellophane, and often thumb-tacked to walls in basement dens. The most prized of collectibles, the front bumpers being too large and garish for home display, were the Edsel gear shift buttons, a complete set of which was almost as rare as a 1909 T206 Honus Wagner baseball card.

A magazine devoted to Ford's biggest flop, *The Big E*, was published five times a year for a while and made the car sound like the company's biggest success. Edsel parades were held in a number of American cities; "Edsel-cades," they were called, and people stood on the sidewalks to cheer at the innocent preposterousness of it.

And then there was the former San Francisco journalist David Mc-Cumber, who

> decided in 1998 to prove that the Edsel was a good, reliable car by embarking on a 10,000-mile journey in one. Leaving his home in Montana, he drove the entire circumference of the United States in his Edsel, getting stares wherever he went. . . . McCumber attended the thirtieth annual Edselcade in Dearborn; met a kid in Cocoa Beach, Florida, who offered him $100 for gas money because he was keeping the "Edsel spirit" alive; and struggled constantly with a broken-down fuel pump, getting stranded on Highway 101 in Los Angeles during rush hour. "It was frustrating at time[s]," McCumber admitted, "but my Edsel survived."

David McCumber, formerly a features editor at the *San Francisco Examiner*, had subjected himself to a form of torture via four-wheel automotive chamber. Driving a poorly made car that was outdated by four decades when his journey began, he added another ten thousand miles of punishment to both his vehicle and his spinal column, while in the process destroying the vehicle's fuel pump.

The Edsel that McCumber drove was too beleaguered an automobile ever to have found its way to Cuba, but other Edsels still could be spotted on the streets of Havana early this century. Not many, to be sure, and not often, but every once in a while one appeared. Behind the wheel would be a bronzed man in a straw fedora and guayabera shirt, and when he passed a pretty lady on the sidewalk, he would shout, "Vamos a mambear!" It is the same thing that Cuban men had been calling out for many years, and the ladies almost always looked at them and smiled. After all, the car was big, ornate, distinctive; it could give the impression that the driver was a man to be admired, or at least taken seriously, on this still poverty-plagued island.

7

Highways to Nowhere

The cars are so plentiful that they might be thought of as characters in the book. To list a few, in no particular order, they are . . .

"a brand-new Buick"
"his old Chevy"
"a '39 Chevy"
"his Texas Chevy"
"a put-together jalopy"
"his old Ford coupe"
"a '37 Ford sedan"
"a '47 Cadillac limousine"
"a mud-spattered '49 Hudson"
"a fag Plymouth"
"a souped-up rod"

Add the "toolshack on wheels" and "the mule wagon," "the weird, crazy Nebraska homemade trailer" and "a brand-new pickup truck," and the "farmer-cars, and once in a while a tourist car, which is worse, with old men driving and their wives pointing out the sights or poring over maps, and sit back looking at everything with suspicious faces." Their gazes manage to penetrate an increasing drizzle, somewhere near Davenport, Iowa, perhaps. That kind of place. But the old men drive on, through the weather, through the night, the car versus the elements and seeming to emerge victorious.

After further thought, though, it might make more sense to conclude that the cars are the setting of the book rather than its characters; to conclude that, taken all together, they are so plentiful that they make up the book's landscape, like the desert in *Lawrence of Arabia*, the ocean in *Jaws*, the mountains in *Alive*. In *On the Road*, the cars are scenery, the places where things happen, in many instances the reason they happen.

In other instances, the vehicles seem to be doing what background music is supposed to do in a movie, reinforcing the story's theme without being so intrusive as to prove a distraction. But, ah, how one longs for distraction in this particular tale. Distraction would be a brief rest from the onerous task of trying to find a purpose for Jack Kerouac's pages, something I tried to do, but without success.

Perhaps the fault is mine. *On the Road*, a controversial volume as far as many are concerned, is not a universally popular one. It *is*, however, one of the three books published in 1957 that commonly are considered classics of twentieth-century literature, *On the Beach* being the first. Forty-one years later, the Modern Library placed the Kerouac opus at number fifty-five on its list of the best hundred books of the twentieth century. And according to *Time* magazine, it is one of the best hundred books in the English language published during the oddly chosen period from 1923 to 2005.

Which, so far, doesn't say much for my judgment.

As for the author, and the life he led before taking to the road himself, it was as unlikely as could be imagined for a man who wrote the kind of books he did. Kerouac gave no early indication that he had a secret longing to be a drifter, an author, or even a Beat (a term preferred by those in the raggedy movement to Beatnik), nor a clue that he wanted to spend a lifetime feeling the nation's highways unroll beneath him. His first goal, antithetical to the purposelessness of Sal and Dean, the two main characters in *On the Road*, was to play football in the Ivy League. He dreamed of being an All-American, maybe even a pro. Kerouac was a talented athlete; the dream was not an unrealistic one. But it died quickly, as so many athletes' dreams do.

For his exploits as a running back in high school in Lowell, Massachusetts, he was offered at least three college football scholarships. After devoting a postgraduate year to prep school at New York's prestigious Horace Mann to boost his grades, Kerouac enrolled at Columbia. But he did not spend nearly as much time on the football field as he had hoped to. "In a freshman game against Rutgers in the fall of 1940," writes social critic Jeffrey Hart, "[he] was the best back on the field, but he broke his leg in the next game, and was out for the year."

He did not give up. He spent the next twelve months working harder than he ever had before or ever would again. Rehabbing his injury meant a long period of rest and healing, and then seven days a week of walking, jogging, running, and then working his way up to sprinting, jumping, doing calisthenics, flexibility drills, and other forms of bodily contortion. He also lifted weights, rep after rep; at times it felt like *eight* days a week. It was worth the effort, though. Kerouac wanted to get his body back, and with it his projected career.

But he couldn't do it. As a sophomore, hopeful of regaining his status as boy wonder, he found his leg still not completely healed, still not capable of lightning-quick stops and starts, the dazzling changes of direction he could execute before his injury. As a result, he started the season on the bench. His physical limitations notwithstanding, he did not think he belonged there. He knew his leg was not back to normal but believed that only by seeing action in games could he loosen it up enough for a return to glory.

His coach, a legendary fellow named Lou Little, disagreed. After a few arguments, Kerouac realized that Little intended to keep him "riding the pine" game after game—this despite the promise he had shown the previous year. Perhaps he would play a few minutes at the end of contests that already had been decided, but his future on the Columbia gridiron appeared to hold nothing more than cameo appearances during what sportswriters today call "garbage time."

This being the case, Kerouac could see no reason to stay in school. He told Little he was leaving, and without so much as a "good luck, kid" in response, the future author left his team, his school, and the Ivy League. His dreams already had vanished.

It did not take long, though, for Kerouac to concede that his coach might have been right; his leg had healed enough for him to get around on floors and sidewalks and lawns, but not enough to permit him to flash down football fields again with light-footed ease. And it did not take long after that for Kerouac to make the sweeping U-turn that would take him to the life for which he is known. No one ever would have guessed the path he would choose.

After a couple of false starts in the military, he finally enlisted in the navy. When he got out, he went home to his parents, settling with them in the Ozone Park neighborhood of New York's borough of Queens. He stayed for an unknown period, leaving, returning, going back and forth almost whimsically. But he stayed longer than one would have expected from the author of such stories of wandering and rootlessness as *The Town and the City*, *The Dharma Bums*, *The Subterraneans*, *Big Sur*, and, of course, *On the Road*, the latter probably more of an address for him than his parents' place was.

Just as Kerouac ended up living a different kind of life than he had expected, so did he produce, in his second and most famous book, a different kind of writing. Its language rhythms are not easily compared to those of other novels, and its plotlessness makes one wonder if *On the Road* can be considered a novel at all. Truman Capote didn't think so. Reacting to all of the fuss about it, he read the book and did not take long to dismiss it. This "isn't writing at all," he lisped, "—it's typing."

Yet the book begins in an almost traditional sense, calling up the nineteenth-century yearning to go west, young man, to cross the continent: the Mississippi and the plains, the Rockies and the desert, and then, the young man finally arriving at the shores of the Pacific, to look out wonderingly at its endless reach. It begins as if the book will be a story about longing for place, rather than the twitchy passion for movement from one place to another simply for its own sake.

On the Road's Sal Paradise has just divorced his first wife and is recovering from a serious, although unspecified, disease. He lives in the East, but it is a difficult time for him, and he longs for activity, some kind of motion. "I'd often dreamed of going West to see the country," he says, "always vaguely planning and never departing." Finally, in the company of his addled idol Dean Moriarty, who "actually was born on the road," Sal rides shotgun most of the way from New York to California as Dean tries to tromp the accelerator through the floorboard. They are basically a couple of harmless young fellows, driving toward the far ocean because they cannot think of a reason to stay where they are. They have no maps, no goals, would not rely on a GPS even if such a thing had existed. They will know where they want to be when they get there.

Or maybe they won't. Maybe what guides them, if they are in truth guided by anything at all, is a wanderlust that permits them to arrive but never settle. Maybe the point of *On the Road* is that there is no point, that nihilism rules.

Unfortunately, that is a difficult kind of story to tell engagingly, and Kerouac's book is not up to the challenge. It reveals nothing profound, and not much that is even interesting, about these people, this first generation of so-called Beats[1]—but how could it? Like various other lower life forms, the Beats seem to be motivated by impulse more than thought. I do not suggest that they are incapable of thought, only that, if *On the Road* is an accurate portrayal, they simply cannot figure out what to think *about*.

---

1. Beat often is thought to be short for "beatnik." But the word might instead be slang for "beaten-down," for those who feel conquered by life and have nowhere to go. Or it might be slang from the drug culture, where it refers to those who have been "cheated, robbed or emotionally or physically exhausted." It is said, though, that to Kerouac, as well as to the poet Alan Ginsberg, "beat" had a spiritual connotation, as in beatitude, although this seems a bit of a reach. More likely, beat is, at least in part, a reference to the free-form musical techniques of jazz, which was evolving into a variety of new forms in the fifties. As far as the word "beatnik" is concerned, it does not seem to have entered the language until the spring of 1958, when, for some reason known only to San Francisco newspaper columnist Herb Caen, he attached the "nik" from "Sputnik" onto "beat."

What is most interesting about the book is Kerouac's style. Its rhythms are more suggestive of jazz—the official Beat music—than literature. Often, the author is able to combine the two, that is to say, he is able to write jive that conveys a genuine grasp of content, a forward thrust of the story, and does so with an intriguingly reckless eloquence.

But more often than not, the author's style seems a disguise for the absence of meaning; the reader finds himself carried along by the beguiling tempo of Kerouac's coffeehouse riffs, cruising with him for a few miles, a few paragraphs or pages, before, stopping with a jolt, he realizes that the author has not given him any worthwhile information about the characters or their destinations or their reasons for the destinations. He rereads the passages, and they still seem a jumble. Kerouac is not even typing, as Capote said; he is playing captivating cadences with typewriter keys rather than a set of drumsticks.

As might be imagined, this one-man verbal jam session soon grows tedious. The rhythms of the vocabulary become random and repetitive. Even progressive jazz pays a kind of respect to melody, to chord structure, to the musical forms and perhaps even specific songs that have inspired it. Kerouac, on the other hand, is at times just running off at the mouth. What seems likely, if not even certain, is that much of his writing was done under the influence of marijuana and wine by the caseload. At the far-too-young age of forty-seven, he would die the alcoholic's death, cirrhosis of the liver.

When Sal and Dean finally alight on the West Coast, without anything much having happened to them en route, Sal wastes little time in deciding that the *East* Coast is the promised land. Sal does not give a reason for this change of mind. Sal does not *have* a reason. Sal does not *do* reasons. Neither does Dean, who, without any reason of his own, is ready to turn around, putting the sunset to his back.

If my calculations are correct—and the way the book is written, it is not as easy to figure out as it should be—Sal makes two and a half round-trips from coast to coast, each a virtual duplicate of the other. He drives, rides shotgun, sits in the backseat after being picked up hitchhiking, and eats as much junk food as he can afford, which is most of the time barely enough for sustenance.

To prepare for writing about Sal's excursions, Kerouac made his own round-trips, three of them by bus from Atlantic to Pacific—by my reckoning a little less than fourteen thousand miles from one side of the United States to the other. He sat in a large, malodorous capsule, cramped and idle, on seats that were not nearly as comfortable then as they are now. Perhaps he was thinking about the touchdowns he would never score. Perhaps he was not thinking at all, but imprinting the country on his consciousness, so that it could one day pass through Sal and Dean's windows. Regardless, it seems that he would have been terribly alone in his seat for all of that time; even if the bus averaged fifty miles an hour, which it could not have done until the Eisenhower Highway Act came into existence, he would have imprisoned himself for twenty-eight hundred hours.

Finally, after one has slogged through most of *On the Road*'s pages, usually at the pace of heavy traffic on a single-lane country road, Sal finds himself in Denver where, according to plan, he teams up with Dean again after the two have had a hiatus from each other. They decide they are tired of going back and forth all the time: from east to west, rest, reverse; west to east, rest, repeat. It is time for something new. Not anything so drastic as a job, certainly, nor a change of heart, not even really a change of mind; it is something far more in keeping with the nature of the two men. This time they will take a new path. This time they will go . . . *south*.

So Sal Paradise and Dean Moriarty, as well as another in-and-out-of-their-lives pal and, a little later, a wanderlusting hitchhiker, pile into a rattling, chortling, lurching automobile that Dean has managed to buy, and "we turned our faces to Mexico with bashfulness and wonder as those dozens of Mexican cats watched us from under their hatbrims in the night. Beyond were music and all-night restaurants with smoke pouring out of the door. 'Whee,' whispered Dean very softly." They are certain they have at last found their Eden.

Of course, Mexico is not as temperate as Adam and Eve's garden; it is hot, dry, populated by lizards, and prickled by cactus. But it has its advantages for a couple of Beats. It is a laid-back land, uncorrupted by ambition, intellectualism, ruthless capitalism, or the wives and children that the two principal characters have left behind. Sal and Dean are, it seems, homeless souls who finally have found their home, finally found the place that will be theirs for the rest of their lives. They are certain of it. The only question is: How soon will they leave?

Having settled in a nameless village for a while, Sal and Dean go out for drinks at night and hear the songs that drown out any sounds of nature; it is as if one discoteca were competing amiably with another, the cacophony of tunes coursing through the bloodstreams of the Americans as if they had been suckled on it since birth. There are, fittingly for this book, melodies such as " 'More Mambo Jambo,' 'Chattanooga de Mambo,' 'Mambo Numero Ocho'—all these tremendous numbers resounded and flared in the golden, mysterious afternoon like the sounds you expect to hear on the last day of the world and the Second Coming."

The experience of being on the road with the characters Kerouac has provided is such that I came across what I believe to be one of the saddest sentences I have ever read. It might not have been so wrenching in a different context, certainly not in a different book. But in Kerouac's work, after more than two hundred pages of roadway, of vacuous conversation among the characters, of emptiness without end, of unreachable horizons, the sentence strikes the reader with a depressing, yet resonant, hollowness.

Actually, it is not even a sentence; it is, strictly speaking, a clause, part of a sentence, in this case the last four syllables of the clause, which comprise the final four words of the paragraph and the chapter.

> It was with a great deal of silly relief that these people let us off the car at the corner of 27th and Federal. Our battered suitcases were piled on the sidewalk again; we had long ways to go. But no matter, *the road is life* (italics added).

When we last see Sal and Dean, ninety-nine pages after the sorrowful words above, with the book now coming to an end even if the road isn't, the two men find themselves north of the border again. Dean is in New York, "three times married, twice divorced, and living with his second wife." Sal seems to have returned to Denver, although it always is hard to tell with him.

Some years ago, a friend of mine, one whose literary judgment became a treasured part of my own career as a journalist, wrote glowingly about *On the Road* for a New York newspaper. Before his encomium, the book was not selling well. Afterward, sales picked up and stayed up, and in some quarters, the late Gilbert Milstein is credited—blamed?—with making Kerouac's volume into the classic it is now thought to be.

When I read his accolade, I could not help but feel that I had slipped into an alternate universe. This was a mentor of mine opining, one of the most knowledgeable literary figures I have ever met and someone with whom I spent many hours discussing how best to write a story for a television newscast. And yet, when he read Kerouac's book, Gil was transported. No pun intended.

I must have missed something. I am still missing it. But I'll be damned, now as then, if I can figure out what it is. The best I can say about *On the Road* is that it was published in the right decade, the right year, for, if such a thing were measurable, it might be that the automobile and its purposes were more on the minds of Americans in '57 than ever before or since.

PART THREE

Little Rock Nine

8

Blacks against Whites

Oliver Brown was tired of it. His daughter, Linda, eight years old, was even more tired—and less comprehending. The white kids in Topeka, Kansas, went to all-white schools that were, for the most part, around a corner or two from their homes. In this era before backpacks, they toted armfuls of books out their front doors, met up with friends along the way, and, in ever-enlarging groups, strolled toward their classrooms, carefree and animated.

But for Linda to get to her all-black school, her school with inadequate supplies, inadequate facilities, and often inadequate teachers, she "had to leave home at 7:40 in the morning, walk through dangerous railroad switching yards, and cross Topeka's busiest commercial street to board a bus that took her to school that opened at 9." All of this to spend the day in a classroom that was steaming in summer and frigid in winter. All of this when she lived a mere seven blocks from a white school that was better in every way. It made no sense to Oliver Brown's daughter. She knew only that it had something to do with the color of her skin.

Her father, who worked as a welder for the Santa Fe Railroad, knew well the dangers of the switching yard, especially for a young girl not familiar with one, and who traversed it in the haze of her early morning hours. Too many cars were being shuttled from one siding to another; Linda had to be careful to avoid them. Too many unsavory characters were stirring from another night's sleep in those cars, with mischief on their minds and cheap alcohol still on their breaths from the night before; Linda had to be even more careful to avoid *them*. So for Oliver Brown's daughter, the trek to a daily education was not just senselessly inconvenient, but potentially hazardous.

To make matters worse, the bus she rode partway to school usually dropped her off early, so that she and her fellow students would arrive before the doors were unlocked. This was not just bothersome; the young black boys and girls sometimes faced the added peril of weather. "On winter mornings," writes Geoffrey Perrett, "[Linda] could be seen on the pavement outside, jumping up and down while she waited, trying to keep warm," a few other black children bouncing alongside her. Sometimes, when not bouncing, they leaned into one another for warmth. And on rainy days, the youngsters, after having squeezed themselves under a short eave of the building, still entered the school soaked. They remained soggy through much of the day, and were still damp, and smelling of wet fabric, when the bell finally rang to dismiss them. By the time they got home, they could change their clothes and finally dry off.

They were exhausted, in other words, before the sound of the first bell. And now they were supposed to learn—put aside the daily evidence that their society regarded them as second-class citizens and educate themselves for better lives. *What* better lives? So that they could do what? So they could *be* what? They can easily be forgiven for not realizing the value of regular attendance at school.

In addition to his employment on the Santa Fe, Linda's father was an assistant pastor and sexton at a nearby Methodist church—a servant of the Lord, as he liked to think of himself. He did not normally participate in the activities of the Topeka NAACP, but when the group asked him to take the lead in legal action against the city's Board of Education, "he came to believe that God approved of his engagement in the case. There was no way that segregationists could paint Oliver Brown as a dangerous radical," and that is precisely the type of man the NAACP was looking for.

In essence, the group was asking Brown to do what the American Civil Liberties Union had persuaded substitute science teacher John Scopes to do almost three decades earlier in Dayton, Tennessee. Both men acted as stalking horses for causes in which they and many others in their communities strongly believed: Brown, for integrated schools; Scopes, the defendant in the famous "Monkey Trial," for the right to teach evolution to his students. Both men and the groups behind them knew they would lose their cases, but that was not the point. What they hoped was that their principles would emerge victorious—through the publicity that the trials attracted, or perhaps through the decisions of higher courts when their verdicts were appealed.

Brown's assignment was to try to enroll his daughter in an all-white school, and he was almost arrested for such a display of impudence. No matter; the starting line for the quest had been reached. On behalf of the Browns and twelve other pairs of parents, who among them had twenty children in Topeka's segregated schools, the NAACP filed suit against the city's Board of Education.

Over the course of the next three years, the focus of the dispute shifted from the classroom to the courtroom. It was a complicated matter, actually a series of complicated matters, because the Topeka suit ended up being "attached" to four other lawsuits filed in four different states, all of them related to race and schools and lumped together for the sake of the judiciary's convenience. But it was the Brown case that stood out, attracting the most publicity, and so when the issue finally reached the United States Supreme Court, it was known as *Brown v. Board of Education*.

On May 17, 1954, the nine justices made one of the most famous rulings in court history, although in the days leading up to it, no one could guess what it would be, mainly because the chief justice was an unknown quantity. After all, Earl Warren, was relatively new to the position, having "been on the bench only six months. At the time of his appointment, lawyers had been appalled by his total lack of judicial experience, and few in Washington had been willing to predict how he would stand in this case . . . Earl Warren was no racist, but he had the reputation of being a staunch believer in states' rights."[1] And civil rights, in the South, seldom meant rights for blacks.

The Supreme Court's decision was read by Warren shortly after 1 p.m., and is here, in part, paraphrased.

> Racial segregation in the public schools violated the Fourteenth Amendment to the Constitution . . . which provides that all citizens have equal protection under the law. The Court ordered schools not just in the South but through the country to be integrated "with all deliberate speed." Said Chief Justice Earl Warren, "To separate children in grade and high school from others of similar age and qualifications solely because of their race generates a feeling of inferiority as to their status in the community that may affect their hearts and minds in a way unlikely ever to be undone. We conclude that in the field of education the doctrine of "separate but equal" has no place. Separate educational facilities are inherently unequal."

In the first blush of victory, the joy among Topeka's black parents, and even some of the whites, was virtually unrestrained. It seemed to many of them, and to supporters elsewhere, that there had been nothing to compare with *Brown v. Board of Education* since the Emancipation Proclamation, and even the latter did not have the same kinds of practical consequences that the former was likely to have in the years ahead.

The journalist David Halberstam, in his history *The Fifties*, joined in the overreaction. He found the court's decision to be "perhaps the single most

---

1. Prior to President Eisenhower's appointing him to be the nation's foremost jurist, he had been the Republican governor of California, and before that, the state's attorney general.

important moment in the decade, the moment that separated the old order from the new and helped create the tumultuous era just arriving." Not to be outdone, fellow journalist Tad Szulc called *Brown v. Board of Education* "[o]ne of the most significant events in American history."

More temperate, and therefore more accurate, was the later assessment of Michael Barone, a senior writer at *U.S. News and World Report* when he wrote the following: "The *Brown* decision was recognized at momentous at the time," he opined; "but it was not as central to the progress of civil rights as many since have regarded it, and it was by no means the most effective advance in civil rights. The idea has grown up that American progress in civil rights was made mostly by the courts. But the historical record shows otherwise."

In the ranks of the NAACP, satisfaction and caution seemed mixed in equal portions. The group had gotten what it wanted but was apprehensive about whether the Eisenhower administration would support the court's decision. If so, would the support be wholehearted, enforced by the might of the federal government? Like his chief justice, the president was not a racist. He probably would have considered himself a centrist, possibly a pragmatist. The year before *Brown v. Board of Education* was settled, he had written in his diary, "The improvement of race relations is one of those things that will be healthy and sound only if it starts locally. I do not believe that prejudices will succumb to compulsion. Consequently, I believe that Federal law imposed upon our States . . . would set back the cause of race relations a long, long time."

Yes, it's the same old states' rights argument. But whereas bigots often called upon states' rights in an attempt to justify prejudice, others, starting with Thomas Jefferson, believed that the rights of the various states to make their own decisions, regardless of the issue, were at the core of American democracy. "The States in North America," Jefferson wrote in 1825, "which confederated to establish their independence of the government of Great Britain . . . became, on that acquisition, free and independent States and, as such, constituted to authorize governments, each for itself, in such form as it thought best."

It is probably a definition of states' rights that serves the thirty-fourth president of the United States as well as it did the third. When asked by a reporter, a year after his diary entry, whether he endorsed the Supreme Court's ruling on *Brown* or merely accepted it, Eisenhower said, "I think it makes no difference whether or not I endorse it. The Constitution is as the Supreme Court interprets it; and I must conform to that and do my very best to see that it is carried out in this country."

The comment was evasive. Upon hearing it, the NAACP was disappointed, if not surprised, that "no word of support came from the White House."

Chief Justice Warren also found the president's response wanting, a meaningless endorsement of the court's decision, if it could be called an endorsement at all—more, it seemed, like a statement watered down as much as possible to fit into the boundaries of the new edict while at the same time suiting Southern sensibilities.

On the other hand, Warren appreciated the president's dilemma. He knew how careful Eisenhower had to be, that he had to walk the finest of lines. If he lost his balance on the one side, tumbling to the South, he would forfeit large pockets of support in the North, which would believe that the country's chief executive was ignoring the law for the sake of political expediency. But if lost his balance on the other side, falling northward, he feared that the court's ruling could prove to be a starter's gun in the South for "excited and racist-minded public officials and candidates for public office [who] proposed and enacted every obstacle they could devise to thwart the Court's decision."

But many in Dixie felt even more strongly. They would be satisfied with nothing less than the president's overruling the Supreme Court, which he would not do, and, according to the law of the land, *could* not do. Reaction to integrated education in the South was "first muted then infuriated." Some officeholders went so far as to announce that because Eisenhower would not defy the court, they would take matters into their own hands, just as their ancestors had done with the Emancipation Proclamation and the various demands of Reconstruction. The South was its own ruling body, these politicians believed—they thought of theirs as a case of *region*'s rights—and they were no more willing to yield their sovereignty to the federal government now than they had been in 1861.

But for the time being, the children of thirteen pairs of black parents in Topeka, Kansas, enjoyed an easier journey to school than they had known before, a journey roughly equal to that of the white boys and girls, one that went unseen by the hobos in railroad cars. The students' relief, however, was matched by the apprehension of many parents. The *Brown* decision was not a popular one in the Kansas capital. Again calling to mind the Emancipation Proclamation, Southerners accused the national government of inflaming resentments with the Brown decision more than settling them. And another similarity, this to Reconstruction: *Brown* was seen by many below the Mason-Dixon Line as a deliberate provocation by its foes on the court rather than a reasoned judicial settlement, one that took into account the long-standing Southern way of life.

In Little Rock, Arkansas, views were especially inflammatory. To the state's governor, what Oliver Brown and the NAACP had done was no less incendiary an act than would have been the burning of the Confederate flag.[2]

Autumn 1957. School was about to begin, but Winthrop Rockefeller, the son of John D. Rockefeller Jr., was afraid it would be no routine academic year. In terms of the way he had chosen to live his life, Rockefeller was a branch of his own on the prestigious family tree. As a young man, he had been a "heavy drinker known for his playboy life style [and] often frequented chic cafes late at night with a movie star on his arm."

But all of a sudden, without the help of Alcoholics Anonymous or any other outside agency, without an "intervention" by friends, he gave up his wanton ways. Even more surprising and seemingly less explicable, he gave up residence in New York, the only home he had known, and fled to the relative privacy and unsophisticated lifestyle of Arkansas.

Or perhaps it is not such a mystery after all. Perhaps he thought that putting more than twelve hundred miles between himself and his previous debaucheries, not to mention the friends who accompanied him on them, would help him reform himself—even *force* himself to do so. After all, chic cafés were few in Little Rock, and actresses for his arm even fewer. Of course, Rockefeller would not be able to avoid booze no matter where he went, but he might have thought that the restrained pace of life in Arkansas would settle him without the need of spirits, helping him to keep temptation at bay. Regardless, he determined that he was up to the challenge. For the most part, he was.

Another reason for Winthrop's drastic change of address might have been the philanthropic strain in his family, its sincerely felt obligation for noblesse oblige. Winthrop's "assessment [was] that Arkansas labored under 'a vast inferiority complex.' He vowed to change that perspective, talking to as many Arkansans as he could—from the most humble farmer to the highest industrialist." His primary interest was improving the quality of education, to make Arkansans realize "that there was a world beyond the borders of the state that could be a rich source of learning and example for all who would tap into it." That included blacks as well as whites. He was, after all, Winthrop Rockefeller. He would not tarnish the family name by making his home in a "separate but equal" state.

In later years, after having held several elective offices, he would succeed with many of his goals. But in 1957 he was still a private citizen, having

---

2. Brown's daughter Linda died in 2018, as this book was being written. "Sometimes it's a hassle," she told a newspaper reporter about her seminal role in the civil rights movement, "but it's still an honor."

resided in the South a mere four years, and not as familiar as he eventually would be with the lay of the land, the psyche of the people. To his surprise, though, he was welcomed graciously, the prestige of his name overcoming his status as carpetbagger, and in time his residence would be the governor's mansion. But with the '57–'58 school year looming, he was already as highly regarded as the man who presently lived there. Possibly even more. So when Rockefeller asked for a meeting with Orval Faubus, it was accurately perceived as a summit of sorts, one that Faubus granted without cavil.

He and the governor were not strangers. In fact, two years earlier, Faubus had appointed Rockefeller to chair the Arkansas Industrial Development Commission, the result of which was that more factories moved into the state and provided a consequent boost to the economy. Faubus was amazed at what he took to be the power of the Rockefeller name, and when the commission disbanded, the governor appointed Winthrop to lead the state's future efforts in industrial development; this was the position he held at the time of the summit. It did not mean, however, that the two of them were friends, only that they shared a goal for the state's financial betterment.

But Faubus's background gave Rockefeller hope that their meeting about race and education would not be as futile as he feared. In his early days in the Arkansas State House, the governor had been a supporter of integration, even enrolling his son in an integrated college. Further: "He had helped open the Democratic party apparatus to black participation and had appointed black leaders to the party's state committee. He had started equalizing the salaries of black and white state employees. *He had overseen the quiet desegregation of the public schools in five districts* (italics added)."

In addition, Faubus "had helped Arkansas to become the first state in the South to open its all white colleges to black. He had appointed a few blacks to state boards. He had also given an Arkansas Traveler certificate, the state's official honor, to Mrs. Daisy Bates, president of the Arkansas branch of the National Association for the Advancement of Colored People."

His good works were widely known, widely discussed, widely praised by blacks. As a result, Faubus was seen "at the very least [to be] a traitor to the southern way of life."

Unfortunately, the governor had another side to him as well. He was also a selfish, bare-knuckled, backwoods-style politician, "a 47-year-old army veteran from the Ozarks," whereas Rockefeller was . . . well, a Rockefeller, despite his past promiscuities. Both men knew in advance the reason for the meeting that the former Northerner had requested. And they knew what the outcome was likely to be—although Rockefeller was daring to hope otherwise. Neither man looked forward to the verbal sparring ahead. But at the least, it was important for each to make his position public, and they had no better way to do so than by each confronting the other.

So the future governor sat with the incumbent in the state's official residence and pleaded with him to allow black students to enter Little Rock's Central High School without incident, which is to say, without violence. In other words, he pleaded with the state's top elected official to do nothing more radical than obey the law.

That Faubus would not do so surprised Rockefeller less than the bluntness with which he explained his reason. "I'm sorry, but I'm already committed," he told his guest. "I'm going to run for a third term, and if I don't do this, Jim Johnson and Bruce Bennett [racists who were opposing Faubus in the Democratic primary] will tear me to shreds." To prevent that from happening, he would call out the National Guard if he had to and form a barricade in front of Central High to keep blacks from crossing the school's threshold. Faubus would not allow a court decision—the Northerners' court, as he thought of it—to disturb the status quo of the South.

That would be "despicable behavior," thought Rockefeller, and he "argued against [it] to the very end, explaining that all the work they had done together in building up industries in Arkansas—which were already providing employment for thousands of Arkansans—was seriously threatened by Arkansas's segregationist stand." It was—or should have been—a convincing argument.

And it is possible, though not certain, that Rockefeller gave his adversary even more to think about. If Faubus did as he threatened to do, Rockefeller might have warned, the nascent television news business might be drawn to town. Should that happen, its cameras would show the country, maybe even the world, the governor of an American state orchestrating defiance to the country's highest judiciary. Microphones would allow viewers to hear the hatred of integration, while cameras recorded its physical expression, whatever that might turn out to be. The governor would blacken the image of Arkansas irreparably. To Rockefeller, the choice seemed a simple one, especially given the civil rights positions that the governor had staked out in his earlier days in state government.

Unfortunately, the choice was simple to Faubus, as well. He was undeterred. The governor's opponents already had seized the low ground in hate-mongering rhetoric, and as far as the governor was concerned, that left him with only one choice: He had to sink lower. His "popularity was waning; he had offended liberal constituents by approving rate increases for utilities and railroads and disillusioned others by raising taxes. His strategy was to build a new base in red-neck racist eastern Arkansas."

But Little Rock was the state's capital and largest city; he would need to set an example here. He also would need a base here, and the cruder and more vocal he became, the more he would blanket the state with his newly formed belief that racism was as American as the Pledge of Allegiance.

Orval Faubus would show himself to be a traitor to the Southern way of life no longer.

All of this, though, was behind-the-scenes politics. For public consumption, Faubus announced that Little Rock was aflame with acrimony against the Supreme Court and its allies; "the evidence of discord, anger, and resentment," the governor stated, "has come to me from so many sources as to become a deluge." For that reason, it would be irresponsible of him to yield to the forces of integration. It might be one of the lesser-known lies in American history, but it is also one of the most vile, a lie that has tainted the reputation of the Arkansas capital ever since.

Faubus spoke of evidence. There was *no* evidence to support his statement. None. It came from *no* sources; there was *no* deluge, except in the imaginations of the governor and those who advised him. In fact, testimony to the contrary showed Little Rock's being at peace with succumbing to the Supreme Court's decision after three rancorous years of ignoring it. It might have been an uneasy peace, but it was peace nonetheless, one that, under the leadership of someone such as Winthrop Rockefeller, could be built upon and even extended.

Those historians who portray Faubus, at least in part, as a greedy and hypocritical man do not overstate; a third term in the governor's mansion—and he eventually would serve six, each of two years—meant more to him than what he believed deep inside, or had once believed, about the relative equality of the races. It also meant more to him than what he should have believed was best for thousands of his state's children. As a result, he was willing to plant seeds of hostility that would grow into prickly flowers with amazing fullness and rapidity. This was not a case of either states' rights or regional rights; it was an *individual*'s rights. The individual was Orval Faubus, and his self-interest was a sanction for violence.

Little Rock's mayor kept a close eye on what was happening in the capital and was outraged. For perhaps the first time since taking office, Woodrow Wilson Mann publicly took issue with the governor. His city was calm, Mann told reporters. No, he said, he had no idea where Orval had gotten the idea that revolt bubbled under the surface, ready to erupt at any moment, nor had he any idea what affirmation to that effect had been presented to the governor. Although left unsaid, Mann's implication was clear. And correct. Faubus was playing politics, and far too much was at stake for play.

U.S. District Court Judge Ronald Davies also thought the state's chief executive was lying or, if not that, certainly exaggerating. And when the governor went so far as to claim that virtually all of the knives in Little Rock had been sold and "mostly to Negro youths," Davies could tolerate such bombast no longer. He ordered the FBI hastily to conduct a survey of close to a hundred stores in the area that carried not only knives but guns and other weaponry. Sales, as it turned out, had not only not increased—they were *below* normal!

Faubus dismissed the count as biased, as bluster. He would soon become known to his foes as "that sputtering sputnik from the Ozarks."

Davies went further to undermine the governor's attempt to undermine the law. His next order to the FBI was for it to assemble a task force of fifty agents to scatter themselves throughout Little Rock, searching for signs that violence was approaching: that people were arming; posters urging insurgency were being prepared; insurrections were being discussed, perhaps even planned; that, at the least, an edginess was in the air, one that perhaps led to the occasional argument, even fistfight. Once again, the agents acted quickly—and this time responded voluminously. In the words of historian William Manchester, "Their 500-page report disclosed not a shred of evidence to support the claim that the peace was threatened."

The peace, of course, *was* threatened, and most insidiously, by the man who sought another term as Arkansas's leader and was willing to continue his courtship with the dark side of human nature to boost his odds of reelection. His most dramatic step, as he had warned Rockefeller, was to summon 270 National Guardsmen and to instruct them to form a cordon around Central High School on the first day of school, September 3, 1957. White boys and girls would be able to enter as they usually did. As for the others, in the words of one guardsman, their orders were plain: "Keep the niggers out!"

What happened next resulted in some of the most bitterly poignant tales to emerge in the 1950s from the tenth circle of hell known as Southern racism. Most readers of this book know what happened in Little Rock in general terms: the brutality, the injuries, the spilling of blood—you have read accounts, seen photographs. The episode that follows has been chosen for the specific purpose of illustrating the horrors of racism even when displayed with a minimum of physical violence. It was still a form of abuse beyond tolerance.

Eight black students admitted to Central High on that September day in '57 made their trek accompanied by an honor guard of ministers, both black and white. They had their missals open and prayed softly as they walked. The procession made up in dignity what it lacked in numbers. But that was the problem, the number. Nine students were supposed to have been in the group.

For some reason, one youngster had not received word of the plan for them to enter together, escorted by clergy; someone had forgotten to call her, or had assumed the task belonged to another. As far as the young girl knew, she was on her own, and when she arrived at school early and saw no familiar faces awaiting, she felt as if she had been deserted.

Elizabeth Eckford, fifteen years old and small for her age, "wanted to be a lawyer when she grew up. Thurgood Marshall was her hero, and although she had never dared to hope she might one day meet the man who had argued and won *Brown v. Board of Education* . . . the African American youngster dreamed of doing the same kinds of daring things for her people." For that, of course, she would need a good education.

Elizabeth got off one of the town's buses, took a deep breath, and willed her body forward, as if it were an object she had to push ahead of her, toward the main entrance of what now was supposed to be her high school. She wore a pair of stylish bobby socks folded over at the top and new shoes that her mother had bought for the occasion, and it was on these that she fixed her gaze.

A throng of white racists lined the sidewalk leading from the street to the school's entrance. Before they saw Elizabeth, they were merely rumbling, making a sound that was like a continuous and throaty buzz, calling to mind a horde of giant insects. But when the little girl appeared, everything changed. This was what the hate-mongers had been waiting for, just as concertgoers thrill at the first glimpse of the show's headliner walking out on stage. They stopped buzzing and started to foam, to curse and threaten, loudly and virulently. Adults these were, grown-ups, citizens of the United States of America behaving in such a manner—100 of them, if not 200 or 250, standing tall and unbowed and defiant, shaking their fists at a single colored girl less than half their size.

Elizabeth continued to look down as she began the longest walk of her life, her concentration appearing so intense that she might have been counting the eyelets on her shoes. It was no consolation that the crowd treated the sidewalk as a boundary they shouldn't cross; perhaps they had been told another of the National Guard's orders to avoid physical confrontation if possible. Regardless, the frothing whites stayed off the pavement upon which Elizabeth forced herself to move with such trepidation.

Still, the throng stood too close for the little girl's comfort, their breaths coming in a single, ill-scented wave. And they were loud—that was the worst part, Elizabeth might have thought, how loud they were. What had she done to be the target of such a horrid sound? Whom had she offended, and why?

For a moment, she glimpsed the soldiers ahead of her; her immediate reaction was to find their presence reassuring. She thought they were there to make sure that she and the other black students would be admitted without incident. She didn't know that their presence had a different purpose entirely.

But the other black students, her friends . . . where were they? It was almost time for the opening bell. Had they decided it was too dangerous to defy the governor? Had they decided to stay home without telling her?

No, surely nothing like that could have happened. She was mystified as well as frightened.

As she got closer to the men surrounding the school, close enough to see the contortions on their faces, Elizabeth began to feel the peril. Something was wrong. She saw the cold eyes of the soldiers staring at her, such unwelcoming eyes, as well as their rigidly unmoving military stances, and she began to think she had been mistaken; maybe they were not shielding the front door to usher her in, but to keep her out.

The thought passed through her like an injection of ice water in the veins. She slowed her pace. The soldiers' eyes never left her; their stony expressions remained in place.

The men and women along the sidewalk kept shouting at her, issuing a constant stream of invective, seeming not to take a moment to breathe.

She continued to approach Central High's front door, but the closer she got, the more slowly she proceeded, and her heart was thumping so hard that she feared it might make her blouse flutter for all to see.

"Here she comes, now get ready!" one of the soldiers is reported to have said. Then another stepped forward and thrust out his rifle, the bayonet at the end of his weapon pointed directly at this threat to Southern life.

Elizabeth stopped, froze; suddenly terrified, she did not know what to do. She was alone, so horribly alone; afraid, but it was a fear beyond fear. According to journalists now descending on the school, although Elizabeth was not crying, she had begun to tremble, all the way from her shoulders to her knees.

She turned her back to the National Guardsmen and began to walk away.

As Winthrop Rockefeller also might have warned Faubus, print journalists would join the TV crews in reporting the story of hundreds of armed men versus the lone Elizabeth Eckford, and they would descend on Little Rock from newspapers in major cities all over the country. The epithets that the media heard that day would have to be censored, both on front pages and on the air.

"Go home, you burr head!"
"Go home, you bastard of a black bitch!"
"Go home before you get hurt."
"No nigger bitch is going to get in our school."
"Lynch her. Lynch her."

Most of the curses probably came from people who were parents themselves, men and women with children of their own whose faces were now twisted into a hatred of someone else's child, a hatred so extreme as to seem anatomically impossible. Again, as Rockefeller had warned, the broadcast crews began recording the scene for posterity, cameras shooting without stopping except to change rolls of film, as they used up one after another after another so quickly that they almost ran out of changing bags. It would be a big shipment back to the developing tanks in New York today. And tomorrow's newscasts, on which the film aired, would be documents of national shame.

The repetition of one of the most ghastly words in American history continued: "Lynch her, lynch her!" Did these people really know what they would do, how they would feel, if they suddenly saw someone among them step forward and begin to tie a rope around the neck of a fifteen-year-old girl already so terrified that just the sight of a rope might cause her to lose consciousness? Would they cheer? Did they really want to tie Elizabeth Eckford to a tree limb to get even with Earl Warren? They were human beings, after all; at some point, the humanity in them had to show itself.

But it hadn't happened yet.

As the whites continued to spew their malignancy at Elizabeth, not all of the journalists gathered around her were situated where they wanted to be.

Television news cameras raced for position, then focused on Eckford and the hostile crowd around her. But the CBS cameraman had gotten into place too late to catch the worst of the contorted on film and the yelling and the Confederate flag waving and the "Nigger Go Home" signs. When [CBS correspondent Robert] Schakne realized he didn't have the footage, he did something that revealed the raw immaturity of this relatively new medium of newsgathering; he ordered up an artificial retake. He urged the crowd, which had fallen quieter, to demonstrate its anger again, this time for the cameras. "Yell again!" Schakne implored as his cameraman started filming.

The racists took their cue. In an act of stupidity so great that the reporters watched with wondering eyes and slack jaws, they did as told and yelled again. And again, and again, as Schakne kept waving his hand to urge them on; he was like a movie director shooting the scene that was his big finale, shooting it from every angle: wide shots, close-ups, head-on, and in profile. Finally he ran his index finger across his throat. Cut! The throng could stop; the director had signaled a wrap. The extras had taken their instructions well and were pleased to stop, if only to catch their breaths.

They didn't know it yet, but they had ignited what would turn out to be nationwide outrage against their deportment and nationwide sympathy for previously unknown Elizabeth Eckford, defying not only the United States Supreme Court, in which they didn't believe, but the Golden Rule, in which, supposedly, they did. They had shown themselves capable of achieving new depths of human behavior, and the CBS News audience would see more varieties of it than their competitors would. The repeat performance orchestrated by Schakne was civil disobedience at its most grim, and he should have known better than to have encouraged it.[3]

All of the preceding probably happened in five minutes, perhaps a little more. But it was enough time for Elizabeth to have retraced all of her footsteps, slowly retreating from the school grounds to the bus stop, hoping she could get there safely and take the next bus home. Then she changed her mind. She did not want to sit in the open, allowing herself to continue to be a target for however long it would take the bus to arrive. Instead, she ran across the street, where a pharmacy already was open for the day. Her intent was to ask the druggist to call a cab for her. Or perhaps to ask him to call the police. Maybe even just to hide.

But the man behind the counter saw her coming. Whatever the young girl's woes were, she was a colored girl, and he didn't want any part of her. He hurried to his door and locked it before Elizabeth could get close enough to knock. He flipped the "Open" sign to "Closed." Then he lost himself in the back of his store, out of sight. She had no choice but to return to the bus stop and sit, unable even to imagine how events would swirl around her.

Bob Schakne decided to approach, his sound man pointing his microphone at Elizabeth, just as the Guardsman had moments ago pointed his knife. The cameraman was rolling. "Are you going to go to school here at Central High?" he asked senselessly. "The girl did not move a muscle." She was "frozen in fear."

Schakne pressed on. "You don't care to say anything, is that right?"

When Elizabeth remained silent, Schakne ended his "cruel inquisition of an innocent victim." Instead. he told his sound man to aim the mike, and his cameraman to aim his lens, at the people slowly squeezing in on them, these citizens of Little Rock who did not realize the power of the ammunition now shooting them.

The segregationist swarm—a tiny minority of the city's population, it should be pointed out, although their views on race probably represented those of the majority—was moving almost as a single person, then fanning out and, gradually surrounding Elizabeth. She had no visible means of escape. But at least the haters were quieting down, their explosive exertions after CBS's extra takes seeming to have left them depleted, at least for the moment. They shuffled off the sidewalk and into the street; the bus driver probably would not be willing, even able, to penetrate them.

---

3. Today, and at least as far back as the seventies, when I worked for NBC, shooting a second take of a news sequence has been forbidden by network news organizations. Even though it might look the same as the first take, and even though viewers would have no way of knowing they were looking at a replay of the event, not the original, a second take is considered "staging" the news and therefore is prohibited.

New York Times correspondent Benjamin Fine was the first to inject compassion into the reportorial ranks. He put his notebook in his pocket, pushed his way through the horde, and sat on the bus stop bench next to Elizabeth. He draped an arm over her shoulder and, smiling, lifted her chin.

"Don't let them see you cry," he said.

Fine's comment "helped the frightened child regain her composure. Now the mob descended on the Jewish New Yorker, shifting easily from racism to anti-Semitism, and threatened the small, appalled newsman that if he did not stop interfering they would castrate him." Fine remained where he was; he would not be dissuaded.

At this point, a woman named Grace Lorch, whose husband taught at a local college for black students, also fought her way through her fellow Arkansans and took a seat on the bench on the other side of Eckford.

"She's scared," Lorch shouted at the hate-mongers. "She's just a little girl . . . Six months from now you'll be ashamed at what you're doing."

They didn't seem to think so. The cries of "nigger lover" thundered down on Lorch like hailstones. She did not acknowledge them. Like Fine, she neither showed any fear or gave a sign that she would yield her seat until the bus came.

By this time, a young John Chancellor and his NBC News crew had approached the bench and begun to film. Years later, Chancellor talked to David Halberstam about that chilling experience, and the latter told Chancellor's story in his book *The Fifties.*

[Chancellor] had watched Elizabeth Eckford's perilous journey with growing fear: one child, alone, entrapped by this mob. He was not sure she was going to make it out alive. He had wanted a story, a good story, but this was something beyond a good story, a potential tragedy so terrible that he had hoped it wasn't really happening. He was terribly frightened for her, frightened for himself, and frightened about what this told him about his country. . . . The mob gathered there in the street was uglier than anything he had ever seen before in his life. It was a mob of fellow Americans, people who under other conditions might be perfectly decent people, but there they were completely out of control. Chancellor wondered briefly where this young girl found her strength. It was almost as if he were praying: *Please stop all of this; please, there's got to be a better way.* He watched in agony and captured it all for NBC.

It was not exploitation, as some people charged. It was, rather, television journalism at its finest. Even Schakne, acting on the spur of the moment, had had the best of intentions.

Finally it happened. The other eight students and their clerical escort showed up, horrified to learn that there had been a mistake, that no one had remembered to call Elizabeth, and she had been there now for ten minutes or more by herself. They could not imagine what she had gone through. They tumbled over one another to reach her.

But it did not matter anymore; Elizabeth's friends finally had found her, and she nestled herself into their midst. They surrounded her with hugs and tears and apologies, anything to acknowledge what must have been her terrible suffering.

After a few minutes, the *nine* students and accompanying men of the cloth proceeded without confidence to the blockade called the National Guard, which had not budged from the Central High front doors since Elizabeth first appeared.

Nor would they budge now. Impervious to the prayers for their white souls spoken by both black and white preachers standing only a few feet in front of them, the Guard made sure the group could go no farther. No blacks would cross their line. After a few minutes, the students and their entourage turned a sad about-face and, for the morning, at least, gave up the battle. There would be no education for the students this day, nor for many to come.

How much of the preceding Faubus learned, and how quickly he learned it, is not certain. For the first few nights of the school year, he had left the turmoil behind him—geographically, at least. He and his wife had departed for the bonhomie and bourbon of the Southern Governors' Conference in Sea Island, Georgia, a sojourn previously scheduled, but one whose timing could not have been better.

Faubus did, however, hear at least the broad strokes of the story at his retreat, and commented for public consumption about the city he temporarily had left behind. "The trouble with Little Rock," he told reporters, "vindicates my good judgment."

But the conference lasted only a few days. At which point, Faubus was forced to return to the place where that good judgment of his was playing itself out, and where he found himself faced with a continuing standoff, one from which he would not back down. The governor kept shipping in National Guard reinforcements, and ABC, CBS, and NBC kept sending in reinforcements of their own, new shifts of correspondents and crews, sound men and producers. They were joined by more from the United States, but from London and other foreign capitals as well. Which is to say that the worse things got in Little Rock, the more people who knew about them, and as commentators both in the United States and abroad began to point out, the racial attitudes of Arkansas were coming to stand for those of the entire country. It was a cruel disservice to the United States, a disastrous misrepresentation, and one whose pervasiveness was greater than even Rockefeller had seen coming.

Meanwhile, the U.S. attorney for Little Rock, refusing to yield an inch to Faubus, had compiled a list of more than 200 witnesses to testify before Judge Davies about the actions of the governor and his minions leading up to September 3. But not that many were needed. After Davies had heard from a mere eight men, each a Little Rock city official, each attesting to the serenity of their city before Faubus stirred the lower levels of the populace into overheated turmoil, he called the hearing to a close and made his pronouncement. He declared that the integration program devised by the Little Rock School Board had been "thwarted by the governor of Arkansas by the use of National Guard troops." Davies also stated, "It is equally demonstrable from the testimony here today that there would have been no violence in carrying out the plan of integration."

In Washington, D.C., President Eisenhower had been watching the coverage every evening. He also had been receiving firsthand reports from Little Rock and began to fear that a state of war might be approaching. He had not wanted his administration to be part of this; he wanted Arkansas to settle its own matters. But Faubus's criminally incompetent behavior demonstrated how unrealistic Eisenhower's support of states' rights had been in this case.

Finally, and with some hesitation, he decided to act. States' rights, after all, could go only so far; the principle could not be extended to opposition toward both the national government and the Supreme Court. No state had a right to do that. After talks between members of the administration and various Southern leaders had failed, the president arranged for a private meeting with Faubus at the Newport Naval Station in Rhode Island. He told him that "there could be only one outcome," if a state took on the federal government; "the state would lose, and I did not want to see any governor humiliated." Afterward, he offered Faubus a few face-saving sops, and, at last, knowing that he had pushed the president as far as he could, the governor accepted his fate and said he would stand down.

But Eisenhower wanted to make sure. He also wanted his administration to provide a massive show of support for an integrated Central High School, one that his top advisers had been telling him was long overdue. He asked the three major television networks for airtime. It promptly was made available.

That night, before an estimated one hundred million viewers, with more than 60 percent of all American sets tuned to him, he announced that he would send a thousand men from the 101st Airborne Division—a racially integrated group, the president emphasized—into Little Rock. "The very basis of our individual rights and freedoms," Eisenhower said, "rests upon the certainty that the President and the executive branch of government will support and insure the carrying out of the decisions of the federal courts, even, when necessary, with all the means at the President's command. Unless the President did so, anarchy would result. There would be no security for any except for that which each one of us could provide for himself."

As for the National Guardsmen who were already in Little Rock and taking their orders from Faubus, they were told that, effective immediately, they were under federal jurisdiction and would be acting in accordance with instructions from the White House, not the statehouse. In a matter of moments, they were to transfer the loyalty of a lifetime. Eisenhower, as most of them believed, had demanded that they turn their backs not only on their fellow Southerners, but on themselves and everything they had grown up believing about the races. But they had their orders, their new orders; they were sworn to obey them.

The nine black high-schoolers of Little Rock finally began their school year. The date was September 24, 1957, exactly three weeks later than scheduled. With tempers on both sides having frayed over that time, perhaps it was inevitable that physical violence would break out at the end. Four young black men who were not students, but journalists, tried to enter Central High with the boys and girls. It was not to be.

> Retreating, they were pursued by about twenty bullyboys, who cut them off and began systematically beating them. One cop climbed on a car to get a better look. Others moved in to stop the mayhem, and as they did Jimmy Karam cried angrily, "The niggers started it." . . . But while the mob had been watching the attack on the black reporters, the nine Negro children . . . walked into the school.

They walked in with caution, though, afraid of facing even more enmity, this time from their fellow students. What would happen now that whites and blacks finally encountered each other under the same roof, in the same classrooms and corridors? The answer, so long awaited, was . . . nothing. Nothing happened on that day, at least. There was the occasional whispered slur, the occasional cold glance, but only occasional. "Most of the white students look at [the blacks] curiously. Some made friendly overtures. None appeared to be hostile." The whites, finally seeing blacks close up, found them interesting sorts, and the same was true in reverse. It is doubtful that enduring friendships were made, but the tension in the air was manageable for all.

Orval Faubus had no explanation for so sudden a turnabout in attitude.

The National Guard remained in Little Rock for nine months—but serving as law keepers now, no longer arrayed as a barrier—until the end of the school year. Their presence for such a long period allowed "[t]he Russians [to use] Little Rock as a counterpoint to Sputnik with a degree of subtlety not common to Cold War animosities. Every day Radio Moscow broadcast in English the moment Sputnik would appear over major U.S. cities and especially over Little Rock."

On graduation night, the National Guard wrapped up its duties in Little Rock in what some people would have considered typical fashion. When Ernest Green, the only senior among the nine black students who went on to be a successful investment banker in the nation's capital, marched out of the auditorium with diploma in hand, he was spat upon. None of the Guardsmen, they claimed, saw it.

By this time, NBC had long since become, in Southern parlance, the Nigger Broadcasting Company. CBS was the Coon Broadcasting System, and ABC the African Broadcasting company.

The *Chicago Daily News* did not acquire a nickname, but it certainly qualified. Reporter Jack Mabley suggested that, because of what he had witnessed in Little Rock, the governor's last name should be converted into a verb.

Fau-bus (faw-bus), v.i.; FAUBUSED, FAUBUSING. 1. To commit an error of enormous magnitude through malice and ignorance. 2. To make a serious error, to commit a fault through stupidity or mental confusion. Syn. Blunder, err, bollix.

For some reason, despite the appropriateness of Mabley's definition, the word never found a place in an official lexicon.

Orval Faubus, the man, not the verb, won reelection for a third term in 1958, and the six consecutive terms he served as governor are to this day still a record in Arkansas.

As I write, Elizabeth Eckford, now in her seventies, is a probation officer in Little Rock.

Ironically, in the same year of her humiliation, in fact within a week of the blacks' first day inside Central High, Congress voted on the Civil Rights Act of 1957, and it was the first such piece of legislation to be approved since 1875, during the Southern revolts against Reconstruction. It was not as comprehensive an act as many hoped it would be, however. For the most part, it concentrated on voting rights for those of African American descent, and the driving force behind it was Texan Lyndon Johnson, a Democrat and the Senate minority leader, who not only fought successfully for civil rights in the fifties, but led the charge for even more sweeping reform in 1964 and '65. On the one hand, he was fighting for the legacy of the slain president Kennedy in the sixties; on the other, he was seeking to establish a legacy of his own. Johnson had been a lifelong advocate of racial equality,

and few were the congressional arms he didn't twist, few the fellow legislators he did not threaten, to get the votes he needed.

In '57, the final score was not even close. The Civil Rights Act passed in
the House, 285–126, and in the Senate, the percentage of support was even
greater, 72–18. It was a resounding victory for racial equality, or so it
seemed.

It wasn't Strom Thurmond's fault, though.

A fiery Democrat from South Carolina, he was so opposed to the notion
of blacks and whites being educated together—or in fact doing anything
together—that he tried to delay passage of the bill by taxing his vocal cords
superhumanly. Somehow, the travesty of a process called the filibuster had
worked its way into the democratic process, and Thurmond believed there
was no better time to use it than now.

When he began to filibuster against the Civil Rights Act, his fellow senators, both supporters and foes, had no idea what an ordeal they were in
for. They would learn regretfully. "Thurmond held the floor for twenty-four
hours and eighteen minutes—the longest one-man filibuster in the Senate's
history—drawling out the Declaration of Independence, the Bill of Rights,
and George Washington's Farewell address." But he was just getting started.

Since it didn't matter what a filabusting law maker said, only that he keep
talking, Thurmond also read the voting laws of all forty-eight states. He
read the United States Criminal Code. He declaimed on jury trials. "He
read a Supreme Court decision, followed by more laws. A friend brought
him a glass of orange juice." He took a few other breaks as well: answering
questions from fellow senators, welcoming a contingent of Italian dignitar-
ies, then pausing to allow them to seat themselves.

Nonetheless, Thurmond gets credit for the entire time he stood on the
podium, and so earned for himself a place of ignominy in the *Guinness
Book of Records*. As far as the efficacy of his marathon is concerned, we have
no reason to believe it changed so much as a single vote. He did nothing
more than delay the right for blacks to vote for another twenty-four hours
and eighteen minutes, during which time no elections were held anyhow.

Although the Civil Rights Act of 1957 opened the curtains of voting
booths to blacks, it was, in reality, something more than just that. Its passage might have been the result, at least in part, of congressional anger at
the extent to which *Brown v. Board of Education* was being ignored or flouted
throughout the South. Three years had passed since the Supreme Court's
decision, and still the majority of school systems in the South were providing separate but *un*equal education—Little Rock having been the biggest
and probably the most intransigent of them. The Civil Rights Act may be
seen, then, as an endorsement of equality in education as well as equality
in the electoral process. To Lyndon Johnson, the act was "a great achievement" and ought to be treated as such.

But, as was the case with *Brown v. Board of Education*, a more measured response was a more accurate one. Even many of those who supported the act, such as the famed civil rights attorney Joseph Rauh, found the legislation weak, flabby, not nearly inclusive enough to deal with all of the problems loaded onto the backs of black Americans. The best Rauh could say about it was the least that advocates wanted to hear: "It was better than nothing." Johnson might have agreed, but being a savvier man than Rauh, he knew what an enormous legislative hurdle integration was, and, as the Chinese proverb, usually attributed to Lao Tzu, has it, "the journey of a thousand miles begins with a single step."

More important by far to the goal of racial equality in the United States were the television networks' newscasts. Viewer outrage at the displays of racism, Little Rock style, as broadcast nationally night after night, were pictures that simply did not look as if they had been taken in the United States, and they changed both hearts and minds. Even vast numbers of people who continued to believe in the inferiority of blacks now came to insist just as firmly that they were children of God and, as such, did not deserve to be treated as horribly as they had been in Arkansas. After all, they treated their aggressors much more decently.

But as "The Little Rock Nine" finally started their lessons, something else was happening outside of classrooms in the South and the judicial and executive chambers in the North. It was something that already had helped to bring the races closer together in some instances, and would continue its good work, even more pervasively, in the coming years. It had been around, this something, in one form or another, for decades, but was just beginning, now that it was changing forms yet again, to assert itself culturally, to play a dramatic role in a society that had never expected such a thing. It all started with a simple four-chord melody and a driving beat.

9

Whites *with* Blacks

Beale Street, Memphis, Tennessee. One hundred forty miles east of Little Rock on Interstate 40, although it could have been another country in 1957, not just another state. There was no place like it back then. It became the black center of Memphis, and starting with the famed W. C. Handy in 1909, it also became the musical center of Tennesee, maybe even of the entire South, teeming with clubs, dives, and restaurants, most of them offering live music. But not just any music.

By the forties and fifties, Beale Street had so many performers that the songs spilled out onto the sidewalks, as old, raspy-voiced black men sat in cane-woven chairs, with the cane ripping here and there, and strummed guitars about as tattered as the chairs were. They played the blues, a kind of music with melodies sorrowful and desolate, hard on the soul. It is a simple kind of music, to be sure, but the emotions it elicits are powerful and often complex.

> Used to be so easy to
> give my heart away.
> But I found out the
> hard way,
> there's a price you
> have to pay.
>
> I found out that love was
> no friend of mine.
> I should have known time
> after time.

Or:

> I'm gonna buy me a pistol with a great long shiny barr'l
> I'm gonna buy me a pistol with a great long shiny barr'l
> Gonna shoot that rounder who stole away my gal.

An occasional white musician might have been sitting in with the blacks, but not often. Most of the audience was black, too; after all, the blues are the black experience in America, the spirit in addition to events. But the music always spoke to a scattering of white folks; they joined the blacks standing in line to get into the more popular joints, such as PeeWee's and the Monarch, never complaining about the wait.

Once inside they made themselves comfortable, sitting wherever they wanted, paying no attention to the skin color of the man or woman next to them. "In the forties and fifties, white music-lovers from all over the world . . . went often and safely to Beale Street to listen to the music," and when the music was playing, nothing more important was on their minds, nothing that could be felt as deeply, as meaningfully.

Most of the music lovers were men, who, in addition to being white, included at least one who might have been underage when he first started frequenting the Memphis joints. He had been born in Tupelo, Mississippi, in 1935, and life there was not easy for him. "After enduring dwindling economic opportunities and downward progression in their already-low social status," writes a biographer of the young man and his mother, "he and his working class family eventually migrated to Memphis. . . . Inspired by entertainers and movie stars [the latter of which he always wanted to be], he developed a penchant for flashy clothes, slicked-back hair, and long sideburns."[1]

The flash, however, was only the surface; within, the boy was a more substantive sort, although his nature was artistic rather than intellectual. At times, though, he was so shy that he seemed to be embarrassed about something, as if he had just spilled a glass of root beer on the pretty young thing who had served him.

But he was concentrating; that's all. Feeling deeply. He wanted to understand the music, its grip on him; just wanted to be alone in the crowd as he sipped his soft drink and listened, trying to feel the songs viscerally, the way they were supposed to be felt, despite his youth, despite his color. Even though the law said he was too young to be in places like this, he had an almost eerie ability to experience what he heard that was older than his years.

Between sets he sometimes talked to the black boys and girls around him. He was comfortable with them. "Poor we were, I'll never deny that," said his father, Vernon. "But trash we weren't . . . We never had any prejudice. We never put anybody down. Neither did Elvis."

As for the blacks, musicians as well as fellow members of the audience, they seemed to take young Elvis Presley seriously, his earnestness and his

---

1. His hair was often compared to a duck's ass, or "DA," combed together, almost making a part, in the back of his head. The style caught on as his music did, but not everywhere. The "DA" quickly became grounds for suspension in a number of American high schools.

gut-level responses to the music. And, of course, that remarkable hair of his, which one day, when he was in his early twenties, would be compared to the tail fins on cars, or the wings on airplanes, especially when a breeze blew past him and fluttered it out to the sides.

But the blues were not just songs for Elvis. Even before they became his music of choice, he was adopting the lifestyle.

> While still in high school, he hung out at Henry's Record Shop in Memphis, where black musicians congregated and proprietor Robert Henry booked acts like Fats Waller and Earl "Fatha" Hines for local shows. As a teen, Elvis bought 89-cent singles by black artists . . . He listened to regional R&B radio programs like *Tan Town Jamboree* . . . and *Red, Hot and Blue*. He greased his hair with Royal Crown Pomade and shopped at Guy and Bernard Lansky's Men's Fashion Store on Beale Street . . . buying the same cool duds as blues artists Jimmie McCracklin and Little Junior Parker.

But the blues were not the only kind of music that influenced Elvis in his early years. He was a regular at another Memphis attraction, the All-Night Gospel Singings at Ellis Auditorium. Sometimes he went alone, at other times with relatives, including his mother and father. Again, it was black music, but at the Ellis the singers were white. It made no difference, though; Elvis was not paying attention to skin color. He was rising up with melodies that themselves soared heavenward, reveling in the energy of singers who boosted the reach of the songs higher and higher. "He sat there mesmerized by what he later described as " 'the big heavy rhythm beats' of some of the spiritual numbers and the delicate beauty of others. . . . Gospel music combined the spiritual force that he felt in all music with the sense of physical release and exaltation for which, it seemed, he was casting about."

The white gospel music he liked most in those days included "the stately harmonies of the Blackwoods, who adapted many of their hits from the new spiritual style of such Negro quartets as the Soul Stirrers and the Original Gospel Harmonettes of Birmington. There were hints of the Ink Spots and the Golden Gate Quartet, and even of contemporary Rhythm and Blues singers like Clyde McPhatter[2] and Roy Hamilton, in their beautifully arranged, precisely articulated styling."

And, of course, growing up where he had and living where he did now, he could not help but be influenced by Western music, which was not called "country and western" back then. Hank Williams: "Your Cheatin' Heart," "Hey, Good Lookin'," "I'm So Lonesome I Could Cry." Jimmie

---

2. McPhatter would later be the first person inducted twice into the Rock and Roll Hall of Fame, as a solo artist and as the lead singer for the Drifters, a group that, that for several years, virtually took up residence on *Billboard* magazine's "Top 100," and a group as influential as it was popular.

Rodgers: "Blue Yodel No. 12," "I'm Free from the Chain Gang Now," "Roll Along, Kentucky Moon." Ernest Tubb: "I'm Bitin' My Fingernails and Thinkin' of You," "You Don't Have to Be a Baby to Cry," "Don't Rob Another Man's Castle."

And that, in terms that perhaps are oversimplified, is the recipe for the artistic genius of Elvis Presley: traditional black blues, white gospel, black gospel, white Western, and a drummer who kept the piano, guitar, and bass driving like a metronome. And more than anything else, the boy had remarkable vocal cords, somehow managing to combine strength and plaintiveness in a style that was a new kind of music in itself, regardless of the type of songs he sang.

But this Elvis, what some of us think of as the *real* Elvis, was not going to last. For he was about to meet a man who called himself Colonel Tom Parker, although he was neither a colonel nor, at birth, a person named Tom Parker. He was, rather, a con man, probably a psychopath, possibly an escaped murderer, and definitely a Dutchman named Andreas van Kuijk. He was also a second-rate P. T. Barnum with a mean streak that the original did not possess.

Somehow, though, the Colonel wormed his way into a relationship with Elvis's unsophisticated father, and the two of them teamed up to persuade the singer to let the Dutchman be his manager. This, with a number of notable exceptions, would be the end of Elvis's art and the beginning of his bad movies, worse soundtracks, overproduced singles, and all of those pitiable nights when he was stuffed like the Michelin man into a jumpsuit on a Las Vegas stage, where the older Americans who once disdained him now were taking him seriously, just as his music became turgid, even sappy at times.

Vegas was the ultimate sellout, and Elvis could not even console himself by having received the ultimate in remuneration: The Colonel probably was taking a higher percentage of his client's gross than any other manager in the history of show business—more, even, than the Mafia would have extorted had it managed to get its hands on Elvis. Parker was the great saboteur of American rock 'n' roll—who knows what Elvis's music would have been like, how it would have evolved, had he not met this so-called Colonel? Consider the Beatles, who started out covering Chuck Berry and ended up producing music that fits into virtually no extant category other than the catch-all "popular." What unnameable categories might Elvis have created?

But the meeting between Tom Parker and Vernon Presley, and its consequences, are a story well told in other books.

The pre-Colonel Elvis was the man for whom Sam Phillips had been looking. A Memphis record producer, Phillips also was something of a visionary, although it was Sam's comanager at Sun Records, Marian Keisker, who recorded her boss's famed comment for posterity, jotting it down as he spoke. "If I could find a white man who had the Negro sound and the Negro feel," Keisker remembers Phillips saying, "I could make a billion dollars."

The kind of music Phillips had in mind was only a few years old when he gave voice to his wish. The first real rock 'n' roll songs probably were recorded in 1951. Among them were "Rocket 88," a number "which extols the virtues of the Oldsmobile 88 convertible as a metaphor for sexual prowess," and the even more sexually explicit "60-Minute Man," by Billy Ward and His Dominoes. *So* sexually explicit is the song that a lot of radio stations refused to play it.

> There'll be 15 minutes of kissing
> Then you'll holler "please don't stop" (don't stop)
> There'll be 15 minutes teasing
> 15 minutes of squeezing
> And 15 minutes of blowing my top
> Top-top-top.

Songs such as these were what Phillips wanted, as new and distinctive as they already were but with a white man's voice making them sound even newer and more distinctive, especially because these numbers had a beat that transformed the sorrow of the blues to something of a celebration. Nothing about Phillips was racist; rather, he was something of a visionary, a man with a good ear for a sound that did not yet exist. He was convinced it would sell. And he wanted to be the man who did the selling.

That is exactly what happened. Until, that is, Phillips made the sale that he cursed for the rest of his days. He sold the contract for Elvis to the crooked Colonel, who already was in league with Vernon, for what seemed like an enormous sum of money at the time. Phillips thought long and hard about the deal, but the Colonel was offering cash in the hand, $35,000 of it* and if Phillips trusted anything more than his instincts, it was the feel of crisp, green bills resting in his palms.

Still, even after he had decided to part with Elvis, Phillips agonized over it, and not just for financial reasons. A personal element was there as well. Sam liked the young man, really liked him. He remembered the day they met, the day Elvis appeared in Sam's studio; a truck driver by trade at the time, Elvis had just gotten off work and was still wearing his T-shirt. Over his shoulder was the only guitar he had ever owned. He told Phillips he wanted to make a "hear-your-own-voice" record, but not for himself, not to audition for anyone; it was for his mother. He wanted to give her music

---

*In today's terms, adjusting for inflation, the amount exceeds $300,000.

as a birthday present. Keisker, sitting in on the meeting, told Elvis how much it would cost, then "noting his name, vocal style, and a phone number at which he could be reached" after the session. Elvis had chosen two rhythm and blues songs, an A side and a B side, for Vernon's wife, Gladys. After the rest of the paperwork was filled out, the singer was told to situate himself comfortably. He dropped onto a stool, adjusted the microphone, and prepared to deliver.

Phillips took his place in the control room, where he started turning some dials and pushing some knobs. When they were properly positioned, he asked Elvis for a level. He complied, and Sam returned the favor with a few more subtle adjustments on the control panel, followed by a jab of the index finger. That was the cue. Elvis gave a few introductory strums on the guitar, then sang.

Side A: "My Happiness," a ballad that first had been recorded nine years earlier and "couldn't have been further from anyone's imagining of rock 'n' roll." Until, that is, Connie Francis recorded it with a beat and an echo chamber in 1958.

Even when he was just giving his level, then idling vocally for a few seconds while Phillips finished tinkering, Elvis caught the older man in his grip. And as the truck driver broke into "My Happiness," Phillips listened in a state almost benumbed. He did not merely hear the sound for which he had been searching; rather, he heard a kind of music almost impossible to describe, virtually a genre unto itself. And Phillips didn't even have to find him; the young longhair had found *him*.

Side B: "That's When Your Heartaches Begin," first recorded by the sentimental black vocal group the Ink Spots in 1941, and also unimaginable as Elvis adapted it.

Although Phillips had not heard the birth of rock 'n' roll that day in his studio, he remained dazed by what he *had* heard, the music's transition from its earliest days into adolescence. It came so unexpectedly—as if anything like that could ever *be* expected, and it came from someone whose name he might not even have remembered as he listened.

Sam Phillips may be considered the anti-Andreas von Kuijk. Although he did not know quite what to make of his customer at first, his instincts told him to let Elvis be Elvis both in the recording studio and elsewhere, and as a result the young man recorded music like none ever laid down on acetate before, blending together those varied influences of his and stirring them into the budding refrains of rock 'n' roll that he also had begun to enjoy. The result was momentous; Elvis pointed the way toward the future of popular music.

At first, though, Phillips feared there might be a backlash that Elvis might be seen as a usurper, a white fellow who was plagiarizing the black songbook, exaggerating the rhythm and adapting the vocals to his own unique and unpracticed style. The men from whom Elvis had learned the blues still were earning a pittance down on Beale Street, which, even in the fifties, had not yet recovered completely from the Depression. Yet in Elvis, Phillips envisioned a multimillion-dollar future. Unless . . . unless there *was* that backlash.

As it turned out, there wasn't, and Phillips should have known. In several ways, musicians are a different breed of mortal from the norm. One of those ways is that they have a history of appreciating originality in their line of work, no matter who demonstrates it, no matter what sources lead to it. Even the best of them sometimes think of themselves as servants of music, not its masters—and so tales of appreciation for talented newcomers greatly outnumber stories about jealousy among vocalists or instrumentalists. See, for one, Louis Armstrong arriving in King Oliver's Chicago. See also the following "argument in reverse" between two white rockers in the fifties who were mutual admirers: Ricky Nelson and Carl Perkins.

Nelson speaks first: "'I really would like to open some shows for you next year, Carl.'

"Carl said," 'You've got your cart before the horse—*I'll* open for *you*.'"

"But Ricky said, 'No way.'"

These are fans of each other, not dueling egos.

In 1956, at the age of nineteen, Elvis had not yet appeared on the *Billboard* magazine lists; had not recorded "Blue Suede Shoes," "Hound Dog," or "Don't Be Cruel"; had not dated any beautiful young music stars. But he had had several regional hits—"Blue Moon of Kentucky," "That's All Right, Mama," and a few others—and was making a name for himself with a never-before-seen variety of live performances throughout the South. It was "his onstage body movements" that set him apart from others, "that really transgressed postwar notions about the supposed differences between 'whiteness' and 'blackness.' Seizing the moves, the poses, the clothes, and the general attitude of various [rhythm and blues] artists, Elvis showed his physical alliance with what people in the 1950s assumed was an authentically black style."

He was, in other words, not yet a national icon but already Elvis the Pelvis when, one night, he sneaked into the Ellis Auditorium and stood in the backstage shadows, not wanting to distract from the performers. They were not, on this occasion, the usual white gospel singers but a variety of musicians playing a benefit for needy black children. Elvis wanted to support the cause, enjoy the music, nothing more. It was just something to do. But B. B. King, one of the singers that night and one of Memphis's top disc jockeys, spied him standing in the darkness and was impressed. He later recalled that "for a young white boy to show up at an all-black function took guts."

And a star-studded function it was, with Ray Charles and the Moonglows among those who joined King in performing.

> During the program, the producer asked [singer] Rufus Thomas to bring Elvis onstage. Thomas was reluctant to do so but finally agreed and asked Presley if he would mind making an unscheduled appearance toward the end of the program. At the appropriate time, they walked to the microphone, and Thomas announced, "Ladies and gentlemen, Elvis Presley!" The singer "was greeted with a screaming ovation from the all-Negro audience when introduced." Nat Williams wrote that "a thousand black, brown, and beige girls in that audience blended in their alto and soprano voices in one wild crescendo of sound that rent the rafters and took off like scalded cats in the direction of Elvis. "You never saw anything like it," Thomas recalled.

Little Richard was surprised to find that the same phenomenon existed in reverse. And, even more, that it was directed at him, among others. "I had this great big head and little body," he said, being too hard on himself, "and I had one big eye and one little eye." His right leg, he claimed, was also shorter than the left. Maybe that was why he became an even more dynamic performer than Elvis; the more he shook, stomped, and whirled onstage, the less likely it was that an audience would focus on, or even be aware of, his handicap.

He could hardly stop himself from shaking, stomping, and whirling—such piston-pumping music did he play, music that coursed through his bloodstream as if shot from a fire hose! His songs "began with piano-driven rock; his boogie-woogie piano recalls the use to which that instrument was put in the big-band music of the 1940s. To this melodic structure, he adds the infectious beat of funk, defined by music historian Anne Danielsen as 'bass-driven, percussive, polyrhythmic black dance music, with minimal melody and maximum syncopation.' "

When Richard found that his music, like Elvis's, was beginning to appeal to a race not his own, he was amazed—at the very least, unprepared. "It would be standing-room-only crowds," he said, and although known for his braggadocio, he was simply being factual here, "and 90 percent of the audience would be white. I've always thought that rock 'n' brought the races together. Although I was black, the fans didn't care. I used to feel good about that. Especially being from the South, where you see the barriers, having all these people who we thought hated us, showing all this *love*."

With Elvis building on the black man's foundation, record sales soared as never before. It was almost as if a new industry had been born. "Aided by the affluence of the time, the invention of the 45 rpm and 33 1/3 rpm records, and the introduction of high fidelity, [which caught on slowly at first] record sales had steadily climbed from 109 million in 1945 . . . then with the arrival of rock 'n' roll [sales] rose to 277 million in 1955 and to 600 million in 1960. In 1956 alone, RCA Victor sold over 13.5 Elvis Presley singles and 3.75 million Presley albums."

But Elvis was not the only white singer following the Negro lead. Others, primarily Nelson and Pat Boone, did the same, although never approaching Elvis's artistry.[3] Ozzie Nelson, Ricky's father, was also a musician as well as a bandleader, but his tastes were those of another generation, and his temper had a trigger on it. As a result, he and his son often were at odds, especially when the younger Nelson picked up his guitar. "You guys have any special arrangements at all?" Ozzie asked as his son headed for rehearsal one day. "No, we just rock and roll." Dad was dumbfounded. "Well, I mean, you can't do that all night. What do you do for a change of pace?" Ricky said, "We just stop playing."

Most of Ricky's hits were songs written for him and originally recorded by him. A few times, though, he did "cover" versions of some of Fats Domino's hits, most notably "I'm Walkin'," and Domino, apparently believing in the maxim that imitation is the sincerest form of flattery, took no offense. In fact, Fats and his occasional doppelgänger became friends, sharing reminiscences together, drinking together, even performing together— and the concert of theirs that appears on YouTube is forty-six minutes and forty-three seconds of unmatched rhythm and reverie.

Nelson's version of "I'm Walkin'" was a bigger hit than Domino's, but its strength on the charts pulled the Fat Man's recording higher than any of his songs had risen before. That is how it was at the start, the white man's cover elevating the black man's original into the *Billboard* empyrean, which meant more whites enjoying the music and, in their curiosity, introducing themselves to the blacks who had originated it. Before long, the black versions began to shoot up the charts on the impetus of their own artistry.

Eddie Ray, in charge of promotion at Imperial Records, Domino's label, saw another advantage to the relationship between Fats and Ricky. "Nelson's hits never sold after their initial success," Ray discovered, "whereas Domino's old hits kept selling, with distributors calling Imperial to request

---

3. Boone could sing a ballad sweetly and cleanly, but about his hard-driving numbers, the less said the better. They were, in fact, driven softly. Nelson, however, remains as underrated now as he was back then. He could switch effortlessly from "Lonesome Town" to "Believe What You Say." In fact, his sound was always effortless; as Bob Dylan would later write in the notes for the *Ricky Nelson Greatest Hits* CD, "He sang his songs calm and steady, like he was in the middle of a storm, men hurling past him. His voice was sort of mysterious and made you fall into a certain mood." Riding the waves of brilliant accompaniment from guitarist James Burton, Ricky Nelson made some of the best music of his time.

500 or 1,000 of each record. 'I could tell what part of the country Fats was working without looking at his itinerary,' says Ray."

Pat Boone also covered a number of black hits, such as "At My Front Door" by the El Dorados and "Two Hearts" by the Charms. In addition, he recorded Domino's "Ain't That a Shame," and Fats was *not* happy about this particular brand of flattery;[4] Boone's pure vanilla voice could not help but take the soul out of Domino's version. Making things even worse, Boone's cover soared to number one on the charts, halting Domino's rise at tenth place.

Once again, though, the black man had an advantage. "Fats had co-written the song with trumpeter Dave Bartholomew, and so Boone's plundering helped subsidize the glittering diamond rings that adorned his stubby fingers."

But Boone's covering Domino was an exception for him, so much so that a more improbable twosome cannot be imagined; it was as if Lawrence Welk had decided to record the greatest hits of John Coltrane. But when Boone chose to cover Little Richard, things got even worse. After hearing Richard's "Slippin' and Slidin'," Boone was inspired; his version thereof, he resolved, would be his next release. According to Richard's biographer, Charles White, it was a lamentable decision, for what Boone produced was "[a]n anemic version in which he reverses the Midas touch and turns gold into dross, managing to sound as though he is not quite sure what he is singing about. It sold a million."

The musical symbiosis just kept happening; Boone's cover, as truly soulless as it is, helped propel Little Richard's raucous original into the top ten. He, too, could buy rings for his fingers, and when he pounded the piano keys his hands glittered like a jewelry case at Van Cleef & Arpels.

Boone also recorded Richard's "Tutti Frutti," and it is not difficult to describe the result. It sounds exactly the way one would imagine "Tutti Frutti" sounding if sung by Pat Boone.

But regardless of the merits, or lack of them, of individual performances, this intermingling of songs from black and white performers, which wouldn't have been possible a decade earlier, led to an intermingling of blacks and whites in the audiences, something else that would have been an impossibility, if not even a crime, ten years to the rear. And this was the magic, the power of rock 'n' roll that shook the culture of the country more

---

4. Boone was an English and speech major in college, and it is music industry lore that he insisted on changing the title of the song, the first few takes thus becoming "Isn't That a Shame." It would have been the worst tribute to good grammar ever recorded. Even Boone had to admit that "it didn't work," and gave his blessing to the destruction of those takes. From then on, he said "ain't," and deposited his checks without embarrassment.

than any other music before or since, the music that transcended the mere uniqueness of its sound.

In 1956, in Annapolis, Maryland, "police had the nearly impossible task of controlling an overflow crowd of between five and seven thousand black and white teenagers attending an integrated concert featuring Carl Perkins, Frankie Lymon, Chuck Berry, Shirley and Lee, Bobby Charles, and the Spaniels. Except for the traffic-tie ups, the show ran smoothly."

But not all black-and-white shows with black-and-white audiences ran smoothly. At another performance starring some of the same singers, the exuberance in the auditorium was something of a chain reaction.

> When Carl Perkins came on and exhorted the crowd, "Let's everybody in here rock and roll," the cops were unable to restrain or contain the delirious and screaming white teenagers [Local deejay and emcee] Hotsy Totsy came back to the mike and, warning the crowd not to have a cop-clobbering incident, told all of them to come on the floor and dance [meaning blacks and whites together]. What happened then sent the [racist] Citizen's Council's members home with the shakes. The crowd got so carried away that the police made the band stop playing thirty minutes before the dance was to close.

It is not too much to call this event a landmark in the history of American race relations. But it was one of many such landmarks of the mid- to late-fifties; it certainly was not common for whites and blacks to share a dance floor, and sometimes even share a partner. Most times, when they did, the occurrences went unrecorded, except for racist diatribes, both spoken and published, that followed in their wake. But they had no effect other than preaching to the choir. As for those who came to see the concerts, they were just bewitched by those moments when the music onstage became so propulsive that no one of any ethnic heritage could sit still any longer. And no one cared about the ethnic heritage of anyone else who was propelled. They were all in it together.

Another story, this one with the ring of urban legend to it, has it that a white girl attending a rock concert, for no reason other than sheer exuberance, was about to dive off the balcony to join the dancing on the first floor. In the nick of time, a black arm wrapped itself around her and saved her life.

To some people, the shame of blacks and whites cavorting together was exacerbated by the fact that people of any race were doing something as ungodly as wiggling their bodies in public. Authors Lois and Alan Gordon tell us that "a Columbia University psychiatrist compares rock dancing to the medieval St. Vitus plague where victims were unable to stop dancing."

Young Ernest Hemingway was not permitted to start. His father refused to allow him to take dancing lessons because such movement "[l]eads to hell and damnation." Even before rock 'n' roll's time, the comically exuberant evangelist Billy Sunday railed at dance, at the notion of a couple in a "voluptuous sexual embrace, their bodies swaying one against the other, their limbs twining and intertwining, her head resting on his breast . . . and the spell of the music . . ." The good reverend seems to speak from fervid experience.

Regardless, everything about rock 'n' roll—the music, the lyrics, the dancing, the racial fraternizing—had its opponents. But none of them, no matter how severe the threats of felony or perdition they issued, had an effect on the rapid-fire beat of the times and the exuberance of those who couldn't sit still because of it.

Irvin Feld, widely regarded as the most powerful rock 'n' roll agent in the business, produced one of the year's most significant events in both music and race relations. Called, accurately "The Biggest Show of Stars for 1957," it played sold-out, one-night stands throughout the country for three months. White performers such as Buddy Holly and the Crickets, Paul Anka, and the Everly Brothers shared stages with black performers such as Fats, Chuck Berry, and the McPhatter-led Drifters. Newspapers wrote a lot about the music, only a little about the performers' skin colors.

An even bigger show of stars made its national television premiere at about the same time and proved to be the greatest single promotional outlet of all for the new music. Prior to '57, *Bandstand*, hosted by Bob Horn, had aired on only one television station, the ABC affiliate in Philadelphia. But just as the *Philadelphia Inquirer* was running a special series on drunk driving, Horn was arrested on the charge and also implicated in a prostitution ring. Dick Clark, a clean-cut rock 'n' roll disc jockey, twenty-seven years old and looking half of that, became *Bandstand*'s new star, and a better choice could not have been made.

Less than a month later, *Bandstand* was picked up by the ABC network, meaning that now, instead of being broadcast on one station, *Bandstand* was seen on sixty-seven, from one end of the country to the other. In honor of its new reach, the program was renamed *American Bandstand*. It quickly became the most influential program for teenagers in the history of the medium.

Airing live every day from 3:00 to 4:30 p.m. in the East, the program played the most popular songs in the country, according to its own survey, as Philadelphia teens danced to them with wonderfully lithesome steps and swirls. We teenagers watching at home tried to copy them, practicing for the Saturday night dances, sock hops, and canteens that we attended in our high-school gymnasiums. Watching *American Bandstand* quickly became an important part of the day for us. It was the homework we did before we did our homework.

Sometimes I took notes on the moves I saw on the show. Sometimes I drew diagrams that only I could decipher. Although I will deny it if asked, I still remember occasions when, in junior high, I was so inspired by the lucky kids who got to dance on *American Bandstand* that I joined them, dancing along in my living room with a broomstick as my partner. "I got a girl named Bony Moronie," went one of the hits of '57, "she's as skinny as a stick of macaroni."

Not long after the program went national, it moved to Los Angeles. Although a few black faces had appeared on the dance floor in Philadelphia, more were visible, and more often, in the West. Too many black faces, feared some ABC executives, and they met with Clark about their concerns. Clark would have none of their timidity. He insisted to both the show's producers and network officials that the program, already integrated to a degree, became even more so. They might not have liked the idea, but Clark already had become a national figure, and if he wanted a black-and-white *American Bandstand*, so it would be.[5] The ratings, which had been climbing steadily before integration, continued climbing afterward. The blacks didn't help the ratings, but they didn't hurt them either, and that might have been the best thing that could possibly be said about mixing the races on national television program. The skin color of the performers and dancers simply did not matter—not, at least, when rock 'n' roll was playing to ease the transition.

To the surprise of many, *Billboard*, the music industry's most influential publication, was among the show's early critics. "The bulk of the ninety minutes," it reported, "was devoted to . . . juveniles trudging through early American dances like the Lindy and the Box Step to recorded tunes of the day. If this is the wholesome answer to the 'detractors' of rock 'n' roll, bring on the rotating pelvises."

It was an unexpected reaction, but even coming from a source like *Billboard* it had no effect. The magazine's censure notwithstanding, "by the end of 1958 the show was reaching over 20 million viewers over 105 stations, and had spawned dozens of imitations on local stations. This was a show about teens, and its consistent high rating and longevity proved that they liked it, regardless of what adults said about it."

Among the solo acts who appeared on the *American Bandstand*, lip-syncing their latest hits, were the biggest names in rock 'n' roll of the time: Sam Cooke, Jerry Lee Lewis, Little Richard, Buddy Knox, Tab Hunter, Marty Robbins, Tommy Sands, and many more, with Freddy "Boom-Boom" Cannon holding the record for the most appearances—110. For reasons unknown, Elvis was never a guest.

---

5. It must be pointed out, though, that the black-and-white program was overwhelmingly white. Blacks comprised about 18 percent of the U.S. population at the time, but they were far less than that on *Bandstand*'s dance floor.

As for the groups performing on the early days of *American Bandstand*, they included Buddy Holly and the Crickets.[6] By this time, their racial identity had been established, but in the summer of '57, they had been booked at Harlem's Apollo Theater under the assumption that, because of their sound, they were black. They were, in fact, a small collection of good ol' country boys from Lubbock, Texas. It was no surprise, then, that "the first couple of shows went as badly as they possibly could. Except for 'That'll Be the Day,' the [all-black] audience seemed indifferent to the Crickets' original songs; apathetic silence turned to spasmodic booing and the creative heckling for which the Apollo was, and still is, famous."

It might have ended catastrophically but for Buddy's equal mastery of a far more acceptable type of material. "When we just couldn't get through with our own stuff, Buddy turns around and says 'Ah, the hell with it, let's give 'em 'Bo Diddley,'" [musician] Niki Sullivan remembers. "He started cutting up and jumping around, giving it everything he had." If the Apollo's audience was intolerant of what it judges to be failure, it was also famous for respecting talent, courage, and chutzpah. The Texans finished their set amid wild applause and shouts for more, which were repeated at every show for the rest of the week.

In the fifties, no integration was like rock 'n' roll integration. It didn't happen everywhere. It didn't happen all the time. But when it did, it was transcendent.

The music, however, was hardly a cure-all for racial discord—in some cases, an even more virulent strain than before, because it was inflamed by the popularity of the new music. To many, rock 'n' roll seemed an act of insubordination, a slap in the face to those who wanted to keep blacks and white separate and unequal. Just as bigotry wasn't going to yield to legislation without a fight, neither was it going to yield easily to music, even if that music, however unaccountably, appealed to many youngsters in the self-perceived master race as well. As popular as their songs had become, the black pioneers of rock 'n' roll were still tormented by the same, ominous figure who had tormented them for so long, the shadowy but powerful specter of Jim Crow.

A story that might be true, but cannot be verified, is worth mentioning regardless, as it captures the strain of hypocrisy that ran side by side with racism at the time. One rock 'n' roll star supposedly remembered the night he was refused service at a diner in the South by a young waitress who could barely bring herself to look at him as she ran listlessly through the

---

6. Of whom two boys from Liverpool, England—Paul McCartney and John Lennon—were such fans that they decided on a name reminiscent of insects for their own nascent rock group.

menu items, telling him that, as far as niggers were concerned, they were out of meat loaf, cube steak, roast beef, and everything else the joint usually served. The menu, as far as blacks were concerned, was a work of fiction. The singer took his leave and, a few hours later, his stomach growling, took the stage at the local auditorium.

He had not even finished his first number when he stepped in front of the footlights and looked out at the audience. In one of the front rows, whom should he see but the waitress, and she was staring at him rapturously, shouting out the lyrics with him; she seemed to know every word, and accompanied her accompaniment by clapping her hands to the beat and smiling at him as if they were old friends, suddenly reunited. It was nice, the singer supposed, but he would rather have had a burger.

A tale that *is* authentic comes from Chuck Berry. "[He] recalled that during a Southern tour in 1956, although he and his bandmates had to reside and dine in segregated facilities, they did perform in front of integrated audiences. Yet there were limitations. On one occasion, immediately before they were to open the doors for the spectators, four of the maintenance guys came out and roped off the armory with white window cord. They looped and tied it to each seat down the center aisle, making it an off-limits zone that neither colored nor whites could tread."

In other words, not only could blacks and whites not sit together as they watched the concert, but there had to be a space between them, a DMZ of sorts, so that the two races were not even close to each other. The problem was that these were the best seats in the house, the most expensive, orchestra center, and they had been turned into a ghost town, occupied by nobody. The proprietors of the armory, whatever their views on race, must have fumed at the lost revenue.

Sometimes, blacks and whites attending a concert, even if they were seated separately, were the victims of abuse as they entered the auditorium. Bigots would gather at the entrance of the venue to hurl both insults and, on the rare occasion, solid objects at them. The taunters were white men and women, fearful of the effects that rock 'n' roll would have on their young and innocent progeny. The music was, after all, the product of "jungle bunnies."

On at least one occasion, a country performer physically confronted Elvis backstage at a theater, demanding to know why he acted like a "white nigger" and sang "nigger trash." As Michael Bertrand writes, "Perhaps no entertainer in history has provoked so violent a hatred in one age-bracket of the public and so fanatical a loyalty in another as Elvis Aron Presley."

Something similar, if not reaching either extreme, might be said of all of the pioneers of the new music—loathing on the one hand, loyalty on the other. The former reaction was expressed in surprisingly vitriolic language by some of the country's most esteemed media sources. Jack Crosby, a highly respected television critic who had written a newspaper column and hosted programs on both radio and television, called Elvis "an unspeakably untalented and vulgar entertainer." He wondered, "Where do you go from Elvis Presley, short of obscenity—which is against the law?" *Look* magazine, a mainstream publication along the lines of *Life* and *Collier's*, asked whether rock 'n' roll was "music or madness?" William F. Buckley Jr.'s conservative magazine, the *National Review*, asked for help from above. "May the Lord have mercy on us." And an unidentified Southerner, who surely did not take his own advice, lamented, "Turn on your radio and listen to the rock and roll death song of the white race."

But the Reverend Martin Luther King Jr., so often a moderating voice in racial matters, a proponent of dignity in addition to integration, was even less restrained. Rock 'n' roll, he asserted, "plunges men's minds into degrading and immoral depths." It was a statement that damaged King's reputation almost as much as later statements urging that blacks abstain from violence in their reactions to provocation. In both cases, he ended up deriding, or at least puzzling, many of the young people who were among his strongest supporters.

As had been the case with the integration of schools, rock 'n' roll sometimes could lead to violence. It was inevitable; the opposition to the songs and those who purveyed them was too great for peaceful resistance from people who were zealous by nature. In Birmingham, Alabama, the Ku Klux Klan decided not to give people the option of listening to music from the jungle's depths. It "knocked black [radio] station WERD off the air by wrecking its broadcast tower. 'KKK' and 'Nigger' graffiti were displayed on the remains." Other stations continued to broadcast, but their walls were defaced with the coarsest language. Often disc jockeys who played the music were threatened in their communities—as they shopped, as they watched sporting events, even as they attended church.

A few television stations offered a new kind of program, a "public service" for those who needed the guidance. A preacher, station executive, or local politician stood in the studio next to a desk. On the desk was a stack of 45 rpm records, and one at a time the fire-breathing fellow cracked the discs into pieces on the edge of his desk, all the while virtually filibustering about the evil that he was also smashing into shards. A public service, indeed; he was destroying the tools of the Antichrist's temptation.

Headlines in various American newspapers, virtually all in the South, reinforced the point.

Beware Elvis Presley
Eight Students Expelled for Attending Elvis Concert
Elvis Presley's Effect on Clothes Deplored
Combat the Menace

In a number of cities, so-called Citizens' Councils combated the menace in their own ways. The largest and most civilized insurrection was probably in New Orleans, where members of the council, most of them well-dressed and polite in manner, patrolled the city's sidewalks passing out handbills that said such things as, "The screaming, idiotic words, and savage music of these records are undermining the morals of our white youth in America."[7]

Ironically, two of the most frequently quoted derogations of rock 'n' roll turned out to be accurate predictions of a future that segregationists were trying desperately to avoid. A man whom history knows simply as a "concerned white Citizen of the Deep South" charged that those who played and listened to rock 'n' roll were "brainwashing the adolescent mind . . . helping to spread the cause of integration."

Yes, as it happened. Things were turning out just that way.

And Ku Klux Klan leader Asa Earl Carter, whose self-proclaimed motto was "Segregation now, segregation tomorrow, segregation forever," warned that the "sensuous Negro music, timed to the jungle beat" would be "the best way to bring young people of both races together." It was a virtual endorsement of racial harmony. One generation's curse proved to be words to live by for the next.

The greatest fear of men such as Asa Earl Carter was that the races would be brought together carnally—after all, wasn't rock 'n' roll black slang for unrestrained, animalistic sex? So, it was asserted by many, especially as the term gained currency in the fifties, and the assertion led to fear that almost reached the epidemic stage in 1952, when a white group called the Ravens recorded a song called "Rock Me All Night Long." According to conservative social critic Jeffrey Hart, "The effect was explosive. This music was no 'Some Enchanted Evening.' This music was about *doing it!*" Hart wrote that songs such as "Rock Me All Night Long," of which there were more and more all the time, were "*The Kinsey Report* set to music."

It is amazing to contemplate that, in 1954, music by black singers accounted for 3 percent of all record sales in the United States. Yet by 1957,

---

7. In writing the previous sentence, I could not help smiling as I thought of Little Richard singing "Tutti Frutti," and several times wailing, "A-wop-bop-a-looma, ba-lop bam-boom." So, the point here goes to the racists. Except that "idiotic words" usually are harmless, hardly undermining morals, and they make one think perhaps of the most famous literary nonsense of all, Lewis Carroll's "Jabberwocky."
'Twas brilling, and the slithy toves
Did gyre and gimble in the wabe:
All mimsy were the borogoves,
And the mome raths outgrabe.
"Jabberwocky" has long been deemed acceptable for the ears of white children.

that figure had jumped to 30 percent, an increase of 1,000 percent in a mere three years! It was a cultural transformation like no other in my lifetime.

In excerpts from *Billboard*'s "Top 100" for the year, I have categorized Elvis as black, which, both musically and in terms of the amount of vituperation he received, is where he belongs. A few other white rock 'n' rollers are similarly, and appropriately, listed. Here, among the most popular songs of the great transitional year of 1957, are listed the following:

1.	All Shook Up	Elvis Presley
9.	Too Much	Elvis Presley
13.	Party Doll	Buddy Knox
16.	Jailhouse Rock	Elvis Presley
18.	Come Go With Me	Del-Vikings[8]
20.	You Send Me	Sam Cooke
21.	Searchin'	Coasters
22.	School Days	Chuck Berry
28.	Whole Lotta Shakin' Goin' On	Jerry Lee Lewis
30.	That'll Be the Day	Buddy Holly/Crickets
38.	I'm Walkin'	Fats Domino
42.	Be-Bop Baby	Ricky Nelson
43.	Short Fat Fanny	Larry Williams
48.	Blueberry Hill	Fats Domino
49.	Whispering Bells	Del-Vikings
50.	Blue Monday	Fats Domino
79.	Rock and Roll Music	Chuck Berry
80.	Jenny Jenny	Little Richard
82.	Keep-A-Knockin'	Little Richard
83.	Valley of Tears	Fats Domino
91.	Bony Moronie	Larry Williams

"In the social atmosphere of the rock 'n' roll explosion of the 1950s," writes Michael Bertrand, "the attachment that southern white teenagers developed toward black culture at least partially obliterated Jim Crow's long shadow. They perceived that which was African American as positive and affirmative." But then he asks: "Did this musical and social process alter southern white perceptions of black people? Did this new social and ideological context make it possible for white youths to look at blacks as equal? Did the rock 'n' roll experience help teach a generation how to overcome prejudice?"

---

8. The first interracial group, although primarily black, to rise to such heights on the *Billboard* charts.

The answer Bertrand provides to these three questions is "maybe." To me the answer is "definitely," but that leads to follow-up questions, some of which cannot be answered as easily.

Precisely *how* were Southern white perceptions of blacks altered by the new music? And who were the most altered? The younger generation surely. Its members were affected more positively than their parents, in large part because teenagers were old enough, mature enough, to allow the joys of music to trump the less meaningful concern of skin shade. As for their mothers and fathers, many of them found rock 'n' roll to be the sound track of cultural degradation, the accompaniment of the horrible decisions being handed down by the American judiciary.

Did the context created by the new music persuade these teenagers to look at blacks as equals? Certainly, in a few cases, but probably very few, at least at the start. A more common reaction, in all likelihood, was that white teenagers held onto their biases, but in more restrained form, one that might be compared to several steps, not just one, leading to the journey of a thousand miles.

Finally, did rock 'n' help teach a generation to overcome prejudice? Not the entire generation, of course; but the new music was one of the most powerful early lessons society ever had provided about the illogic of racial bias. Before rock 'n' roll worked its magic in the fifties, young people of both races had been wary of each other at best, violent at worst. They never aligned themselves at any time for sheer enjoyment. In fact, it may be that they had never aligned themselves peacefully for any reason, except on a dismal day ninety-two years earlier when the train carrying Abraham Lincoln's coffin passsed through Baltimore.

"White and black side by side in the rain and the mud, with eyes strained upon that coffin, with eyes running over, and with clasped hands, and with faces drawn and distorted, or set in marble fixedness. White and black leaned forth from the same windows . . . and there seemed to be no consciousness of any difference of color." If racism is a many-layered quantity, rock 'n' roll managed to peel away at least some of those layers, the beginning of a long, still-evolving process. Today there might be as many white hip-hoppers as black.

In the photo section of Bertrand's book, *Race, Rock, and Elvis,* is a reproduction of a poster for "1 BIG ROCK AND ROLL SHOW," starring, among others, B. B. King, who appears on the poster. The caption beneath it, which is placed in quotation marks but not attributed, reads: "Rhythm and blues and rock 'n' roll shows are 'doing a job in the Deep South that even the Supreme Court hasn't been able to accomplish.' "

The statement sounds extreme. It is not. Law is coercion, sometimes successful. Rock 'n' roll is a choice; those who sang along and danced together were volunteers. With the law providing support for the music, the pressure to lynch Jim Crow was greater than ever, but it was not until the comprehensive Civil Rights Acts of 1964 and '65 that the will of Congress made its biggest impact on attitudes. These also were years when blacks and whites kept swapping positions of prominence on the *Billboard* listings, as they had done ever since '57.

More than anything else, in summing up the insufficiently appreciated effect of rock 'n' roll on race relations in the fifties, I am drawn again to a bit of conversation Carl Perkins recalled. One day he thought back on something Chuck Berry had said to him when the two men were touring the South.

> There was an integration problem in this part of America, a pretty severe problem back then. But there was no [segregation] in music. When you walked up to an old '54 or '55 model Wurlitzer jukebox, it didn't say "Blue Suede Shoes," Carl Perkins, white, "Blueberry Hill," Fats Domino, black. No. There was no difference. Kids danced to Little Richard, Chuck Berry, Elvis . . . Chuck Berry said to me one time, he said, "You know Carl, we might be doing as much with our music as our leaders are in Washington to bring down the barriers."

Just two men, talking at their ease. Each a singer and guitar picker and composer. Each a pioneer. Two men who were not aware that they were in the process of making history, nor that they were analyzing history so astutely. But yes, Carl, Chuck was right. Music, *their* music, was chipping away at obstacles that, almost a century earlier, were the primary cause of the deadliest war in the history of their country.

> Just let me hear some of that rock and roll music
> Any old way you choose it
> It's got a back beat you can't lose it
> Any old time you use it
> It's gotta be rock 'n' roll music
> If you wanna dance with me.

But music wasn't chipping away at the racial obstacles all by itself. It had help from another cultural force, the assistance of which, like the assistance of rock 'n' roll, would not have been possible in the recent past.

PART FOUR

Robert Meses, "Emperor of New York"

10

Moving Stories

To Floyd Patterson, unlike anyone who ever preceded or followed him in the ring, boxing evoked Eros. "It's like being in love with a woman," he mused about his sport. "She can be unfaithful, she can be mean, she can be cruel, but it doesn't matter. If you love her, you want her, even though she can do you all kinds of harm. It's the same with me and boxing. It can do me all kinds of harm, but I love it."

In the first few days of 1957, Patterson was a twenty-one-year-old black man who reigned as the youngest heavyweight champion in the history of his sport.[1] He was not the first of his race to assume the title; among others, Jack Johnson was probably the most powerful puncher, and Joe Louis the most popular and accessible of the champs, both during his career and afterward, even through his embarrassing days late in life as a punch-drunk glad-hander at Caesar's Palace.

But something set Patterson apart from these two men—a dignity, a composure, and a degree of self-restraint that demonstrated his respect for himself and his assumption that others should respect him in return. He was not an easy man to dismiss with a racial epithet. He also was not an easy man to understand.

If a poll had been conducted of both African Americans and whites, he and Jackie Robinson would have ranked highly among the most admired black men of the era they shared—Robinson a firebrand, Patterson more restrained and at times difficult to picture as a champion pugilist. But he was more than just the latter. Says the former journalist Janet Langhart, "Floyd Patterson was one of the heroes who gave 'the Negro' a sense of power, a conviction that, in spite of prejudice and hatred, we could compete and triumph."

---

1. On January 4, he turned twenty-two.

For Patterson, triumph was the end of a winding path, a long journey to claim his crown. It started in the town of his birth, a map blip called Waco, North Carolina, a place that today has a population of 321 and yesterday had too few to mention. From there, it proceeded to the radically different environs of Bedford-Stuyvesant, one of the toughest neighborhoods of Brooklyn, where Robinson later would play his baseball and the Patterson family would move when Floyd was a toddler. The youngest of eleven children, he was a troubled boy and a thief in both places.

In Bed-Stuy, he stole food on occasion, although it is not certain that the family needed it. He also stole an armful of dresses one night, believing that his mother deserved better attire than what she had; she deserved the kind of clothes worn by the schoolteachers from whose classes he often played truant. "When my mother asked where I got the dresses," Floyd said, "I told her I found them."

For his most ignominious performance as a thief, the boy chose to steal a case of soda pop from the plant that bottled it. But he was only ten at the time; whatever the weight of the case, it was too much for him, especially when the police began to give pursuit. After a block or two he dropped the case but kept two of the bottles. He ran as fast as he could, but the cops, in adult-size strides, were gaining on him. He even threw away the two bottles. They didn't lighten his load enough to matter. He was captured and taken back to the plant, where one of his captors demanded a confession. Floyd refused, claiming some other boy had given him the sodas. The cops knew it was a lie, and one of them started slapping the child as if he were a mosquito trying to bite.

He also accused Floyd of hurling the two soda bottles at him. When Patterson began crying, the patrolman picked up an empty wooden crate and smashed it over the little boy's head. In that moment, or so it seemed in retrospect, everything changed; Floyd went from a reclusive, shy, quiet kid to being "crazy mad," as he later described it. "Snatching up a crate himself, he attacked the officer. The patrolman . . . [had] never seen anything like it. Floyd had become a miniature wild man, screaming and fighting. It took two or three more cops to subdue him, and he was bloody by the time he was subdued."

Still just ten years old, he was sent to reform school. If the same thing had happened today, of course, there would be justified uproar in the streets. And if proof could be offered in a courtroom, the officer who administered the violence to the black child would have spent more time in jail than Patterson had in reform school. But this was a long time ago; that kind of justice was distant, still a dream.

Young Patterson did not just challenge authority but expectations. He was "a tall, straight stick of a boy, slender except for big shoulders. He had a long, straight nose and wore long sideburns: there was something humorously dandified about his appearance. Outside the ring, his favorite position was horizontal. If he saw a bench, he would lie on it rather than sit on it." He was not lazy. He was, rather, a thinker, a fantasizer, and sometimes, lying on that bench, he would lose himself in reflections about what it was like to suffer a boxer's greatest indignity.

> It's not a *bad* feeling when you're knocked out. It's a *good* feeling, actually. It's not painful, just a sharp grogginess. You don't see angels or stars; you're on a pleasant cloud. After [Sonny] Liston hit me in Nevada, I felt, for about four or five seconds, that everybody in the arena was actually in the ring with me, circled around me like a family, and you feel warmth toward all the people in the arena after you're knocked out. You feel lovable to all the people. And you want to kiss everybody—men and women—and after the Liston fight somebody told me I actually blew a kiss to the crowd from the ring. I don't remember that. But I guess it's true because that's the way you feel during the four or five seconds after a knockout.

After those four or five seconds, Patterson admitted, the pain of being flattened became unbearable both physically and emotionally. His description of the initial feeling, though, as well as his comparison of boxing to an unfaithful woman, revealed the poet in the boxer, and there had not been a combination quite like that before—not, at least, at the top of the heavyweight boxing rankings. By the time a fellow named Cassius Clay came along—Clay, who was much more the entertainer than a thinker like Patterson—the position of poet laureate of boxing had been filled and probably closed forever.

As a result, Patterson attracted a kind of fan who previously had shown little interest in men who earned a living with their fists. "Indeed, among contemporary boxers," wrote the novelist and fight aficionado Joyce Carol Oates, "no one is so articulate as Floyd Patterson."

Other literary fans of the fighter included James Baldwin and Gay Talese. The two men visited the young champ at his training camp one day in 1963, and Baldwin would later state, "I remember the glimpse I got of him then, a man more complex than he was yet equipped to know, a hero for many children who were still trapped where he had been, who might not have survived without the ring, and who yet, oddly, did not really seem to belong there."

Patterson's career record was fifty-five wins and eight losses, and two of the losses cost him the heavyweight championship. It was those fights he remembered most and that mortified him so much so that he could not stand to be seen in public afterward. When he lost his crown the first time, to the Swede Ingemar Johansson, he started wearing a disguise whenever he had to leave home. As if he were auditioning for a small-town vaudeville show, he applied a cheap set of whiskers and a mustache to his face, and according to the journalist Talese, writing while Patterson was still active in the ring, "he has carried [them] with him in a small attaché case into each fight so he can slip out of the stadium unrecognized should he lose."

Certainly not a typical pugilist was Floyd Patterson, nor a typical man. Nor, indeed, a typical father.

The Pattersons lived in a $100,000 house in the upper-class white suburb of Scarsdale, New York. It was not so much a place where the champ wanted to live as a place where he thought he *should* live, a place where he was *entitled* to live. After all, despite his apparent shyness, his occasional aloofness, "he considered himself socially superior to white men [the reference is probably to white boxers], to a Colorado roustabout like Dempsey or the son of an Italian shoemaker like [Rocky] Marciano or even a purebred Aryan like the Swede Johansson," the latter of whom he fought three times for the heavyweight title, losing the first bout, winning the next two.

But his self-confidence was TKOed almost every time he made himself visible in Scarsdale. His neighbors would have been amazed to know he felt such a thing. They didn't stare at him on the sidewalks, often pointing him out to their children, solely because he was a black man; they did so because he was a champion, and perhaps because he was a combination of both. Regardless, they were pleased to see him up close. Scarsdale had little overt prejudice.

But Patterson seemed constantly wary of what lay beneath the surface. There is something that only a black person can sense, a judgment in the gaze, a vibration in the air, conveying the realization that only the white person can feel true comfort, a true sense of belonging, in a white society. Although he would have been stared at almost anywhere in America, Scarsdale was turning out to be uncomfortable for him, despite the fact that he combined wealth and fame to greater degrees than any of his neighbors.

And Patterson's seven-year-old daughter, Jeannie, was even more uncomfortable. She was, on occasion, bullied. One day, Patterson's wife, Sandra, called him at his training camp in upstate New York, and she must have had a good reason; Sandra knew not to interrupt his workouts for an ordinary reason. This wasn't. She told him that some white boys, the usual suspects, were at it again—picking on Jeannie, and, as had not happened before, bringing her to tears. She told her mother she could stand it no longer.

At the time, Patterson was in the midst of preparing for an important fight. Of course, they were all important, and he readied himself for them intensely, setting goals for each day's workout, the most important of which was to exceed the day's goals.

But not today. Today his wife's phone call made the champ forget his upcoming challenge and decide that he should take on a new opponent, a crowd of seven-year-old boys. He summoned his pilot, Ted Hanson, and they sped six miles in his car over rutted and twisting country roads from his camp in Orange County, New York, to a tiny airport, where a single-engine Cessna awaited. From there, with Patterson at the controls as much as Hanson, they flew to Scarsdale as fast as the headwinds would allow. "I'm not going to work out today," he had told a friend at camp as he prepared to depart. "I'm going to fly down to Scarsdale. Those boys are picking on Jeannie again. She's the only Negro in this school . . . and some of the older boys tease her and lift up her dress all the time."

" 'How old are they?' he was asked.

" 'Teenagers,' he said. 'Old enough for a left hook.' "

Which he never delivered.

The plane landed, and the day continued to unfold like a sequence from an adventure movie. Patterson leaped into a cab that already had been summoned, going straight to the school and, as would be the case in a film, getting there just as the day's final bell was ringing.

By the time the students began pouring out the doors, departing for home, Patterson had learned the identity of his daughter's chief tormenter. He found the boy and pulled him aside from his buddies. But the two of them, the heavyweight boxing champion of the world and little boy of privilege, did not remain by themselves. A circle of the boys' friends formed loosely around the pair. Other students gathered behind them. All wondered what was going to happen.

But the world's most powerful man, and one of its most famous, had a hard time thinking of anything to say. The circle continued to form, not just students now, but even more, white parents, waiting to pick up their children. They appeared to be in awe of Floyd Patterson the boxer, many never having seen him before and some, perhaps, never having been so close to a black man in their lives. But they also were wary of Floyd Patterson the black man, the one who lived in their shiny white town, and the feelings were hard to separate. The air crackled with violence, but perhaps that was something only Patterson could sense. Or control.

Finally, he began to talk to the privileged child. The champ was used to large crowds watching him throw punches, but he never had attracted a crowd for being a righteously indignant father. His anger seemed suddenly to dissolve, "so his voice went soft, and he said, finally: 'Look, boy, I want you to stop it. I won't tell your mother—that might get you in trouble—but don't do it again, okay?'

'Okay.' "

The boys calmly turned and walked, in a group, up the street.

And that was all. It was that simple. Patterson was that gentle. The movie ended anticlimactically, but more to the point, Jeannie Patterson's skirt never was lifted again.

Although maybe, just maybe, without thinking, Patterson had been curling his fingers into and out of a left hook as he spoke.

Patterson was not nearly so kind to his opponent in the only title defense he made in '57, holding onto his championship with a technical knockout over Tommy "Hurricane" Jackson. He dominated the bout from beginning to end, dropping Jackson to the canvas three times. "He went to the floor the first time," it was reported, "just before the bell ended the first round. He went down again in the second and was up at the [referee's count of] two . . . And he was down a third time in the ninth, when he took a count of four." Jackson wanted to continue fighting, but the referee stopped the fight, ruling that the challenger had taken enough punishment.

It was the first time Patterson had defended his heavyweight crown, and he had won. It would have been something nice to daydream about while lying on a beach. Perhaps he did, although he was not the kind of man to whom victories brought peace of mind.

Two years later, Ingemar Johansson beat Patterson, becoming the first man to strip him of the title. In later life, though, it was friendship that mattered most to the one-time combatants, not rivalry, and the connection between the two men, white and black and different in so many other ways, became a strong one. In alternate years, Patterson flew to Sweden and Johansson to New York. Suddenly they were the Fats and Ricky of boxing, although knowing Patterson, one guesses that the two did not engage in shop talk. Patterson would not have enjoyed reminiscing about old bouts, memorable punches received and taken. He would more likely have been more at ease talking about Sweden, its politics, topography, history, so much to learn.

Johansson might have talked about his businesses. No less an intriguing figure than Patterson, his onetime foe starred in a couple of movies, bought a boat that he named "Ingo's" for his fishing expeditions, and later moved to Pompano Beach, Florida, where he bought a hotel. His friend Floyd visited often. In 1985, at the age of fifty-seven, Johansson started—and finished—the Stockholm marathon. The two men were so much more intriguing out of the ring than within its confines.

When Patterson died in 2006, he was suffering from prostate cancer and, according to biographer W. K. Stratton, "lost in dementia's fog," unable to remember names, places, and events, including his own matches. The champ had taken too many punches to the head, a subject of little medical knowledge back then and no societal concern. "Punch-drunk," the term that I previously, and disrespectfully, used to describe Joe Louis was, we now know, a form of concussive damage, and Patterson probably ended up suffering from it as much as, if not more than, Louis.

Just as they lived in friendship during their post-boxing years, so did Patterson and Johansson die in a similar manner. The latter was the oldest ex-heavyweight titleholder up to that point, passing away at seventy-six years of age, three years after Patterson's death at seventy-one. The Swede, too, was lost in "dementia's fog" at the time, with the official cause of death being Alzheimer's disease.

At the end, Patterson's trophies and belts were just bright, shiny objects to him, and as such could hold his attention for no more than a few seconds; he fingered them like an infant with toys. But they were of no particular meaning, stirred no memories. In a forlorn way it is fitting, because Patterson, so unlikely a figure to have excelled at so violent a pastime, is himself barely remembered today.

Nineteen fifty-seven was not a memorable year in American sports—not on the field or court, on the rink or in the ring. In baseball, one of the most exceptional, if ultimately meaningless, feats of marksmanship ever seen was performed by Philadelphia Phillies' outfielder Richie Ashburn. Elected to the Hall of Fame after his playing days, Ashburn had 2,574 hits during his fifteen-year career, and a batting average of .308. He was the fastest player in the National League for at least some of his years, and his speed helped him chase down fly balls that others could not reach as a result, he led the league in fielding percentage several times and was one of baseball's top base stealers.

Still, despite these accomplishments, Ashburn gave no hint that he could achieve what he did on August 17, when he hit one woman two times with foul balls in the same at bat. And, of all people, the victim was the wife of the sports editor of the *Philadelphia Bulletin*. Ashburn's first foul hit her in the face, and she toppled forward in her seat. Help was summoned immediately.

Then, as her rescuers carefully made their way up the steps of Roosevelt Stadium, carrying her stretcher to a waiting ambulance, Ashburn fouled off another pitch that hit her again, although this time lower on the body. Mrs. Alice Roth, stunned as much as pained, was taken to a nearby hospital, where her broken nose was mended and other injuries were treated and bandaged. She would recover completely, her headaches ending after a few days and her nose resuming its previous configuration after a longer period of time.

In time, she and Ashburn became friends, and it was he who arranged for her son to serve as a batboy for the Phillies.

More substantively surprising, Jackie Robinson was traded from Brooklyn to the New York Giants on January 5, 1957, and the deal shocked the sporting populations of both boroughs, as well as baseball fans all over the country. Robinson, the consummate outsider only ten years earlier, *was* the

Dodgers now. Fans no longer shouted abuse at him; rather, they cheered, applauded, waved pennants and signs, acknowledging what he had over-come as much as what he had accomplished. Don Drysdale could pitch, Roy Campanella could catch, and Gil Hodges and Pee Wee Reese formed half of an All-Star infield. But none of them meant Brooklyn baseball the way Jackie did. How could the Dodgers let him go? After all he had done for them! It was the team's general manager, Branch Rickey, who was responsible for bringing Robinson to Ebbets Field in the first place; how could he now evict him? Would the Yankees have rid themselves of Mickey Mantle?

Unhappy about the deal, Robinson refused to report to his new team, instead retiring to begin a second life in the business world. A proud man, Robinson had not even been consulted about the trade and would not allow himself to be treated in such a manner. As chattel, he might have thought. Few baseball players are summoned to discuss a possible change of teams, but more than any other player in the majors back then, Robinson had earned the right. His major league career had lasted a decade, from 1947 to 1956, and had shattered precedent and shaken the earth.

His best year had been 1949, when he hit .342, with sixteen home runs, 124 RBI, and 122 runs scored. Always daring afoot, he also stole thirty-seven bases, and although the latter is the only category in which he led the National League that season, his excellence in so many categories made him unique. The fans voted him the league's starting second baseman in the All-Star Game, and, at season's end, he won one of baseball's top awards, being named the Most Valuable Player in the National League.

But by 1956, his second mediocre season in a row, his batting average had dropped to .275, with ten home runs and a mere forty-three RBI. He had lost much of his fleetness, stealing only twelve bases and being thrown out more than ever before. Part of his decline, as might be expected, was due to age. He was thirty-six that year, and his body no longer carried out his instincts with the alacrity it had shown before. Further, the abuse that no longer plagued him from the bleachers now plagued him from within, albeit of a different nature. He was beginning to feel the onset of diabetes.

When the 1957 season began, a quiet black man named Jim Gilliam, known as "Junior," took over second base for the Dodgers, a startling sight for the team's fans. And a startling experience for Gilliam, following in his sport's biggest footsteps. He did not do well his first season, hitting .250, with two home runs and thirty-seven RBI.

As for Robinson, he now had a desk in the executive suite of the New York coffee manufacturer, Chock Full o' Nuts.

Everyone knows the story of Robinson's having been the first black to play major league baseball, and how he suffered, in the din of ceaseless vilification as a result. Less known is that, in 1947, Robinson's first year with the Dodgers, the color barrier was also broken in the American League, although "[t]he trials of Larry Doby in Cleveland that same year were never as well covered as Robinson's in New York." And, less than two weeks after Doby started his career as the Indians' pariah, the same league's St. Louis Browns (later to become the Baltimore Orioles) made Hank Thompson their third baseman. After all of those solid-white years, suddenly three African Americans showed up on professional diamonds in a single season.

To say that sports combined with music to do more to advance racial equality in the United States than statute is not to disparage either the legislative or judicial branches of government, both of which did what they could for the cause after enough pressure was applied. It is, rather, to say that, although ours is theoretically a nation of laws, it is in many ways governed by cultural influences; these often determine the country's course, the personal decisions and activities of an individual's daily life. It is fair, then, to insist that, at least in the fifties, Sam Phillips and Branch Rickey were no less responsible for the limited racial progress in the United States than Lyndon Johnson and Earl Warren.

In professional football, several years before the Super Bowl was even a gleam in a merchandiser's eye, the Detroit Lions beat the Cleveland Browns in one of the least interesting championship games ever played in any sport. Final score: Lions 59, Browns 14—and this even though the Lions played the game without their starting quarterback. Hall of Famer Bobby Layne had been injured, but his backup, Tobin Rote, completed twelve of nineteen passes for 280 yards and four touchdowns.

As for the colleges, their season ended inconclusively, as the Auburn Tigers, voted the nation's top team, were prohibited from competing in a bowl game. The NCAA had added an enforcement division only five years earlier, "and it determined that an Auburn assistant coach had paid twin brothers $500 apiece as an enticement to play for the Tigers. Auburn got the harshest punishment that had been handed out until that point—a three-year bowl ban."

It was one of the few times that such a transgression had been revealed in those days; now, of course, reports of such incidents are as common as weather forecasts. And, as no one but the terminally naive can doubt, far more of them occur than are exposed by the press.

Pro basketball was somewhat of a minor sport at the time, with only eight teams enrolled in the NBA's 1956–57 season. The all-powerful Celtics, led by six-eleven Bill Russell, defeated the St. Louis Hawks, whose star was the sweet, six-nine jump-shooter Bob Pettit, four games to three. The Celtics were in the midst of dominating their game for a longer period of time than any other team has ever dominated a professional sport—and it is no wonder. In addition to Russell, the '56-'57 Celtics would place four other players in the Naismith Memorial Hall of Fame: guards Bob Cousy and Bill Sharman, and forwards Tom Heinsohn and Frank Ramsey—and Ramsey wasn't even a starter. As per coach Red Auerbach's innovation, he was instead the sport's first great "sixth man."

College basketball was promoting no such thing as March Madness in 1957, another concept not yet having occurred to merchandisers, and the field of entrants in the NCAA tournament was twenty-four rather than today's rabble of sixty-eight. In the championship game, one of the best ever played, the University of North Carolina beat Kansas University, 54–53. The game's leading scorer was the first seven-footer ever to play basketball at a high level for a major university. Kansas's Wilt Chamberlain had twenty-three points and fourteen rebounds against the Tar Heels, impressive numbers for any other player, but in this particular game's context they spoke more highly of the North Carolina defense than of Chamberlain's offense. For his college career, Chamberlain averaged thirty points a game and eighteen rebounds, and as a pro once scored one hundred points in a single night's exertions.

Nobody of historical note captured any of golf's four "majors," and one of the year's most gifted athletes, the Thoroughbred Bold Ruler, crossed the finish line first only once in a Triple Crown event. The year's star on the tennis court was the American woman Althea Gibson, who lost in the Australian Open finals and then became the first person of African American descent to claim the title at Wimbledon. "She is one of the greatest players who ever lived," said Robert Ryland, who made history himself by becoming the first African American to play tennis professionally; and, for a time, served as the coach of Venus and Serena Williams. "Martina [Navratilova] and the Williams sisters couldn't touch her," he said of Gibson.

But if 1957 was not a memorable year on the playing fields, it was a year of seismic importance behind closed doors. When they finally opened and an announcement was made of what had been decided, the news far transcended the feats of athletes, although people would be slow to understand the true breadth of its significance.

Baseball has inspired more elegiac writing than all other American sports combined. In fact, because of its pastoral nature and relaxed tempo of play, which is generally tranquil and sometimes thoughtfully deliberate, it is the only sport to which the word "elegy" is even applied. A few decades after Ernest Thayer produced the light-hearted poem "Casey at the Bat" in 1888, F. Scott Fitzgerald and William Faulkner put their pens to paper to effuse about baseball more artistically. So did Jack London, George Orwell, Irwin

Shaw, James Baldwin, and the Lardners, both Ring and his son John. Even the unlikely duo of Irish poet William Butler Yeats and the Spanish poet and dramatist Federico García Lorca saluted an afternoon of finesse and strategy at the ballpark.

More recent rhapsodies have been written by George Will ("Baseball is Heaven's gift to mortals"), Anne Tyler, Don DeLillo, Norman Mailer, John Updike, and Philip Roth. In the latter's uproarious novel *Portnoy's Complaint*, Roth digressed from such topics as masturbation, priapism, and Jewish motherhood long enough to muse on the joys of playing center field. He had done so for only a few years in a childhood softball league, but both the memories and the possibilities lingered.

Roth wrote of a child who would chase after balls hit to him, "and the farther I had to run, the better. 'I got it! I got it! I got it!' and [I would] tear in toward second, to trap in the webbing of my glove—and barely an inch off the ground—a ball driven hard and low and right down the middle, a base hit, someone thought . . . Or back I go, '*I* got it! *I* got it!' and back gracefully toward that wire fence, moving practically in slow motion, and then that delicious DiMaggio sensation of grabbing it like something heaven-sent over one shoulder. . . . Oh, the unruffled nonchalance of that game!"

If there were such a thing as an authorial Hall of Fame, all of the preceding would have been first-ballot entrants.

But the home of the Dodgers was a better subject for musing than it was a home for baseball. Buzzie Bavasi, who succeeded Rickey as the Dodgers' general manager, would write in his later years that "Ebbets Field was a great place to watch a game if you were sitting in the first 12 rows between the bases. Otherwise, we had narrow seats, narrow aisles, and a lot of obstructed views." Further: "By 1957 the right field screen hung in tatters, the bathroom odors were stifling, and parking was available for only 700 cars."

Which was indicative of a worse problem, the most serious for the Dodgers. On all too many occasions, space for seven hundred cars was almost enough. The more the stadium deteriorated, the more the fans stayed away, even though, throughout the fifties, the Dodgers were the best team in the National League.

Brooklyn reached its all-time attendance high in 1947, when 1.8 million people came to see the team integrate professional baseball—and, not incidentally, win the National League pennant. But from then, it was all downhill in terms of fan interest. Throughout the fifties, the Dodgers won more games than any other National League team, not to mention achieving more postseason glory, as they collected another five pennants, although only once in those five years did they win the World Series. Three other times they just missed a trip to the Series, finishing in second place.

Yet their attendance figures were those of a cellar dweller. "On the last Wednesday of the 1956 season, with the defending World Champions [the Dodgers] one-half game out of first place, the day after [Brooklyn pitcher Sal] Maglie had thrown a no-hitter, the Dodgers drew 7,847 to Ebbets Field." Meaning that more than twenty-four thousand seats were vacant.

But it was not just the decaying state of the stadium that kept people away, with the place resembling a setting for one of Stephen King's novels more than it did the inspiration for his free verse. A rumor was circulating, whispered in newsrooms and local taverns since 1953, that might have been damaging Dodger attendance more than anything else. The team, people were saying, was looking for a new home. It was planning to move, to leave Brooklyn behind. Some people believed it; most didn't. To the majority, the Dodgers playing in some other city seemed an even more unlikely prospect than Jackie Robinson's eventual employment by a coffee company. Just as Robinson was the Dodgers, no less so was Brooklyn.

But change was on the way, even though it was not what Walter O'Malley, who owned the team, had in mind. It is true that he wanted a new stadium for the Dodgers, but in Brooklyn, not elsewhere. He insisted, however, that it be a large, modern facility. Only such a ballpark, he believed, would enable his team to attract enough fans to make enough money to stay in the city where the Dodgers had started, where they belonged. It was not, however, to be. One of the most powerful men in the history of New York had made his own decisions about the Dodgers' future, and they did not mesh with O'Malley's.

Robert Moses was not an easy man to like, even to tolerate. His scowl was built in, his voice seemed to scold no matter what he was saying, and his smile was cold; he was all business, too full of purpose—whatever the day's purpose happened to be—for amenities such as civil behavior. In fact, on one occasion, commemorating the opening of a controversial stretch of highway that Moses had superintended, he spied a "little old character— just a minor functionary in government," and said to a newspaper reporter, " 'Wait'll you see what I do to this guy.' He went over and grabbed him and almost literally picked him up by the scruff of the neck and shook him. It was very embarrassing. I said, 'What did he do?' [Moses] said, 'He hasn't done anything yet, but I just wanted to head him off.' " Other altercations between Moses and men of lesser stature, and always lesser physical stature, were also witnessed by the press.

Moses had never held an elective office. He disdained the idea of his fate being decided by the whims of a public vote, especially when the public consisted of people for whom Moses had no respect. Which was virtually everyone with whom he came in contact. Rather, he hid behind the scenes, at least at the start of his career, and carefully climbed the ladder of appointed positions; as New York's commissioner of parks in the thirties, he built sixty new parks, "seventeen outdoor swimming pools in congested neighborhoods, added two hundred tennis courts to the city's plant, and almost doubled the number of public golf courses."

By 1957, while still serving as commissioner of parks, he was also the supervisor of a dozen other public works agencies, a remarkable total. The results were no less remarkable. Without him, there would have been no Shea Stadium, no Lincoln Center, no United Nations headquarters. He built more than a thousand apartment houses, in which more than half a million people resided. And he built bridges: the Henry Hudson, the Throgs Neck, the Verrazano Narrows, the Bronx Whitestone, and the Triborough (now known officially as the Robert F. Kennedy Bridge). He built parkways: the Merritt and Hutchinson, among others. He built throughways: the Bruckner, the Major Deegan, the Cross-Bronx, and more. He built the Robert Moses Causeway and the Robert Moses State Park. He was the chairman of the New York State Power Authority when it "was building gigantic hydroelectric power dams, some of the most colossal public works ever built by man, hundreds of miles north of the city, along some place with the romantic name of the 'Niagara Frontier.'" Robert F. Wagner Jr. might have been the mayor of New York and W. Averell Harriman the governor, but Robert Moses was omnipotent.

Poor Walter O'Malley just owned a baseball team.

In addition to an unyielding arrogance, Moses brought a mean-spirited genius to his various supervisory roles, with the result that his will became the city's way. He did not seek such trinkets as money, even if the trinkets added up to a fortune; he was not a man who could be bought. Rather, it was eternal life that Moses craved, and only he could grant that to himself. Remarkably, he did, at least to an extent, in part by working harder than any other man in New York.

Moses turned the big Packard limousine [in which he was driven] into an office. With [fellow city official Arthur] Howland sitting beside him on the rear seat, three other engineers swiveled around on the jump seats and another two crammed in beside the chauffeur, he held staff meetings in the limousine—

while another limousine trailed behind so that when Moses was finished with his men, he could drop them off and they could be driven back to [his office] while he continued on to his destination. The door pockets in the Packard were crammed with yellow legal note pads and sharp-pointed pencils, and he spent his hours alone in the car writing letters and memos that his secretary could type up later.

But in addition to creation, Moses also had a knack for destruction. Robert Caro, the greatest American biographer of my lifetime, who wrote the now-and-forever definitive work on Moses, says that "[t]o build his expressways, he evicted from their homes 250,000 persons, in the process ripping out the centers of a score of neighborhoods, many of them friendly, vibrant communities that had made the city a home to its people. To build his non-highway public works, he evicted perhaps 250,000 more."

Moses tore apart some of Central Park, a public location, to build a parking lot for a private enterprise, an overpriced restaurant called Tavern on the Green. In addition, he tried—but failed—to raze much of Greenwich Village for what he called the Lower Manhattan Expressway; and for no earthly reason, he attempted—this time succeeding—to bring an end to one of the city's cultural masterpieces, the series of free performances called Shakespeare in the Park. Fortunately, the series later resumed.

Caro compares Moses to J. Edgar Hoover. He was able "to keep many city officials in fear . . . he hired skilled investigators he called 'bloodhounds' who were kept busy filling dossiers. Every city official knew about those dossiers, and they knew what use Moses was capable of making of them . . . They had seen him dredge up the dark secrets of men's pasts and turn them into blaring headlines."

This was the man who held the key to the Dodgers' future.

O'Malley discussed the topic with Mayor Wagner, but the time he spent with Moses is better described as a series of confrontations, one that left O'Malley wondering whether Moses wanted the team to stay in New York or vacate the city permanently. And wondering whether, in the process, for no reason that could possibly be imagined, he wanted to punish the entire metropolitan area.

Moses insisted that if a new stadium were to be built, it would have to be in the borough of Queens.

O'Malley was caught completely off guard. Queens? Why, for God's sake? Moses had no ready answer. Reasonably enough, O'Malley wanted to stay in Brooklyn, so that the esteemed name of his team could remain as it had been, as all had known it; he wanted to keep tradition alive. Further, he wanted to save a small fortune by eliminating "Brooklyn" from uniforns and documents, souvenirs, and memories. Point: O'Malley.

Moses decreed that the Dodgers' new playing field be enclosed in a multipurpose arena, which would have meant additional income for the city during winter months—perhaps concerts and other cultural events, perhaps football or hockey games.

O'Malley insisted on a stadium for baseball only. Point: Call it a draw.

And in a curious reversal of the roles that one would expect, a reversal that might in time have cost New York untold millions of dollars, Moses demanded that the new facility be funded by the taxpayers.

O'Malley was willing to finance the stadium privately. No charge whatsoever to taxpayers. Point: O'Malley.

These were just a few of the issues on which the team owner and the city "owner" could not agree. The only thing now that stood in the way of the Dodgers and a new home was a gentle nudge from the far less tyrannical West . . . and it was on the way.

At the other end of the country, a twenty-seven-year-old Los Angeles councilwoman named Rosalyn Wyman, ambitious beyond her years, signed her name to a bill that was, in effect, an invitation for O'Malley and his players to move to her city, for the Brooklyn Dodgers to become the Los Angeles Dodgers. In the East, the notion made no sense. Nor did the sound of it. How could there possibly be a baseball team called the *Los Angeles* Dodgers? It was even a more discordant notion than the *Queens* Dodgers.

The first of those possibilities, however, made perfect sense to Wyman. "A city never grows," she said, "if we don't have major league sports and major league arts. I went out and never thought I'd end up with the Dodgers. That was the best sports team in America at that time, in any sport."

Wyman was pregnant while bargaining for the Dodgers, in which enterprise she was joined by her fellow council members as well as officials in Brooklyn. But make no mistake, despite her condition, she was the driving force behind the effort to abscond with the Dodgers, the clean-up hitter. She was relentless, and particularly upset that New York, the mere existence of which was a bête noire to Angelenos like her, had three baseball teams— the Giants and Yankees in addition to the Dodgers—while her city had none. A missive she wrote to O'Malley, which aimed to change those numbers, was brief and deceptively simple. (Note the friendly comma, instead of the formal colon, ending the salutation.)

Dear Mr. O'Malley,

On numerous occasions the City Council has voiced its interest in obtaining a Major League Baseball club for the local populous [*sic*]. We have been authorized by the Los Angeles City Council to discuss the matter with you.

Very truly yours,
Rosalyn Wyman

According to the 1960 census, if Brooklyn were considered solely on its own, rather than as one of New York's five boroughs, it would have been the third largest city in America: population, 2.6 million. Barely behind it, in fourth place, was Los Angeles, with 2.5 million residents. But the latter had more to offer O'Malley than the former, starting with a privately owned stadium that would seat fifty-six thousand people.[2] Moses had proposed a seating capacity of thirty-two thousand, which was a mere ninety-two more people than Ebbets Field housed.

Even more enticing, Los Angeles offered O'Malley a thriving, fast-growing metropolis all to himself; he would not have to share the fans' attention with two other baseball teams. In fact, the deeds to several parcels of that metropolis, invaluable downtown real estate in a booming city, probably were slipped into O'Malley's goody bag after one of his visits to L.A. What was good for the team might well have been a fortune for the owner, even before the first pitch was thrown.

Early in 1957, as such a measure required, Walter O'Malley asked permission from the seven other owners of National teams to move his franchise to the shores of the Pacific. He met resistance at first; why would the Cincinnati Redlegs, for example, be willing to cross the country to play three or four games in Los Angeles, then fly back again? It would be exhaustive and costly.

But O'Malley's fellow owners didn't care about tiring their athletes; that was the players' problem, and they were young and vital and would regain their energy quickly, especially with a day off either before or after the trip. Or perhaps both. As for the other concern, travel expenses, teams that visited the Dodgers would be playing before tens of thousands more fans in Los Angeles than they had in Brooklyn. Thus, the visitors' share of the gate would be an additional five figures per game; the trips west, rather than being expensive, would be entered in the ledgers in black ink.

---

2. For Brooklyn, O'Malley had proposed a structure seating fifty-five thousand fans, covered by a Plexiglass dome designed by the futuristic architect Buckminster Fuller. Wyman figured a Los Angeles team wouldn't need a dome and upped the seating ante by a mere thousand fans. Still, in these days before big television contracts, the money was more important than it sounds.

Besides, as O'Malley realized, moving his team to the West Coast would spread Major League Baseball's publicity web over a greater distance, and although hard to quantify, this meant even more income and goodwill for the sport. As is true for any economic enterprise that is gaining in popularity without expanding its base, it was time for baseball to think of itself as more of a business than a sport. To think of itself as a national venture, no longer regional. And that would have a dramatic effect on the entire country.

On May 28, 1957, the National League voted unanimously to allow the Dodgers to play their home games in Los Angeles the following season. The effect in Brooklyn was also seismic.

Some fans were enraged, writing letters to the editors of newspapers, sending threats to the Dodgers' offices, uttering streams of invective in workplaces, barrooms, on front stoops. Good-bye letters—more like good-riddance letters—were taped to the outside of Ebbets Field, and obscene graffiti was painted on the walls; people who had bought Dodgers' baseball paraphernalia made a show of throwing them away. To these fans, the very word Dodgers became a synonym for traitors.

But such examples notwithstanding, the public outcry was not as great as expected. Privately, though, it seemed to be a different matter. Apparently something was different about Dodgers' fans, something in their reactions that would not have been found elsewhere, a profound kind of resignation, almost a martyr complex. "We just suffered," said one of them, many years later. "It was absolutely devastating. I think Brooklyn never recovered from that loss because you lost your identity."

Dodgers' pitcher Carl Erskine, who won thirteen games in the team's last season in the East, understood the feeling, "I always kind of related our departure in Brooklyn to a young person who dies too early in life."

Even today, more than sixty years after the Dodgers uprooted themselves, those who remember the sting of the surprise still have hard feelings. Jerry Reinsdorf, a little boy in Brooklyn at the time who now owns the Chicago White Sox, and owned the Bulls in Michael Jordan's glory days, says, "I'm still ticked. There's no way an iconic franchise should have been allowed to move." And another boy in the borough in '57, his name not given, told the *New York Times* in the spring of 2018, "It was a disaster. Walter O'Malley, his name remains in infamy."

When the Dodgers played their last game in Brooklyn in 1957, they failed to score a run, losing to my hometown team, the Pirates, 2–0. It was an appropriate score for an event that was more like the end of a summerlong wake than an athletic contest, and the between-innings music could not have been more appropriate. It had been chosen by Gladys Goodding, the team's organist, and included such numbers as "'Am I Blue,' 'After You've Gone,' 'Don't Ask Me Why I'm Leaving,' 'When I Grow Too Old to Dream,' 'How Can You Say We're Through,' 'If I Had My Way,' and 'Que Sera, Sera.' As the fans filed out, Goodding played 'Auld Lang Syne.'"

The process of filing out, however, did not take long. Only 6,702 fans attended the last game, the last display of the "supreme performing art" of baseball to be played by the Brooklyn Dodgers. After eighty-six years, baseball in Ebbets Field would be no more.

In fact, before long there would not even be such a place as Ebbets Field. By 1962, the stadium would be torn down, and the Ebbets Field Apartments would occupy the site. A decade later, in the year of his death, the residences would be renamed the Jackie Robinson Apartments.

May 28, 1957, was an even worse day for New York baseball fans than has so far been portrayed. The National League owners had not just approved the Dodgers' move to Los Angeles; the Giants also were permitted to cross the country, packing their bats and gloves and uniforms and departing to San Francisco. Like the Dodgers, they were leaving behind a shrinking fan base and an antiquated stadium. In fact, the Giants were playing in the Polo Grounds, in upper Manhattan, after it officially had been condemned by the city of New York. Five years later, in 1962, the New York Mets were born—their uniforms featuring orange to commemorate the Giants and Blue for the Dodgers. The Polo Grounds were glued together more securely, and the Mets played their first two seasons there, before moving to their longtime home, Shea Stadium. Robert Moses finally had his team in Queens.

In the autumn of 2017, Rosalyn Wyman was eighty-seven years old. Her health was fine, but she was not in the best of spirits. Her Dodgers had just lost the World Series to the espionage agents who played for the Houston Astros, being outscored in game seven by five runs to one. But she was not so dispirited that she couldn't look back on what she and her city had accomplished so long ago.

"Brooklyn fans still don't like me 60 years later," she cackled. "I can go to a dinner party today and somebody will say, 'She took the Brooklyn Dodgers.' They hate me. But you know, I said, 'What a dumb city. They not only lost one team, they lost two teams.' How dumb can you be?"

Ms. Wyman obviously had reached an age at which she no longer felt the politician's need to moderate her language.

But the event in which she played such a major role was far more than a mere sports story. Prior to '57, Major League Baseball was played in only two cities west of the Mississippi, and these just barely west: St. Louis and Kansas City. Only one pro basketball team was on the west bank of the river, the Minneapolis Lakers. And of the twelve NFL teams, only two were situated on the country's far edge: the Los Angeles Rams and San Francisco 49ers.

The latter two sports, however, didn't really count, not back then. They played forty-one and half a dozen home games, respectively, during their relatively short seasons, whereas a baseball team occupied its diamond seventy-seven times—and most of these on soft summer days when a seat at the ballpark to watch nine innings unfold was like a small vacation.

The moves by the Dodgers and Giants opened the gates to further westward expansion for Major League Baseball—to Denver, Phoenix, and San Diego, then eventually to Arlington and Houston, Texas. For a time, MLB also planted a team north of the border in Montreal. As for the National Football League, it now has outposts in Dallas, Minneapolis, Denver, New Orleans, Jacksonville, Nashville, Seattle, and Las Vegas (formerly Oakland). And the National Basketball Association has spread out in even more directions, also settling in Oakland, as well as Los Angeles, Sacramento, Portland, Denver, Salt Lake City, Oklahoma City, San Antonio, New Orleans, Houston, Charlotte, Miami, Orlando, Memphis, and even Toronto, Canada. Professional sports cover the map today and thus are agents of national consciousness and consensus more than ever before. They are billion-dollar-a-year enterprises that have become year-round passions for tens of millions of Americans.

In '57, replicas of players' jerseys were not yet part of the nation's standard wardrobe. Now, no matter how short and fat you are, no matter what your age or how much hair remains on your head, or whether you know what a moving pocket is, you can wear a replica of Ben Roethlisberger's jersey in public, and in your psyche stand six-foot-five and weigh 240 pounds—so satisfying an experience is it for so many people, if a difficult one to understand for the rest of us. And some of those Roethlisberger jerseys are worn in Omaha, some in Salt Lake City, some in other places to which Pittsburgh Steelers' fans have moved. To remain devoted to a sports team from which one has had to take his leave is to maintain a comfortable hometown identity for a population that has become ever more mobile.

And as professional sports have relocated, so, in its own way, has integration. Dak Prescott jerseys now sell as many in Dallas as Roger Staubach's used to; Stephen Curry's jerseys are more popular in Oakland than Rick

Barry's ever were; and the late Tony Gwynn remains more popular than anyone else in the half-century history of the Padres.

In '57, there was no such thing as a sports bar, with half a dozen events playing simultaneously on half a dozen TV screens, giving strangers a chance to meet other strangers and strike up a rapport for parts of four quarters or nine innings. Nothing equals sports for ease of communication. Baseball and football, basketball and hockey—they are important enough to engage the viewers' attention, inconsequential enough to keep them smiling through disagreements, the perfect topic for small talk that is not really small. As they became more pervasive geographically, sports became more pervasive socially, and something changed, or expanded, in the dynamic of American intercourse. To a society of individuals was added a new binding agent.

In '57, there was no such thing as all-sports radio. Now you can wait on hold for hours to tell the host that you've been giving the matter a lot of thought recently and have concluded that the Yankees will go down as one of the best baseball teams in history. And when the hosts of the program hang up on you and start ridiculing you for the obviousness of your statement, you will not care; you were part of the sports blather experience, sometimes fifty thousand watts' worth of it, and in all of the cities of which I know, these programs are pots of gold for both the stations and the sponsors. In addition, you can be part of the experience in New York by calling from Cheyenne, part of the Los Angeles experience by picking up a phone in the Mississippi Delta. Long-distance calls usually are free these days, and radio stations hundreds, even thousands, of miles away, can be heard on computers. The country is smaller, and the teams are everywhere and, as a result, more of a priority than ever before.

In '57, there was no such thing as all-sports television. Now, for millions of Americans, there is no such thing as life without it; it is always there, always broadcasting, ready for you whenever you want to tune in. It does not just quench the desire for information; it presents so much in the way of mind-reeling trivia that it creates a hunger for more such particulars, the quirkiness of them proving not only irresistible, but more perversely pleasurable than other facts with which we are bombarded daily—political facts, for instance, which so often are examples of the worst in human nature. On its various channels, ESPN, the reigning monarch of all sports television, provides a blend of scores and silliness that is like a 24/7 time-out for the brain.

Because of these kinds of shared experiences, which inevitably have led to a more uniform nationwide character, the Dodgers' and Giants' moves west may be seen as first steps in making a sprawling country seem more inclusive, the beginning of a national culture of sports. No matter where you live now, a professional sports team is close enough for you to care about it. And even distant teams have local relevance. Red Sox fans now have reasons to concern themselves with the strengths and weaknesses of the Tampa Bay Rays; they are, after all, in the same division, one's fate tied to the other.

The United States remains, as ever, a union of states, but starting in '57 we became a union of leagues as well.

11

The Man Who Believed in God

The Reverend Billy Graham died on February 21, 2018, at the age of ninety-nine at his mountain retreat in Montreat, North Carolina. A person born in the twenty-first century is likely to think of Graham, if at all, as a relic. Not to mention something of a mystery, for his place in the American archives is singular, and thus his ascension to that place is difficult to explain. It depended, surely, on the context of his times, but on what particular elements of the context? It is not easy to understand the man's prominence; it is, however, impossible to deny it.

Graham was "America's pastor" and was the first person ever to be so regarded; he was the "national clergyman," and no one had been called anything like that before, either. Nor is there likely to be an America's pastor or national clergyman again. According to his obituary in the magazine *Christianity Today*, Graham "was perhaps the most significant religious figure of the twentieth century," and if he truly reached that stature, he eclipsed nine popes in the process.

He was not the pastor of a particular church; rather, he was a "tent speaker," or so men like him were called long ago, itinerant agents of God whose venues changed from week to week, enabling them to bring their message to greater numbers of people than could clerics bound to a single building. Crusades, this road-show religion was called, and their lessons always were simple ones, the texts of virtually every Southern Baptist preacher, rooted in the infallibility and literalness of the Bible.

Numerous tent speakers were about as the twentieth century turned. Most lived hand-to-mouth, Sunday-to-Sunday existences, unable to put money aside for an unholy day, seldom able to attract the leading citizens of a community to their services. On days when they were not preaching, they were toting their tents and makeshift altars from one town to another, then posting notices to announce their arrival and the hours at which they would save souls the following weekend. They would talk to funeral directors to find out whether their services might be needed for a burial. They would talk to preachers to find out whether a young couple planned to get married in the next few days. Usually, though, these duties were performed by the pastor of a local church. As for the vagabond, he was dependent almost solely on the money he raised under his tent. It was not an easy life.

And then, a few decades into the twentieth century, along came Billy Graham. That there was something out of the ordinary about him cannot be gainsaid, something not only plainly visible but captivating, without his even trying to bring it forth. It was in his manner, his presentation; he tempered the fieriness of evangelism with the restraint of a gentleman, and with a degree of intelligence uncommon in clergymen who spoke with his fervor and decibel level. That easy-on-the-ears North Carolina drawl of his softened the occasional excesses of his fundamentalist style, making him a more acceptable figure to those who preferred some moderation in their holy pyrotechnics.

As his reputation grew, more and more leading citizens of a town *did* drift into his tent on a Sunday morning. And they told their friends, who told other friends, and brick by brick Graham built the edifice of a reputation.

He was, in other words a charismatic figure, and part of that charm included a dignity that seemed, at times, almost like diffidence. He was not really a showman. He was a man who spoke with conviction, not with schtick.

His appearance was striking. In his prime he was a handsome man, six feet-three and weighing about two hundred pounds. His body was an athlete's, and his long, wavy, sandy-brown hair could have belonged to a movie star.

A man who had turned his life over to the Almighty as a boy of merely sixteen, his stature eventually became such that tents no longer could hold all who wished to see him. He traveled around the country in cars, then vans, then trains, commercial airliners, and finally private planes, and every night for several days or sometimes weeks at a time he would decamp and fill the kinds of venues that rock stars would fill for shorter periods: Graham would set up shop for a week at this baseball or football stadium, another two weeks at this arena or auditorium; the crowds kept growing, and had it not been for logistical problems, he might have been able to conduct services at the Grand Canyon—Sunrise Sunday at a venue more than two billion years in the making.

It is believed that, before he stopped preaching in 2005, he personally had carried the word of God to 210 million people, not counting a much greater number who saw him on television.

William Franklin Graham Jr. was born on November 7, 1918, on a farm near Charlotte, North Carolina, where he woke up at 3:30 in the "black starless mornings" to begin tending to the animals for the day. And he did so, he later recalled, the memory clearly a happy one, "as soon as I could walk." When his chores did not engage him, and that was seldom, he spent much of his time alone, tramping through the woods, often barefoot and followed by the members of his first congregation, a tiny assembly of goats. His thoughts about the Almighty were just beginning to form; it was an exciting time in the life of a boy.

> He grew up . . . in a regimen of diligent pieties in his household; by the time he was ten, he had memorized all the 107 articles in the Shorter Catechism. We had Bible reading and prayer right after supper, even before I cleaned up the kitchen," says Mrs. Graham. "We all got down on our knees and prayed, yes we did, sometimes from twenty to thirty minutes. That was the main event [of] the day in our house." They attended an Associate Reformed Presbyterian church, a somewhat formal fundamentalist sect . . . On those Sundays, Billy was forbidden to read the comics in the newspapers, to play ball, to venture into the woods—the only diversions during that day being the perusal of Scripture and religious tracts, with Mrs. Graham collecting the children into the front room in the afternoon to sit together listening, on their radio console, to Charles Fuller's *Old-Fashioned Revival Hour* from Long Beach, California.

Among the most treasured moments for many a lad is a trip with his father to see his first major league baseball game. For Graham, perhaps *the* most treasured moment was a drive to Charlotte to take in a former major league player: centerfielder, Chicago White Stockings, "a great thrower, a fair hitter, and one of the finest base runners in the profession." But that was then. Now the outfielder had become the most famous preacher of his day, the maniacally twitchy Reverend Billy Sunday. "Wide-eyed, [young Billy Graham] took it all in—the spectacle of thousands gathering in a tent to sing and pray and the scintillating sermon delivered by the athletic evangelist who pranced around the tabernacle platform like a circus performer."

If the boy had been inspired before by the Almighty, he was positively enraptured now. Unlike Sunday, Graham did not become someone who treated the altar like a stage, did not in the least call to mind a performance under the big top; it was not his nature. But preaching surely was, and Sunday had fired the boy's enthusiasm to spread the word of God in his own, more restrained way. He began by preaching to small groups of neighboring farmers even before his conversion at sixteen.

The conversion, however, was what assured that he would remain on the path of devoutness for the rest of his life. It happened one night in an unlikely location, "with the shyest hint of autumn's cool quiescent weather, after hours of walking the golf course, [when, although carrying no clubs and striking no ball] he sank down on the edge of the eighteenth green, at the crest of the fairway's long moon-pale inclines." He was in the midst of a religious crisis of which it is said all holy men must at one time or another endure.

One of the elements of Graham's crisis was a young lady, the first to win his heart: Should he give his life to her or to Jesus? Should he be a man of the Earth or of realms celestial? Or should he postpone a decision of such magnitude until he was older? What was it that even urged him to ask, let alone answer, the most important question of his life when he had lived so little of it?

Graham had no idea how long he sat there on the golf course. But he did remember, for one thing, that "his head hung. And then he was breathing in light rapid shallow pants, as if his lungs were stunned by some sudden blow, and looking up, his eyes blurred, starred, and in an instant, his gaunt jaws were wet with tears . . . 'That's when I surrendered,' he declared. His hands twisting together, he called out in a hoarse voice, 'All right, Lord! If you want me, you've got me. . . . You can have all of me from now on. I'm gonna follow you at all cost.'"

And follow he did, to such world-bending distances that the good Lord must have had trouble keeping up with him at times. But Graham kept pushing on with unwavering belief in the purpose of the journeys. At the start, he had to work out his ideas, making sure they meshed with one another, that they led into and out of one another consistently, not contradictorily—his was the growth of a young intellectual no less than that of a young clergyman. But it was a process he found as enriching as it was challenging.

As for the young lady who, for a time, stood in the way of his conversion, he reclaimed his heart from her, while in the process breaking hers. Instead, when he was older, more ready, he married Ruth McCue Bell, and their partnership lasted for sixty-four years, 'til death did them part.

Precisely what was it that went into the making of a man such as Graham, a man as faithful to his wife as he was to his Lord, a clergyman with such great secular appeal? The question perplexes, resists an easy response. It is a struggle to understand all of the steps he took, a struggle to understand how the farm boy who was sweating by dawn managed to grow into so captivating a presence across the globe. The further problem is understanding the steps taken by those in his congregations over the years, how they fell more and more under his spell. But perhaps it makes for a more compelling story *not* to seek answers, simply to relate what is extraordinary rather than attempt to analyze it.

Near Big Bear Lake in southern California is a memorial that marks the spot where Graham converted, dedicating his life to the Almighty. Less than a decade later, he was sitting in the White House, telling President Harry Truman that the end of the world was coming. Truman said he didn't believe it, and their meeting, arranged by a couple of Democratic congressmen, went downhill from there.[1]

But no harm was done by the failure of a Truman-Graham detente. Shortly afterward, "Billy Graham drew over 300,000 Californians to his shrine and converted 6,000 of them, including a crooner, a cowboy, a racketeer, and a professional athlete." And, with the sole exception of Truman, the rest of the presidents of his lifetime would be, if not Graham's converts, at least his confidants. It is almost accurate to say that the presidents served under the preacher, rather than the other way around.

During the Eisenhower years, in a rare act of public irresponsibility, as well as a rare expression of explicit political views, he seemed to be quoting from the Joe McCarthy playbook when he warned that there were "over 1,100 social-sounding organizations that are communist or communist-operated in this country. They control the minds of a great segment of our people. . . . education [and] religious culture is almost beyond repair." He never uttered such a preposterous statement again—not for public consumption, at least.

Graham and Eisenhower became friends on their first meeting, starting with the first grip of their hands, and it was with Ike that the minister began a surprisingly uncontroversial and long-lasting alliance between church and state.

In the years to follow, when there was no longer much conversation, either public or private, about communist infiltration of the United States, Graham became a common sight in the Oval Office, at Camp David, on Air Force One and various golf courses leading up to the reign of non-golfer George W. Bush. Eleven presidents were his friends, and he had at least a small degree of influence with them all, representing, as he did, such a large constituency of churchgoers.

When Graham passed away two years into the Trump presidency, one of the latter's predecessors, William Jefferson Clinton, said of him,

---

1. Many years later, when Truman was older, crankier, and less astute, he composed an oral biography and claimed, "It used to be you couldn't go downtown in the evening without running into a half dozen evangelists ranting and raving and carrying on . . .

"But now we've just got this one evangelist, this Billy Graham, and he's gone off the beam. He's . . . well, I hadn't ought to say this, but he's one of those counterfeits I was telling you about. He claims he's a friend of all the Presidents, but he was never a friend of mine when I was President. I just don't go for people like that. All he's interested in is getting his name in the paper."

> I will never forget the first time I saw [him], 60 years ago in Little Rock, during the school integration struggle. He filled a football stadium with a fully-integrated audience, reminding them that we all come before God as equals, both in our imperfection and in our absolute claim to amazing grace.

With his good looks, easygoing ways, and unwavering devoutness to his faith, Graham could have fit anywhere in the twentieth century, by the side of any chief executive. By nature a modest man, he was courtly and decent and if, like Truman himself, his judgment was sometimes questionable, it always was well-intended; he never took advantage of his proximity to power.

As part of its tribute to him upon passing, the BBC published "Billy Graham: Six things he believed." They are, in my paraphrase, as follows: treating blacks and whites equally, extending a helping hand to strangers, avoiding the appearance of sexual impropriety, finding hope even in one's darkest hours, believing that no one is beyond the redemptive power of Jesus, and further believing, with regret, that he had devoted so much of his life to politics, the counseling of presidents. *Time* magazine's White House correspondent once wrote that, regardless of a president's faith, "[Graham] came with the office like the draperies."

Maybe so, but unlike several others of his calling, he brought no shame to his mission, remaining untouched by the evangelistic scandals of the late twentieth century. He was not an adulterer like Jim Bakker and Jimmy Swaggart, not a racist like Billy James Hargis, and not a snake-oil salesman like the cheaply wigged Peter Popoff who, as late as 2018, was doing television commercials for free tubes of "Miracle Water"; just drink one small tube of the stuff—or wash your hands with it, rinse your hair, brush your teeth, maybe even mix it with your scotch. The result? The commercial suggests that you will receive a check in the mail from someone or other, for some reason or other, in an amount ranging from $4,000 to $40,000. No reason given. Just get the water and pay off your mortgage, buy a boat, thank the Lord.

Isn't there still a Federal Communications Commission in this country?

Although Graham did not indulge in the previous excesses, he had his share of critics, several in addition to Truman. Among the most cogent was a fellow preacher who spoke out in the early seventies. He is cited by Graham's most thoughtful biographer, Marshall Frady, who, oddly enough, does not provide the man's name. It is a notable omission; nonetheless, as one of the rare skewerings of Graham ever published, especially by a fellow clergyman, and one who seems a thoughtful sort, it deserves to be published almost in its entirety.

The unnamed man of God points out that

it's supposed to be the obligation of the church to pronounce the judgments of God on the state—that's been true ever since the Old Testament prophets, Nathan, Ezekiel, Hosea. But what is Graham doing? . . . What we have right now is the most powerful man religiously in this nation, Billy Graham, giving the government and its policies and the power community in this country his conspicuous blessings . . . What we've got is almost a Graham-Nixon axis. I don't mean to sound intemperate. But the truth is, Jesus went to the cross because he alienated the powers of his day. Not for nothing do the coming do the Scriptures say, *"Beware when all men speak well of you."* . . . You ask me if there's anything finally tragic about Graham in all this? Lord knows, it's tragic.

But one does not have to wait until Nixon's presidency to find reasoned disapproval of Graham. As Frady points out, "by the time of Graham's epic exertion in Manhattan in 1957, his crusades and his message had already begun to occasion a certain deep unease among some Christian thinkers— principally, that it propagated a pious simplicity that finally flattened the true dimensions of good and evil in life, impoverished all the true possibilities of human character and human struggle."

The epic exertion in Manhattan to which Frady refers was indeed that, a "monumental ninety-seven-day stand . . . that still constitutes the classic performance of his crusade system." The most epically exerting of sites in Graham's visit to New York were Madison Square Garden and Yankee Stadium, and it wasn't just the size of the venues that proved so daunting; it was their reputations, their prominence in the popular culture, not just of New York but of the entire country. Once Graham mapped out his itinerary for the nation's largest city, his publicist said that "the name of Jesus Christ will be for many the biggest topic of conversation on the streets, in factories and offices, and on the dimly lit night circuit of such spots as The Stork Club and Toots Shor's."

As an epithet, the son of God frequently was mentioned in the latter two locales; but as a topic of serious conversation, as even part of a complete sentence, the name Jesus Christ was probably never uttered. The good Reverend Graham had his work cut out for him.

His New York encampment, all three-plus months of it, would be the longest period during which he had ever maintained the same base of operations. And Manhattan had so many sophisticated people: rich, powerful, and famous—it would seem to have been a daunting prospect for a thirty-eight-year-old country boy. Was he ready for a showdown of this magnitude? Especially given Graham's opinion of the so-called Big Apple, which he repeated all the more as the crusade date approached.

"For his part," Frady states, "Graham now began casting New York both as the Sodom of modern civilization and as 'our Jerusalem. It is the center of art, culture and entertainment. The world watches New York, how it eats, drinks, dresses, looks.' For much of the year of prelude [to '57], though, Graham himself was withdrawn into the high solitudes of his new mountainside home in Montreat engaging in what had becoming his chronic pre-crusade agonizing: 'We face the city in fear and trembling,' he would periodically proclaim. 'I'm prepared to go to New York to be crucified by my critics, if necessary.' "

But it didn't happen. As usual—and Graham knew that it probably would be so—his pre-crusade agonizing was an overreaction, a ritual, like a compulsive fellow stepping over the cracks in the pavement. In one of the most consistently star-studded of Manhattan's arenas, Madison Square Garden, he managed to attract, over the course of several nights, such luminaries as

> Sonja Henie, Pearl Bailey, Gene Tierney, Ed Sullivan, Dale Evans, Dorothy Kilgallen, [and] Walter Winchell. Surveying from the celebrity box this whole huge Noah's Ark pageantry of revival that Graham had brought to pass in the Garden, Perle Mesta effervesced, "Isn't it fantastic! I think he is just wonderful! Certainly we need this. It's all that's going to save the world."

Similar reactions came from others. Whether they were sincere, or merely being appropriate to the occasion, as well as Graham's ever-growing reputation, cannot be said with any certainty.

After Madison Square Garden, Graham preached in a few of New York's churches, shared the word of God in a number of open-air spaces, and even made an appearance at the New York Stock Exchange, where he rang the opening bell without pronouncing blessings on mammon. His very presence, though, gave the trading floor a patina of piety for a day, a feat not easily achieved.

However, the most challenging of New York's venues for the country boy from North Carolina was in the Bronx, where Yankee Stadium stood as the city's grandest of secular temples. It was the last engagement of the tour, and the temperature "would reach a sweltering 105 degrees in the shade that day . . . but as early as 10: A.M., nine hours before the service, buses began arriving."

The stadium presented three times as many seats as Madison Square Garden. Could he possibly fill all 67,200 of them? As it turned out, his agonizing on the eve of his most largely attended service ever was even more of an overreaction than usual; Graham not only matched the stadium's normal capacity, but far exceeded it.

100,000 Fill Yankee Stadium to Hear Graham

So read the front-page headline in the following day's *New York Times*, and below it was a photograph that seemed to contain most of those people, a teeming mass of humanity, shoulder to shoulder and, for at least one midsummer's night, faithful to the Lord and courteous to one another.

Below the photo were facts at which Graham would never have guessed.

> One hundred thousand people jammed Yankee Stadium last night to hear the Rev. Billy Graham call sinners to repentance. It was the largest crowd in Stadium history.
>
> More than 10,000 others were turned away.
>
> At 7 P.M. when the service began, every nook and cranny in the arena was filled. Standees lined the aisles at the triple-tiered stadium.

Others, however, decided not to confine themselves to the stadium's seats, but overflowed to the foul areas behind home plate and along both baselines all the way from home to the outfield walls. They covered most of the infield and every blade of grass in the farthest reaches of left, center, and right. Some brought lawn chairs, some folding chairs, and some made do with their derrieres. There wasn't enough room left over for Bobby Richardson to have dropped down a bunt.

The *Times* continued its report:

> The only open space was the carefully manicured greensward of the infield. A four-foot picket and wire fence circled the bases. It was the only barrier between the speakers' platform and a sea of faces.
>
> Among the 300 persons sitting on the platform with Rev. Graham was Vice President Richard M. Nixon.

The previous record for Yankee Stadium attendance had been set twenty-two years earlier, when an estimated "83,150 sports fans watched the Joe Louis-Max Baer heavyweight fight. In 1953, a meeting of Jehovah's Witnesses drew 81,000 in the stadium itself, with 7,500 assembled outside."

It had happened. Billy Graham, the country boy, had conquered Yankee Stadium, just as his hero had conquered it so many times before. One night during a previous summer, just as he had started his procession to the stage at a crusade in Charlotte, North Carolina, someone gave him a news bulletin. He kept walking but could not contain his enthusiasm. "Mickey Mantle hit two home runs today," he whooped. "Boy, what a guy."

Looking back on Gotham in the weeks after he had departed, Graham gave the credit for his jubilant ninety-seven days to his Savior. It is probably the oldest of bromides for a Christian holy man to express his gratitude and attribute his successes to Jesus Christ, but Graham did so with a sincerity that could not be mistaken. He was but the messenger, he said; it was the message that found resonance in the hearts of his listeners.

But what gave special resonance, and thus a special degree of success, to his New York crusade, especially on the night of July 20, when the temperature reached three figures and the attendance six, was that he did not try to adapt himself to the big city. Rather, he allowed the big city to adapt itself to him, and his much simpler ways.

For all of his anticipatory precrusade pronouncements posing Manhattan as the great Byzantium of America's cultural and civilized life, once he arrived there, he mostly remained an undeflectably resolute provincial. . . . Greenwich Village, the evening lobby at the Algonquin, the Guggenheim Museum, the Actors Studio, O'Neill and Ionesco and Arthur Miller on Broadway—it all might as well have been five thousand miles away. The sensibilities out of which he preached were still those of Charlotte . . . [his] resolve and commitment persevered still impervious and intact, delivered now to New York with an eye-blazing jaw-clapping finality.

If he could make it there, he could make it anywhere.

12

The Woman Who Believed in Man

She might have been the anti-Billy Graham. As profound an atheist as he was a Christian, she wrote the most controversial novel of the twentieth century, although despite the millions of copies the book has sold, its title would not come readily to most people's minds as having been so popular. It was, in fact, the most controversial work of fiction since Harriet Beecher Stowe's *Uncle Tom's Cabin*, published almost exactly a century earlier. Which of the two was the more controversial cannot be said; the judgment would be a subjective one, based on how one defines the term and how one views the times when the books were published. But both stimulated conversation and roused contentiousness to degrees that no other novels had done before in our country. In addition, both raised issues that still are unsettled.

What can be said objectively about the two books is that they deal with entirely different subject matters. It also can be said that the plot of *Atlas Shrugged* covers more ground than does *Uncle Tom's Cabin* and is more complex in its philosophical underpinnings. This is hardly an insult to the latter; it is simply to say that the impact of Stowe's book is largely emotional, and its plot is thus relatively simple, its focus on a single topic. The impact of Ayn Rand's volume, on the other hand, is intellectual and deals with a number of topics, albeit related ones. And it further can be said that Stowe's novel is regarded almost unanimously as a classic, whereas some reading these words already are irate that I have spoken so highly of Rand's magnum opus.

Nonetheless, three decades after it was published, *Atlas Shrugged* was selling three hundred thousand copies a year, and it continues to sell at a similar pace. If the *New York Times* calculated its list of best-selling novels differently, the Rand epic almost certainly would have found a place on it every week in all six decades-plus since its publication. It would appear today along with the latest works of King, Grisham, Patterson, Michael Connelly, Daniel Silva, and Nicholas Sparks. In some weeks, the Harry Potter novels would have outsold it, but they have not had time to prove themselves the same kind of enduring phenomenon.

Atlas Shrugged, on the other hand, made its debut in bookstores in the first year of Dwight Eisenhower's second term in the White House.

It is, of course, a momentous accomplishment for any work, but almost inconceivable for one so serious—not to mention lengthy. *Atlas Shrugged* is a reader-daunting 1,169 pages (my copy is divided into two volumes) that devotes sixty of them, a mighty chapter, to a speech by a single character. The speech, in effect, is a doctoral dissertation on Objectivism, which is what Rand named her philosophy, although the speech is not recognized as academically grounded—among other reasons, because she allowed fictional characters to stand in for real ideas. And because she is Ayn Rand, and nobody in the academe pays any attention to her, neither as an author nor a philosopher. In fact, whereas Stowe preached what virtually all Americans today consider conventional morality, Rand is charged by many foes with being a cheerleader for *im*morality.

And not just because of her atheism. Billy Graham's night at Yankee Stadium and the publication of Rand's fourth and final novel may be said to represent the extremes of belief in the big picture of the twentieth century.

"In a 1991 survey sponsored by the Library of Congress and the Book-of-the-Month Club, Americans named *Atlas Shrugged* the book that had most influenced their lives, second only to the Bible." It is an amazing dichotomy in American reading tastes. From the angels to Satan, Rand's foes would say, and she would laugh at the notion of grown-up men and women believing in either angels *or* Satan.

Seven years after the survey, the Modern Library conducted a referendum of its own, asking its readers to choose the best novels of the twentieth century, and Rand's book finished an unsurprising first. But that is only the beginning of the achievements bestowed on the author by Modern Library subscribers. Its poll of best novels produced results that are almost impossible to believe, all the more so because of the vast number of people these days who know so little, if anything, about the author. Not to mention those, even including some of her fans, who do not know how to pronounce her name. It is *Ine*, not *Ane*, not *Ann*.

Despite its occupying 741 pages in another two-volume edition of mine, *The Fountainhead*, another classic work of American literature, finished second in the Modern Library poll. Considered by Rand to be her "practice" book for *Atlas Shrugged*, *The Fountainhead* is the saga of Howard Roark, a brilliant architect with a Randian ego. Accepting a commission to build a housing project only after being assured that it will be constructed strictly according to his vision, that there will be no tampering with it whatsoever, he finds that the finished product has in fact been corrupted. Geegaws have been added to the starkness of the design. Doodads have been piled onto the geegaws. Roark is appalled. He believes that he has been violated and destroys the project, dynamiting it to rubble. He is arrested, tried, and found not guilty after a stirring courtroom peroration about the sanctity of artistic vision. It is a verdict with which few people would agree.

And, as if it were not enough that Rand occupied the top two places in the Modern Library's survey, two of her lesser works, *Anthem* and *We the Living*, much leaner volumes, finished seventh and eighth, respectively—this despite the fact that most Americans haven't heard of either one of them. Still, according to a number of American readers, Ayn Rand, who has only four novels to her credit, has written four of the ten best works of fiction in the century. The mind reels at such a showing by tomes of such weight—both in their poundage and in their messages.

In this postliterate era of the United States, we are a people who seek beach reads. We are a people who seek books one can read in a single sitting. Ayn Rand does not write for us. She writes for herself.

Millions of readers would have it no other way. They are people whose minds click into a higher gear when they read her, the process an automatic one. They are not academics. They are persons described nicely by Rand biographer Anne Heller as "the largely abandoned class of thinking non-intellectuals." They do not read Rand to improve their academic standing, for they have none. They do not read them to impress their friends, for their friends probably will be disapproving. They read her because she affects them viscerally, which is yet another coup for this author who some-how manages to combine relative anonymity on the one hand with un-precedented fame and impact on the other.

And yet—there is always an "and yet" when reporting something favor-able about Rand—as Heller points out, "in a corresponding list of critics' literary choices, Rand's novels are entirely absent."

It is Objectivism that provides the motive force for her writing, yet the most authoritative philosophers of the twentieth century never granted her a chair among them. They are more likely to pull out a chair from under her as she sits. And Objectivism, as far as they are concerned, might as well be a communicable disease. Such men as Alfred Adler, Theodore Adorno, Mortimer Adler, Walter Benjamin, and Roland Barthes, most of whom are masters of incomprehensible prose, refused to lower themselves by even acknowledging a mere novelist, especially one who believed selfishness to be a virtue and altruism a sign of weakness.

And yet: "In a certain sense, every novelist is a philosopher," Rand once said, making calm and perfect sense, "because one cannot present a picture of human existence without a philosophical framework." However, in her case, "In order to define, explain and present my concept of man, I had to become a philosopher in the specific meaning of the term."

Rand is surely the most engaging philosopher of my lifetime—not only because her prose is accessible, though hardly candified, but because her ideas are concrete, directly related to the workings of the world and their deepest underpinnings. In fact, many of the topics about which she writes are the very substance of the quotidian. One does not have to read Rand to become acquainted with her subject matter; it is the very air we breathe.

The kind of philosopher who so despises Rand, on the other hand, is usually an esoteric sort, like the fellow about whom I recently read who was watching a football game on television when it struck him that, in order to score, Team A has to cross Football Team B's half of the field, thus sanctifying "the property-seizing principle" of imperialism.

Should a book ever be written called *Philosophy for Dummies*, I submit the preceding for chapter 1.

Meanwhile, Rand has come to conclusions about rational matters in a rational manner and written them into stories so gripping that the public, her thinking nonacademics, can comprehend them and react with either praise or disdain. She is, in other words, an outlier in philosophy, a woman whose literary style, although clunky at times, adds action to the deliberations of thought.

The book you are now reading, let it be clear, does not endorse Rand's entire philosophical canon. There is much in Objectivism with which I disagree, in many cases profoundly. For instance: Better by far that Howard Roark be upset and well-paid for his grief than that much needed new housing be blasted to smithereens. But Rand is an all-or-nothing ideologue. One cannot pick and choose, she has said, among her tenets; one must agree with all upon which Objectivism insists; take it whole, or be censured as an apostate.

Which makes me the latter. At times, when reading her books, I want to scream at the pages: You have overlooked this! You have undervalued that! You have discounted the role of emotion in developing your characters, in determining their actions!

But even when Rand makes me fume, she makes me think, is always worthy of discussion, always deserving of attention. And that is her gift to the reader, as true of *The Fountainhead* as it is with any of her other volumes.

Today, Ayn Rand's readers are young and old, blue collar and white, athletic as well as physically challenged, college dropouts as well as postdocs. Hundreds of thousands of them meet in Ayn Rand study groups, in coffeehouses and living rooms, in libraries and even around picnic tables in public parks.

More formally, they assemble under the aegis of an Ayn Rand institute that promotes her work and is called the Center for the Advancement of Objectivism. Headquarters: Santa Ana, California. The Center gives an Ayn Rand scholarship on the basis of an Ayn Rand essay contest, and teaches Ayn Rand courses, hosts Ayn Rand speakers (formerly including Ayn Rand), sends Ayn Rand books free of charge to schools, and sponsors Ayn Rand Conferences every summer in different American cities. They treat Rand, as she is worthy of being treated, as a thinker who matters.

And yet: Look at the philosophy texts and literature texts in a university library today. You will not find the word "Objectivism" in virtually any index.

As a child, Rand seemed to be in a hurry to grow up so that she could get started on the work of her mature years. Having been born and raised in Russia, she found the schools there insufficiently challenging for someone such as she. Biographer Heller points out that Rand once was assigned to write a paper on the joys of childhood.

> Rand didn't agree that it was joyous and shocked her classmates with "a scath-
> ing denunciation" of childhood, she recalled. At the top of the page, she cop-
> ied quotations out of an encyclopedia from Descartes ("I think, therefore I
> am") and Pascal ("I would prefer an intelligent hell to a stupid paradise") to
> make her point, which was that children couldn't think as clearly as they
> would be able to once they had grown up and learned more.

Rand had grown up and learned enough to start writing in her mid- to late-twenties, when she began to take notes for *Atlas Shrugged* while working on the first draft of *The Fountainhead*. She also started on the even lengthier process of untying the knots in Objectivism, which she had begun to think about in her teens. Once she accomplished the latter to her satisfaction, assuming she ever did, her philosophy would be too nuanced for summary in a book that has as few pages and as many other goals as this one. Even the sixty-page speech near the end of *Atlas Shrugged*, the most concise exposition of Rand's views to be found anywhere, is too detailed for encapsulation.

But its last sentence must be cited. Somehow, John Galt, the flesh-and-blood character who is a pervasively ghostly presence throughout most of the book, a subject of whispers and speculation, manages to hack into the nation's radio networks. People who are expecting their favorite programs are bewildered. They do not hear the western *Gunsmoke*, do not hear the vocal stylings of the Andrews Sisters, do not hear the comedy of Groucho Marx, the Great Gildersleeve, or Andy Devine. Instead, if they have stayed with Galt for his entire address, they listen to him conclude as follows: "I swear—by my life and my love of it, that I will never live for the sake of another man, nor ask another man to live for mine."

The reason it takes Galt sixty pages to get here is that the statement is not as straightforward as it seems, was not arrived at without building blocks that are many and varied and, to my way of thinking, often coldhearted.

Although the numerous themes of *Atlas Shrugged* defy a précis, the same is not true of the plot, the main point of which is revealed in the book's working title, "The Mind on Strike." For it is Galt's notion to enlist the finest intellects and artists and businessmen in the country, the men and a woman or two who are America's prime movers, and persuade them to leave behind their current lives, disappearing into a remote valley in Colorado that, because of its perpetual cloud cover, cannot be seen from the air. Galt has turned the valley into a Shangri-La for prodigies, a refuge for those whose competence, like Roark's, constantly is being undermined by the mediocrity that dominates so much of American government and culture.

Before his hijacking of the nation's radios, Galt already has met with many of the people he thinks of as colleagues and told them of the barbarism that will ensue without them. Products of genuine quality no longer will be manufactured because of a lack of raw materials. Trains will neither run on time nor remain on their tracks; when trucks break down, they will stay broken, as there is a lack of good people to fix them, and the factories that once made parts for them are in business no longer. Without the distribution systems these vehicles made possible, clothing will be stacked in warehouses, food no longer will be available despite gluts of production; houses no longer will be built because of shortages of plumbers, electricians, bricklayers, carpenters, furniture makers, and telephone linemen. Art no longer will inspire, if it is even created. Education will be the domain of the uneducated. This is but some of what will happen when the mind goes on strike.

And yet Galt *wants* to bring about conditions like these! Could anything be harsher, crueler, more destructive?

Galt has no patience for reactions such as these. He explains that he is a man of reason, and that reason has failed time and again against the types of people now in charge of the world's workings. So he convinces his recruits that only by deliberately darkening the horizon for a time can a lasting dawn come, one in which the citizens of the valley finally are appreciated for the people they are, the skills they possess. Only then will they be able to break the fetters of servitude that have been imposed on them unjustly by the regulations of inferior minds. Only then, by denying the world their services for a time, can these people assert their right to rule because of expertise.

"Men do not live by the mind, you say?" Galt announces early in his radio talk. "I have withdrawn those who do. The mind is impotent, you say? I have withdrawn those whose mind isn't. There are values other than the mind, you say? I have withdrawn those for whom there isn't."

Among those who have withdrawn because of Galt are Francisco d'Anconia, the copper magnate, and in time the efficient mining of the malleable metal, used in literally hundreds of products, comes to a halt. No one of d'Anconia's ability is there to take over the business. Nor is anyone of Hank Rearden's ability there to take over the steel industry when the hordes of little men finally defeat him; when their pointless mandates and decrees, often supported by the government, result in the quality of steel dipping to so primitive a level that it cannot be used for many of its previous purposes. Galt also persuades Ellis Wyatt, the oil baron, to join him, and the raw material that once gushed from the Earth begins to trickle, and even much of that is lost because of faulty equipment and the lack of proper storage facilities.

Galt further brings to his valley Midas Mulligan, the underappreciated financier; Quentin Daniels, the underappreciated engineer; Hugh Akston, that most underappreciated of philosophers, a man whose ideas arouse rather than befuddle; and Richard Halley who, despite his being the most transcendentally inspirational composer of his time, also is the least admired—despite, or because of, his being a creator of music for the soul.

They all agree to put their minds on strike, to live together beneath the mysterious cloud cover in a manner they never had imagined, to spend their days performing the most menial tasks, happy to be devoting themselves to honest labor. Such a welcome change is it for them to work as gardeners and housepainters, mechanics and librarians, cooks and electricians—with no bureaucrats telling them how to do their jobs. They breathe deeply of the valley's unsullied air, delighting in the company of their overqualified coworkers, with no one telling any of them how to go about their tasks.

Rand herself is among them, for she does a cameo in the book, the old Hitchcockian trick. She is a minor figure known as the fishwife, and her job is to see that the valley's grocery store always is well stocked with quality seafood. She would rather do this, one cannot help but believe, than write novels that do not matter.

But all is not what it seems for the man who organized the strike. Someone is missing, not only from his valley but from his life: a woman who has managed to resist Galt's charismatic ways so far, continuing to run her railroad despite ever-decreasing numbers of passengers and products to haul. Which, of course, means continuing financial losses. She has soldiered on through the Taggart Tunnel disaster. She even has kept the John Galt Line running, without quite knowing why she has named the line as she did in the first place; knowing only, somehow, that it was the right thing to do.

Eventually, though, and inevitably, Dagny Taggart gives up. She yields to Galt's entreaties, and he transports her to a place she never knew existed and a peace of mind she never believed she would feel. But Dagny is more than just Galt's most valued conscript. He has espied her from afar for a long time, hiding in the shadows as he admires her dedication to work, her refusal to give in to the incompetence that surrounds her, the single-mindedness of her valor. And her body, her hypnotizing, sculpted handsomeness. He has determined that she is the love of his life. And he quickly becomes the love of hers.[1]

As Galt has predicted, the world begins to unravel when the work stoppage begins, becoming virtually inoperable, subject to the governance of men too inferior either to issue or follow orders; men who, no matter what their careers, have had only one goal throughout their working lives—to be able to say "It wasn't my fault" whenever anything goes wrong. Before long, the entire planet is hovering on a precipice, a globe balanced on a pyramid's point of extinction.

And then it is that Galt and his posse mount up and ride back into Tombstone, agreeing to save the day. The conditions upon which their leader has insisted for their return are draconian, but, out of necessity, have been accepted. Those of exceptional vision, exceptional intellect, and the proper experience and training will be granted total freedom in their domains. No restrictions will be imposed on them; no government entity will question either their output or methods. The ignorant populace finally has come to its senses.

"'The road is cleared,' says Galt, bringing the epic tome to a close. 'We are going back to the world.' He raised his hand and over the desolate earth he traced in space the sign of the dollar."

Which, lest the author's imagery escape the reader's eyes, is Ayn Rand's version of a priest tracing in space the sign of the cross.

It was, said Rand, not surprisingly, the most difficult of her books to write. "It takes all of my intellectual circuits," she explained, while in the midst of it; "it requires my full capacity." And she made an interesting confession, one that reveals the true nature of her work. For the characters she admires are not the type one runs into on the street. And they certainly are not the cardboard variety, found in so much pop fiction, as many critics continue to charge. Rather, they are representatives of different points on Rand's personal spectrum of ethics and worthiness, carefully shaded, so that she can describe her versions of good and evil in their various permutations. It is

---

1. Notice the hard sounds of Rand's heroes, names that belong to men who tolerate no compromise, accept no weakness. Her villains, on the other hand, include Wesley Mouch, Claude Slagenhop, Cuff Meigs, Ellsworth Toohey, and Balph Eubank.

one of *Atlas Shrugged*'s major accomplishments that the reader can so clearly distinguish Wesley Mouch from Balph Eubank, even though both are alike in the vile mindlessness of their misdeeds. And, similarly, it is an accomplishment that the reader so clearly can distinguish d'Anconia from Rearden, even though both are alike in their matchless capabilities.

The novel, then, may be looked at as a modern, more sophisticated version of the old-fashioned morality tale, in which the characters are named directly after their traits. In the prototypical work of the genre, *Everyman*, written by an unknown author in the late fifteenth century, are people such as Justice, Equity, Strength, Fellowship, Beauty, Knowledge and Good Deeds. Rand does not make her names so obvious, but their attributes easily are discerned (as were those of Dickens, who created such villains as Smike, Mr. Gradgrind, Seth Pecksniff, Uriah Heep, Ebenezer Scrooge, the Artful Dodger).

However, so concerned was Rand with the philosophical nuances of her characters, as well as lengthy expositions of their ideas, that she ignored some of the other requirements of a good novel. And deliberately so. Hence, her confession: "The need to communicate moods, emotions, sensory perceptions feels like it's impeding what I really want to say." It was quite an admission for a novelist to make; she is saying that what retards her writing are the same ingredients that propel so many other works of fiction, that give them their impact. She is not interested in creating well-rounded characters. The majority of hers are either all virtue or all vice.

Usually, when an author finishes writing a book and bringing a sheen to the prose with a copy editor's assistance, the manuscript is turned over to a publisher. But not so in this case. For a reason I have not been able to discover, Rand hung onto *Atlas Shrugged* for a few additional days before turning it over to Random House, perhaps wanting to think some more about passages with which she wasn't entirely satisfied. Whatever the explanation, it was a risky thing to do. In this day before photocopying machines, there were no duplicates of the manuscript, except mimeographed sheets, which often were smeared and difficult to read. This being the case, Rand determined that security for her opus must be tight, all loopholes closed, DEFCON 1.

On the day before Rand would release her masterpiece, she left the 1,169 pages with her husband, Frank O'Conner, and, rather than stashing it at home behind a locked door, O'Conner took it with him to a neighborhood delicatessen. "It was in a case attached by a chain to his wrist, like a handcuff . . . 'He uncuffed it for dinner,' said a young woman who accompanied him, 'I think with a key. We ate. . . . He locked it to his wrist again, and left.' "

Atlas Shrugged was published on October 10, 1957. The price was an offputting $6.95. Now it was time to wait for the reviews.

Rand hadn't expected them to be good; after all, literary critics were among the kinds of people she least respected, and the feeling was mutual. But her notices were not just negative; they were vitriolic, and she was stunned by such depth of hostility.

The *New York Times*: "[As] loudly as Miss Rand proclaims her love of life, it seems clear that the book is written out of hate."

Los Angeles Times: "Is it a novel? Is it a nightmare? . . . It would be hard to find [another] such display of grotesque eccentricity outside an insane asylum."

The *New Yorker*: "the globe's two billion or so incompetents, having starved to death, will know better than to fool around with businessmen."

National Review: "Miss Rand. . . . plumps for a technocratic elite . . . And in reality, too, by contrast with fiction, this can only head into a dictatorship . . . From almost any page of *Atlas Shrugged* a voice can be heard, from painful necessity, commanding: 'To a gas chamber—go!' "

Few, if any critics, pointed out the novel's fundamental flaw. As Rand acknowledged in different words, just cited, her humans are not quite human enough; by placing ideology above all, she created characters who seem programmed, incapable of making a decision without the author's firm hand on their shoulders. John Galt, Dagny Taggart, Francisco d'Anconia, Hank Rearden, *The Fountainhead*'s Howard Roark and his lover Dominique Francon—all of them, each in his or her own way, calls to my mind the Tin Man in *The Wizard of Oz*.

"If I only had a heart," Jack Haley sings, playing the role in the movie.

Well, if *they* only had hearts.

But to denounce *Atlas Shrugged*, as did the *Chicago Daily Tribune*, which made a comparison between Rand's principles and those of Adolf Hitler, is shameful. And there is the equally indefensible line in the *National Review*: "To a gas chamber—go!"

No character in *Atlas Shrugged* so much as hints that an adversary be gassed. Or killed in some other way. Or physically harmed. Rand does not even have one of her heroes scratch a foe with a fingernail. She wants to defeat her bad guys philosophically, not physically; she wants to deprive them of power that she believes they do not employ productively and thus do not deserve. Objectivism versus Collectivism, a subject for mature debate.

As for the mention of Hitler, nothing, *nothing* in *Atlas Shrugged* is reminiscent of the man, not a single character, not a single character trait, not a single snippet of dialogue. One must be a hater of irrational proportions to find comparisons between Rand and a genocidal maniac such as Hitler. Stalin will do, as will Mao, Idi Amin, Saddam Hussein, and their heinous brothers in the commission of unspeakable acts. John Galt and his own brothers will *not* do—and shame on those literary critics, so mindless in their vituperation as to find similarities between John Galt and mass murderers.

"I had told Bennett [Cerf, the head of Random House] not to expect a single good review," Rand admitted. "If there were any, fine, but we couldn't count on it—although I did think I'd get more intelligent smears, I didn't expect them to be such abysmal, stupid hooliganism, to contain such self-contradiction and such total distortions of what I said."

Actually, Rand did get a few intelligent reviews, and they were far from being smears. For example: John Chamberlain, writing in the *New York Herald-Tribune*, called *Atlas Shrugged* a "vibrant and powerful novel of ideas," comparing it to Dostoevsky's *Crime and Punishment*. And Ruth Alexander, in the *New York Daily Mirror*, said, "Ayn Rand is destined to rank in history as the outstanding novelist and most profound philosopher of the twentieth century."

But these opinions, and a few others, however welcome, were not enough to erase the sting of so much vituperation. The result was that Rand fell into a "black agony of depression." And there she took up residence as the initial sales figures came in. *The Fountainhead* had started slowly; *Atlas Shrugged* started even more slowly. But not for long. "As always in Ayn's professional career," writes Barbara Branden, whose husband was a Rand colleague, lecturer, and then lover, "it was predominantly word of mouth that caused the sagging sales of her novel to pick up—then to soar—then to skyrocket through printing after printing and edition after edition for year after year. Speaking of the success of *Atlas*, Bennett Cert later remarked, 'In all my years of publishing, I've never seen anything like it. To break through against such enormous opposition!' "

The increasing sales, and the flood of effusive fan mail that she received, pulled Rand out of her mire, so much so that she was able to proclaim herself "the most creative thinker alive" during a television interview with Mike Wallace. She was bragging, of course. She might also have been right.

As a young man, I wanted to be part of an intelligent dialogue about Rand's works. It was my twenty-third year, and I was living in Boston at the time. Having by then read all of her novels and a collection of philosophical essays, I had decided to attend one of Rand's lectures at Symphony Hall. I had so many questions I wanted to ask, although I knew I would be lucky if I were called on even once.

I left early to buy a good seat for myself, perhaps a couple of hours before starting time. It wasn't enough. I could get no closer to the venue than two blocks, and it was another two hours until the lecture began at 8 p.m. In these days before computerized ticket sales. I had no way of knowing that even standing-room admissions were gone. After not being able to move so much as a single step closer to my goal for at least half an hour, I gave up and returned home.

The only person with a drawing power comparable to Ayn Rand in 1957 was probably Billy Graham.

Rand was, in many ways, a surprising woman. To me, the biggest surprise was the discovery that she had a heart after all. Yes, despite all I have written to the contrary, Ayn Rand had a heart. But I was able to find evidence of it only in her correspondence, not in her novels, her lectures, or her philosophical publications. It was the personal Rand who demonstrated humanity, not the author, not the thinker.

Christmas is not usually one of an atheist's favorite holidays; Rand certainly did not believe in its religious significance. But as a social event it delighted her, and she never failed to send cards to friends. One year her message read as follows: "With Loads of Good Wishes, For Christmas, For New Year, Forever." The printed signature was: "Mr. and Mrs. Frank O'Conner (Ayn Rand)." The card showed a cartoon locomotive—the John Galt Line?—puffing merrily around a track that framed her good wishes.

To give but one of many examples of the Tin Lady's heart in a letter to friends, there is this, in a message to her husband's niece, Mimi Sutton:

August 21, 1948

Dear Mimi:

I was very interested to hear that Connie [Mimi's daughter] intends to be a writer. Tell her for me that if she really wants to be one, nothing on earth can or will stop her. When she is ready for it, let her write me about her career and her plans. It's one profession in which I can help her and will be delighted to help. If she is serious about it, I can teach her many short-cuts, save her a lot of time and teach her a lot of things a young writer usually takes years to discover.

Thank you for the nice things you said about me and *The Fountainhead*. To tell you the truth, I really didn't know how you felt about my book. Give my thanks to the people in the bookstore who told you that.

The Fountainhead will always be current fiction. I appreciate that very much. . . . Frank and I have been rushed like mad, alternating between the studio and the ranch. Frank has had to neglect his flowers and chickens a little, but he is enjoying it tremendously, and it is all very exciting at the moment.

It is a charming missive, and there were many more, to many other people who responded in kind. She also could be charming in person, sometimes with a wry skepticism, even if the person to whom she spoke had dared to be critical about her work.

At one point before *Atlas Shrugged* was published, an exasperated Bennett Cerf read the manuscript and was aghast. He said, about Galt's speech, " 'Ayn, nobody's going to read that. You've said it all three or four times before [in the book] and it is 30-odd pages long. You've got to cut it.' She looked at him calmly, he said, and replied, 'Would you cut the Bible?' Like many others who disagreed with Miss Rand before and since, Mr. Cerf gave up.' "

And the speech, Galt's dissertation, not only wasn't cut, but ended up being twice as long as Cerf had dreaded.

The success of the book, however, not to mention its longevity, ended up being more than he or his author had dreamed.

Ayn Rand died on March 6, 1982. She was not expecting to be greeted by Saint Peter. Among a small percentage of Americans, all of them devotees of the author, Objectivism lives on. Her criticisms of mediocrity live on as well, and in some ways seem more pertinent now than ever. The only difference is that Rand found intolerably inept behavior primarily in the business world; today, it seems fair to say, it is in the realms of politics and government that the lack of intelligence and decency have reached a nadir.

13

Gang Wars on Broadway

It was not an opera, not in the traditional sense. Not all of the dialogue was sung, and the orchestra did not play throughout the entire performance. It was, rather, a Broadway musical, but of a different kind, one that had never been seen before. For one thing, it did not have a happy ending. For another, it brought to the stage such untheatrical deeds as fisticuffs, knife fights, and virtual rioting in the streets, combining the "classic and the hip," as one observer put it. It opened on September 26, 1957. But the idea for *West Side Story* had been planted much earlier.

It is believed that William Shakespeare wrote *Romeo and Juliet* three years before the end of the sixteenth century, based on an English poem that itself had been written a few decades before Shakespeare was born by a man named Arthur Brooke. It was another Arthur, though, Arthur Levine, who wrote the book for *West Side Story* hundreds of years later. But afraid that so obviously Jewish a name would lead to anti-Semitism, even in the world of the arts, he previously had become Arthur Laurents, as whom he made a fundamental change in Shakespeare's tale. In *West Side Story*, the two warring factions are not families, the Montagues and Capulets; they are street gangs, the Jets and the Sharks, the latter Puerto Rican.[1] That was an easy problem to solve.

More difficult was the show's language, a kind of obstacle that Laurents had not encountered before, and not because he was forced to update old English. A simple renovation to modern English would have been easily

---

1. Ironically, the tenements of New York's Puerto Rican west side would be torn down the following decade and replaced by Lincoln Center, a set of showcases for the arts that was not only the grandest in New York, but probably in the whole world. Sometime afterward, a Lincoln Center stage would host a revival of *West Side Story*.

accomplished. However, the original Shakespearean dialogue contained curses sprinkled throughout the plot specifically to amuse the least cultured folks in the audience, the "groundlings," men and women who could afford admission to the Globe only if they sat in the dirt up front, packed against the stage apron. But curses that convulsed the unwashed three and a half centuries ago would not have been tolerated, and in many cases not understood by an audience in 1957. They were too obscene, even in the old tongue. And so among Laurents's challenges was to create his own curses—or rather language that sounded like cursing but was, in fact, meaningless. It is a more difficult challenge than it sounds.

At one point in the play an angry Shark says to a Jet—or is it vice versa?—"Cut the frabba-jabba." The word could have been reminiscent of something Goldie Hawn uttered goofily on the old TV program *Laugh-In*. Or, several decades later, an expression blabbed meaninglessly by one of the characters on *Seinfeld*. But because "frabba-jabba" is spoken with such derision in the play, and because an ominous silence follows, a crackling in the air, it does in fact sound like a curse.

Shortly afterward, a fight ensues; the meaning of "frabba-jabba" remains a mystery, but its connotation becomes clear enough. It leads to teeth gnashing and fists forming and bodies bouncing.

About his two main characters, Laurents wrote, "Just as Tony and Maria, our Romeo and Juliet, set themselves apart from the other kids by their love, so we have tried to set them even further apart by their language, their songs, their movement. Wherever possible in the show, we have tried to heighten emotion or to articulate inarticulate adolescence through music, song or dance."

Laurents was an eminent figure of stage and screen. He wrote the book for *Gypsy*, as well as the screenplays for *The Way We Were* and, previously, Alfred Hitchcock's classic *Rope*. Nothing, though, wore him out like *West Side Story*.

Perhaps the lyricist felt the same way. He was a young, headstrong fellow named Stephen Sondheim, making his Broadway debut and facing his own distinctive set of problems. On one occasion, for instance, he had to work the phrase, "A boy like that who'd kill your brother" into the requirements imposed by the melody. "Put on a Happy Face"—now *that* was a Broadway lyric. But killing your brother? Sondheim sweated over the murderous locution for a long and stressful time.

On other occasions, simply for the sake of the audience's being able to comprehend what was being said, Sondheim had to make the young hooligans who comprised the cast sound more lucid than they really were. But he had to do so with street lingo still intact. It was another challenge that seemed impossible, even oxymoronic. Yet Sondheim succeeded again.

Dear kindly Sergeant Krupke,
You gotta understand
It's just our bringin' up-ke
That gets us out of hand
Our mothers are all junkies
Our fathers all are drunks.
Golly Moses, natcherly we're punks!

But the score of *West Side Story* is no less memorable than the lyrics. In addition to "Gee Officer Krupke," a novelty number, the play's tunes include "Something's Coming," "Maria," "America," "Tonight," "I Feel Pretty," and "Somewhere." Very few musicals, if any, can boast so many numbers that still are being recorded and performed today and that stir such feeling. And yet they descend from a musical that, with its operatic overtones, perhaps demands more of its performers and audience than any production preceding it on a Broadway stage.

As for the dances, it was they, even more than the sophistication of the songs, that made *West Side Story* a one-of-a-kind theatrical experience, going even further than *Oklahoma!* to change the nature of the American musical by telling so much of the story through choreography. It was dance, not as a series of interludes whose main purpose was to break up stretches of conversation and accompany songs, but dance as an element of plot, an inherent part of the story, dance accomplishing what dialogue usually does. *West Side Story* was, indeed, in the words of Walter Kerr, a "truly epochal" feat.

Kerr, who wrote for the *New York Herald Tribune* and was the eminent grise of New York theater critics at the time, continued his review by writing of "the most savage, restless, and electrifying dance patterns" he had ever seen on a New York stage, going on to say that "it was the 'danced narrative' that took precedence over the evening." It was, he believed, the physical movement more than any of its other elements that moved the plot.

Kerr was not the only person who had not seen anything like *West Side Story* before; neither had sold-out audiences, night after night, and if Kerr is right, the credit belongs primarily to choreographer Jerome Robbins, perhaps the most talented man ever to create movement that so enhanced a theatrical story. Among his previous credits were such landmark productions as *On the Town, Peter Pan, The King and I, Gypsy, The Pajama Game*, and *Fiddler on the Roof*.

One cannot imagine *West Side Story* without Robbins, but his assignment seemed an intimidating one, even to a man as gifted as he. He was to create dances that were part ballet, part free-for-all fracas between the Jets and Sharks—in other words, he was to create graceful violence, suitable for the stage and a sophisticated audience, but calling to mind a backstreet rumble.

He wasn't sure he could do it, and as rehearsals got under way, he was sure he *couldn't*.

So, he quit. Just like that; turned his back on rehearsals one day and walked out of the theater. He was emotionally drained. He couldn't pull it off, he insisted—not, at least, according to the theatrical custom that allowed four weeks to invent and polish the dances for a Broadway production. Maybe that was enough time for an ordinary musical, Robbins said, but not for this one, this half-operatic hybrid. This show relied so heavily on dance, and the dance was more unusual in concept and complicated in execution than ever had been attempted before.

Producer Harold Prince demanded a meeting with Robbins. Both men were adamant. Prince simply could not, *would* not, lose his choreographer. Robbins simply *would* not do what he was supposed to do in so little time. To Robbins's surprise, Prince said he could not agree more. A certified Broadway legend even though still shy of thirty years, Prince saw precisely the problems that Robbins saw and told his choreographer he could have eight weeks. Twice the usual time. Robbins, delightedly, was back on the payroll. Not only that, so was someone else. Prince said that he would assign an assistant choreographer to the production. Anyone Robbins wanted.

His choice was a young man named Peter Gennaro, who would go on to a distinguished career of his own, mapping out the pivots and whirls, the leaps and lopes, for such musicals as *Fiorello!*, *Annie*, and *The Unsinkable Molly Brown*. He was also a performer, with credits for his dancing that included *Kiss Me Kate*, *Guys and Dolls*, and *The Pajama Game*. Further, he choreographed television shows for Judy Garland and Ed Sullivan, as well as such programs as *Your Hit Parade*. In his spare time, he put the Radio City Rockettes through their paces.

The result for Robbins of being given so gifted an assistant and twice as much time to prepare, was one of his five Tony awards. But it was *West Side Story*, more than any of the other four, that memorialized the most extraordinary of his accomplishments—sometimes startling, sometimes ferocious, at all times unique for an American stage. "No previous Broadway musical," writes Robbins biographer Deborah Jowitt, "had ended Act I with two dead bodies onstage and Act II with a third. There had been ambitious dances integral to a show's plot before . . . but I attended none in which dance is a way of defining character from the outset."

Leonard Bernstein, perhaps the first native-born American to be acclaimed around the world for his skill as a conductor, was much more than that: he was "one of the most prodigiously talented and successful musicians in American history." He wrote the music for *West Side Story*, and his classical training was everywhere apparent in the intricacy of his melodies. He did not set out to find a middle ground between a Broadway show and an opera; his songs just happened to fall that way, the result of his musical upbringing, his artistic sensibilities. The Bernstein melodies, it has been said, transported "the American musical idiom where it was left when George Gershwin died."

But some of those melodies could be difficult to play, and even more difficult into which to fit the proper sentiments. Even *im*proper sentiments, such as murdering a sibling. Bernstein was aware of the problem; in fact, it was he who had written the first draft of the lyrics for many of his tunes, and they were so inept, thought Sondheim, that he laughed in Bernstein's face when he heard some of them. The older man was furious. He might have thought Sondheim was "a charming, gifted boy." But it was not a boy whom he wanted as a collaborator—certainly not a boy of such insolent behavior. It was a man, and an accomplished one.

So the two of them became antagonists almost as soon as they became colleagues. It was inevitable, believes Sondheim biographer Meryle Secrest, because they "could not have differed more sharply, Sondheim's response to an unpromising situation being to withdraw to an impenetrable distance, and Bernstein's to presume a superficial intimacy that Sondheim would have mistrusted, attuned as he was to any display of humbug."

Robbins, too, had his problems with Sondheim at the start, complaining that one of the show's most famous songs, "Maria," was impossible for him. Secrest explains that the lyrics "gave him nothing to play with visually. It's a love song. A guy met a girl. He's radiant with tenderness and hope, so he stands there and sings.

"So Robbins says, " '*You* stage it.' "

It was not a promising beginning for young Sondheim, who was not only making his Broadway debut, but doing so in the daily company of, and with daily pressure applied by, some of the greatest names in American theater. Some of his insolence, then, can be attributed to nerves, some to insecurity, and probably all of it to his childhood, as his early years were a series of nightmarish experiences.

His parents divorced when he was ten, and, as Secrest points out, he became a withdrawn, emotionally stunted boy, one who had gotten a head start on solitude by being an only child. Although his father, rather a cold man, sought custody of Stephen after the divorce, the boy was sentenced to his mother, an even colder human being who took out her hatred of her ex by constantly excoriating their child. As far as she was concerned, Sondheim could do no right, and she told him so daily, often in the tones of a banshee.

To prepare for his future vocation, however, Sondheim did something very right as a boy. He became best friends with James Hammerstein, the son of Oscar Hammerstein II. Along with Richard Rodgers, the younger Hammerstein was responsible for such classic musicals as the previously mentioned *Show Boat* and *Oklahoma!*, in addition to *South Pacific*, *Carousel*, *The King and I*, and others that made the two men the most brilliant pair of contributors of their kind in American theatrical history. James Hammerstein's father took a liking to Sondheim and appointed himself the lonely boy's mentor, a gardener of a sort who recognized the youngster's talent and helped bring it to full bloom. As a young man under Hammerstein's tutelage, Sondheim became thrilled by the theater and its possibilities. As an adult, by the time Hammerstein had passed away, he had mastered them.

Eventually, though, Sondheim settled down and all was resolved to the satisfaction of his *West Side Story* mates, all parts managing to mesh. And as the different elements of the show came together, and everyone associated with it began to see what a masterpiece they were creating, the egos also began to mesh.

The following are some of the phrases that appeared in various reviews of *West Side Story* the morning after opening night:

"profoundly moving"
a "bold new kind of musical theatre—a juke-box Manhattan opera"
"the action with the momentum of an inter-continental missile"
"poignant to a degree almost unheard of in the popular musical theatre"
"most exciting"
"theatrical beauty"
"freshness" [with regard to the lyrics]

The reviews were rare in their effusiveness, almost breathtaking. But it was Alex Ross, the music critic of *The New Yorker*, who noted specifically what Bernstein was up to. In his book *The Rest Is Noise*, written many years later, Ross concentrated on the song "Somewhere," saying that

the main theme of the slow movement of Beethoven's *Emperor Concerto* becomes the love song of a white boy in love with a Puerto Rican girl in the gang-ridden neighborhoods of Manhattan's West Side. It was a theft with a political slant: Beethoven Americanized and miscegenated.

West Side Story is a beautifully engineered piece of pop theater, fueled by bebop melody, Latin rhythm, and old-school Tin Pan Alley lyric craft. It is also a sophisticated essay in twentieth century style.

But just as the musical's melodic structure drew praise, so complaints surfaced about the complexity of some of the songs, as well a lack of beauty in its settings. This was not what one expected of The Great White Way.

Yet it could not be otherwise. Rodgers and Hammerstein's music does not accompany street gangs, nor do Park Avenue penthouses provide them with habitation or Saks Fifth Avenue with wardrobes. *West Side Story* tells about the underside of life in New York, the wilderness of tenement neighborhoods, where the risk of battle constantly lurks, and sometimes the best that can be hoped for from life is to survive it. That a story with such a setting be beautiful and tuneful as well is too much to expect.

Brooks Atkinson, drama critic of the *New York Times*, was one of those not persuaded by such a rationale.

> Instead of glamour, [*West Side Story*] offered the poverty-stricken lives of Puerto Rican street gangs, and it did not conclude with romance and the cliché of living happily ever after. It concluded with the violent death of the chief male character. Although it was deliberately patterned after *Romeo and Juliet*, it dispensed with the wit, poetry, gentility, and ceremoniousness of the Shakespeare drama.
>
> In the beginning, some theatergoers were repelled by the ignobility of the *West Side Story* and complained that Broadway had betrayed them. But enthusiasm travels fast and infects theatergoers everywhere, and it was not long before *West Side Story* was recognized as an achievement of the first order.

In 1947, a full decade before opening night on Broadway, Robbins had suggested an updated version of *Romeo and Juliet* to Bernstein and Laurents. All agreed the idea was a good one, but they were tied up with other projects at the time. In a log he kept while touring the country, conducting a new work by the Russian-born composer Serge Koussevitsky, Bernstein wrote, "Columbus, Ohio, April 15, 1949. Just received draft of first four scenes [of *West Side Story*]. Much good stuff. But this is no way to work. Me on this long conducting tour, Arthur between New York and Hollywood. Maybe we'd better wait until I can find a continuous hunk of time to devote to the project. Obviously this show can't depend on stars. being about kids, and so it will have to live or die by the success of its collaborations, and this remote control collaboration isn't right."

Eventually, however, the collaboration would *not* be remote; it *would* be right, it would be *more* than right. Although Bernstein was correct in rejecting stars for the original cast of the musical, never before had such a glittering assembly of celebrities been assembled behind the scenes.

But before they could gather and work out their differences, several more years would pass. During that time, Bernstein's accomplishments would include the songs for his first motion picture musical, the joyfully uplifting *On the Town*, starring Frank Sinatra and Gene Kelly, with the latter making his directorial debut.

Among other musical feats in the interim, Bernstein would conduct the New York Philharmonic and several more orchestras, teach at Brandeis University, and begin a series of widely acclaimed television lectures on the CBS program *Omnibus*. I was an aficionado of doo-wop at the time. But I listened as raptly to Bernstein as if I were learning a new language.

Finally, though, it would be time for *West Side Story*. Bernstein would be able to write in his log, "Jerry [Robbins] loves our gang idea. . . . Here we go, God bless us!"

Two years later, both God and the critics did just that, and through the application of alchemy and art to the dross of real life came musical drama suitable for La Scala, dancing suitable for the Bolshoi, and a combination that lit up Broadway not only in '57 but in numerous revivals since. In fact, as I write this chapter of my book, tickets already are on sale for the latest reincarnation, scheduled to open at the Broadway Theatre on February 6, 2020.

West Side Story is, as well, constantly illuminating regional theaters; at some time or other, the show seems always to be playing somewhere. It is part of the Broadway canon, and yet no musical of such prestige was so daringly unusual for its time.

Those who selected the winners for the Antoinette Perry awards, however, did not bless Robbins, Bernstein, Sondheim, Prince, and company. In one of the most surprising votes ever taken by the selectors, the Tony for best musical of 1957 went to Meredith Willson's *The Music Man*—a much more conventional work than *West Side Story*, although a good one nonetheless.

Innovation can be easier to respect than to enjoy.

14

The Youngest Monster

The story for the movie already had been written, and hopes were high. It was the same old thing in most ways, except for a difference in casting the lead role, and that is where the optimism lay. But it was also where the problem lay—and another problem as well, the same one the Ford Motor Company was facing in '57.

No one could think of a title.

Everything else for the movie, though, seemed to be in place. The credit for the tale went to two men writing under one name, and the producing credit went to the same two fellows also sharing a nom de plume. In both cases, Herman Cohen and Aben Kandel had pooled their efforts under the pseudonym Ralph Thornton, and although they had produced films before, this was the first time they had collaborated on a screenplay.

They had started producing movies together in 1952, and their first three efforts were *The Bushwackers*, *Kid Monk Baroni*, and *Bela Lugosi Meets a Brooklyn Gorilla*. Among movies they produced later in their careers were *Berserk!* and *Craze*; and their writing credits, in addition to the screenplay that didn't have a name yet, included *How to Make a Monster* and *Headless Ghost*, for both of which they traded in their Ralph Thornton alias for the slightly more dignified Kenneth Langtry.

Dignity, however, was not their strong suit. Their skills were limited. They were craftsmen more than artists, and they knew no *Citizen Kane* or *Godfather* was in their future. Rather, Cohen and Kandel's goal for their nameless movie was not to make a significant step forward aesthetically, but to take a reasonable step forward financially, to put product in theaters and earn a good return on their investment. They usually did. They would do so again this time.

The screenplay tells of a mysterious young high-school student named Tony Rivers, sweet natured but with an occasionally ferocious temper. "I guess I lost my head," Tony tells a cop, after throwing punches in the schoolyard fight that opens the movie. "I burn easy"—and one can imagine a twenty-year-old Jack Nicholson sneering out a line like this in his old B-movie days. One can see the glint in his narrowed eyes and hear his chilling cackle. In fact, Nicholson was a candidate for the role, and many thought he would have been a perfect choice.

Instead, the casting decision was a surprise, as the lead role went to twenty-one-year-old Michael Landon, better-looking than Nicholson and able to project an innocence not in Nicholson's repertoire. It was an important consideration; Cohen and Kandel wanted the audience to feel at least a modicum of sympathy for their protagonist, even though he was capable of inflicting deep scratches and even deeper bite marks on his victims.

One night, for instance, Tony dines on raw hamburger. Fortunately, though, he satisfies his appetite off camera, with the audience finding out about the meal only because Tony's father makes a quick reference to it. He tells his boy it would be better for him in the future to cook his meat. Tony says he will, and the subject is dropped. Regardless, an important hint has been dropped. At this point, we do not know what, if anything, Tony's eating habits have to do with his "easy burn," but we sense a grisly connection coming.

The fight that begins the movie is not especially violent; no one is seriously injured, and blood does not flow. But Tony does not have a stake in the fray; he has no reason to enter it, and that is his problem: he *never* needs a reason to throw a punch. Rather, he needs only to see others engaged in combat for him to join in. He doesn't take sides; he will slug whomever is closest to the end of his arm. No backstory explains Tony's uncontrollable rage; Ralph Thornton did not do things such as backstories. That was for people who had taken screenwriting classes.

But after school one day, following a reprimand from the principal, Tony proves himself capable of a more garish form of violence than mere fist-fighting. Walking past the door of the gym, he stops and looks in. It appears to be empty. Looking more carefully, though, Tony sees a pretty young gymnast in a far corner. Her body is slender, flawless; her breasts, although not pendulous, tug at the fabric of her one-piece outfit as if they might rip through fabric. He watches her appreciatively for a few moments as she works gracefully on the balance beam. Then appreciation turns to lust, his own particular brand of lust, and he loses his mind. According to Samuel Z. Arkoff, soon to be introduced in this chapter: "by the sound of a ringing school bell, he grows fangs and a blanket of facial hair and brutally devours the girl in the Rockdale gymnasium. No wonder he has trouble making friends."

This attack, more offensive by far than eating a primitive version of steak tartare, is not shown on camera, either. But the girl's shrieks pierce the afternoon air, and for a few seconds, Tony is frozen in place by the ghastliness of what he has just done. Then he flees.

The police are called, and Detective Donovan (a character not given a first name), who somehow knows that Tony is "a person of interest" in the crime, tells the teen that he needs help—in particular, the kind of help that can be provided by Dr. Alfred Brandon, a psychologist who works at the local aircraft plant. Tony does not agree at first, but eventually his rage reaches the point at which he frightens even himself. Warily, he makes an appointment with the esteemed doctor.

It turns out to be one of the worst pieces of advice in the history of cinema. For Dr. Brandon is not only the tale's villain, but its resident crackpot, possessed of a notion for ministering to Tony that will, in fact, prove antithetical to the young man's chances of recovery. It seems that the doctor has begun experiments with a serum known as scopolamine.

Before he became a best-selling author, the late Michael Crichton graduated from Harvard's medical school. In an essay about his experiences as a student, he relates a conversation with a resident physician about the uses of the drug. He tells us that scopolamine was "famed in World War II movies as truth serum." It also was used as a painkiller for women in labor, "but it wasn't a painkiller at all."

Crichton studied medicine in the sixties. More recent sources have listed scopolamine as a treatment for nausea, vomiting, and motion sickness—making it seem an all-purpose elixir. In this movie's version of pharmacology, though, it seems that "scope," as it's known in the profession, can do even more; it has the power to regress people to their most primal states of existence, their most animalistic selves. But for a reason never made clear, and which defies common sense, Dr. Brandon believes scopolamine will make Tony, the schoolyard bully, behave *less* primally, *less* animalistically.

The young man, unaware of this, hoping merely for relief, submits to an injection.

After he leaves, Dr. Brandon's assistant, Dr. Hugo Wagner, expresses his chagrin. He disagrees with the treatment, insists that, rather than helping Tony, scope could end up killing him. Dr. Brandon tells him, in effect, to mind his own business. That difference of opinion suggests the violent ending toward which the film already has begun to build.

But it is not just the ending . . .

Later, after a small party at a haunted house that did not need to be haunted because nothing otherworldly has ever happened in it, nor do any frightening characters—save one—make an appearance in the movie, Tony and his girlfriend Arlene offer a friend a ride home. The friend declines. He prefers to walk through the eerie darkness of the woods that surround the house. He needs the exercise, he says.

So Tony and Arlene leave him to it. Still in his gentlemanly mode, Tony drops off his girlfriend at her home, making no untoward physical contact with her, then drives away. Arlene assumes that he, too, is going home. He isn't.

Cut to the friend tramping through the woods, now beginning to hear strange sounds in the distance. He seems unconcerned. But then the sounds get closer, and more frequent, and louder. The boy stops, turns around, but despite the fact that he sees no one in pursuit, he begins to run. Someone—or something—is chasing him; he knows it, knows it is dangerous and that he has to escape its clutches. He doesn't quite make it. Again, the ensuing violence is not shown to the audience.

The next morning, the friend's body is found. It has been mauled so viciously, left in such a bloody heap, that it seems an animal has had at him; he is barely recognizable as once having been mortal. But no animals are nearby that could inflict such terrifying damage on a human being. As the last two people to have seen their friend alive, Tony and Arlene are questioned by the police. Both seem horrified, unable to talk. They can't even guess what has happened. But is Tony faking his ignorance, or is it the real thing? Even he doesn't seem to know. What he does know is that something is wrong with him, very wrong, although it seems he doesn't yet realize how bad it is.

His friend's body is taken back to the police station and examined thoroughly, but with no luck; no one can figure out how Tony's pal has reached such a savage end. No one, that is, until the building's janitor, a fellow named Pepi, shuffles into the frame. Pepi was born and raised in Europe's Carpathian Mountains, a huge range that covers parts of Slovakia, Poland, the Czech Republic, Hungary, Ukraine, and Romania. It is some of the most haunted land on earth, Pepi says. Further, he believes, it is the home of werewolves. Yes, Pepi insists; such things actually exist.

Of course, nobody believes the janitor; werewolves are mythic creatures, fictive figures—even a simple fellow such as Pepi should know better than to think they are real. His companions in the police station scoff at him, but something about his stoic manner mutes their derision.

And no wonder. It happens that Carpathian janitors know more than one thinks they do, especially about werewolves. When it is discovered that Tony Rivers had not returned home the night of the most recent murder, the police promote him; no longer "a person of interest," he is now the primary suspect. They issue an All-Points Bulletin. Tony, as it happens, has Carpathian blood in him. Although it goes against all reason and rationality, the boy might be part lycanthrope.

The next morning, however, with the werewolf having escaped yet another police dragnet and Tony now having returned to his clean-shaven, non-werewolf version, he goes to see Dr. Brandon again. But the mad scientist is now madder than ever. He still believes he can cure Tony, or claims he can, but first he wants him to undergo his horrible transformation one more time: from teeth to fangs, from skin to fur, from talking sensibly to growling incomprehensibly. From classmate to monster. Dr. Brandon wants to witness the process for himself, to take notes that he can leave for posterity. He wants to leave a visual record as well, to take photographs of Tony's change of beings for the advancement of science.

Returning to his werewolf state is the last thing Tony wants, but before he can stop the doctor, he has been punctured with two more shots of scope's black magic. He begins quickly to fall under the drug's spell.

But the villain has made a miscalculation not only serious but fatal. When Tony turns into a mindless, hirsute creature this time, no one is nearby upon whom he can practice his viciously fatal arts except Dr. Brandon (a worthy victim) and Dr. Wagner (who deserves a better fate). Tony kills the two men—the most gruesome of the deeds revealed only by the victims' horrified facial expressions—then destroys the camera, exposing the film to light; there will be no pictorial evidence of what Brandon has done to Tony. And vice versa.

But before the young werewolf can escape from the doctor's office, Detective Donovan and one of his most trusted deputies burst in with guns a-blazing. Killing Tony takes more bullets that a normal teen would require, but both men's weapons are fully loaded. They fire until empty. Tony staggers toward the two cops but falls lifelessly to the floor before he can reach them.

"Upon dying, Tony's normal features return," says the voice of an off-screen narrator, and one final time we see the handsome, innocent face of Michael Landon. As Donovan and his partner watch this impossible alteration, the narrator brings the screenplay to a close, providing the movie with a moral, ruing the arrogance of "man interfering in the realms of God."

The movie that knew no name, like the other movies previously mentioned, was a product of American International Pictures, a purveyor of low-rent entertainment for the big screen, founded by Jim Nicholson and Samuel Z. Arkoff in 1954. Years later, Arkoff wrote a biography of his early days in Hollywood and recalled the conversation between Nicholson and himself about finally deciding what to call their werewolf movie. He thought back on the problem they were having with one word in the title, which turned out not to be a problem at all.

" 'Listen to this one.'

"Jim Nicholson was tossing out titles one morning in 1957 during our morning meeting.

" 'Sam, I came up with this title last night: *I Was a Teenage Werewolf*. What do you think?' "

"I was stunned. 'My God, it's terrific,' I told him."

> At the same time, however, I wasn't sure quite how middle America would react to it over their morning cup of coffee. There had never been a teenage horror picture before; during the twenties and thirties, when these kinds of movies were thriving, Bela Lugosi and Boris Karloff and Lon Chaney, Jr. and the other stars of such films had always reached adulthood before growing fangs. Usually, there weren't even any teenagers in the cast, let alone in a featured role. Maybe they had a good reason. My wife echoed the advice I received from a lot of people. "It's a great title. But don't you dare use it."

Initially, Arkoff agreed. But the title was not that easily dismissed, either by Arkoff or Nicholson, or, for that matter, by the theater owners who showed American International pictures. Just as the two founders of AIP were the kinds of men willing to take a chance when nothing more was at stake than the possibility of being offensive, so were the men who ran the theaters that showed AIP products.

Arkoff and Nicholson called some of them, conducting an informal poll. They *loved* the title. And so it was, despite the objections of Mrs. Edith Arkoff, that the new movie finally had its name.

S. A. Desick of the *Los Angeles Examiner* could not have been more pleased. So pleased, in fact, that Arkoff and Nicholson were left shaking their heads: "To take first things first, the title is a magnificent piece of composition," Desick wrote. "It has a haunting quality about it, and I ought to caution you that if you let it pierce your consciousness it will echo in your brain in a constant refrain—*I Was a Teenage Werewolf. I Was a Teenage Werewolf.* The title is, in other words, by way of being a little monster itself."

Most others who heard the title did not go so far as to regard it as "a magnificent piece of composition" but found that it echoed in the brain regardless. It was, in fact, the attention Desick paid to the title that started the film on its path to the tipping point.

"[S]till weeks before the movie was shot and eventually released, AIP's phone began ringing off the hook," Arkoff wrote. "Newspapers and magazines across the country were calling us for stories and interviews with the people behind the movie. Comedians on TV shows were doing jokes based on the *Teenage Werewolf*. Overnight, the picture was getting millions of dollars' worth of free publicity, long before it had ever reached the theaters. *Time* did a story on the movie. So did *Look* and *Life*. Bob Hope and Jack Benny joked about it in their acts. . . ."

AIP prided itself on making movies quickly. *I Was a Teenage Werewolf* was a virtual sprint. From first shot to the final call of "That's a wrap," not even a week had passed. In six days—*six days*—the studio was able to stop film-ing and start editing and performing other postproduction chores. Five months later, mostly spent preparing a publicity campaign, *Teenage Were-wolf* was scheduled to open.

Because the film belonged to the so-called exploitation genre, and because it appeared more often in drive-ins than in theaters with carpeted floors, few "respectable" publications deigned to review it. But *Variety*, the show business trade paper, was compelled to acknowledge the latest AIP opus. "Another in the cycle of regression themes," said the paper's critic, "is a combo teenager and science fiction yarn which would do okay in the Exploitation market . . . Only new thing about this . . . production is a psychiatrist's use . . . of a problem teenager . . . but it's handled well enough to meet the requirements of this type film . . . good performances overcome deficiencies. Final reels, where the lad turn[s] into a hairy-headed monster with drooling fangs are inclined to be played too heavily."

Which, of course, raises the question: How does one play such scenes with subtlety?

Although Arkoff, who, like Ayn Rand, did not expect favorable reviews for her very different kind of work, he was a savvy enough businessman to realize that the cleverness of Jim Nicholson's title would make up for doz-ens of condemnations. But he had not expected one of the latter to come from the halls of Congress. Paul Douglas, a highly regarded senator from Illinois, as well as a respected economist, wrote to Arkoff, "*I Was a Teenage Werewolf* is of considerable concern to me. At a time when the country is sensitive to the problem of juvenile delinquency, we need the motion pic-ture industry to take a responsible stand in the movie it makes for young audiences, rather than making movies that are scandalous and immoral."

Arkoff was stunned. The movie contained no sex, no titillation, no foul language, and virtually no violence on camera, certainly less than *West Side Story* displays on stage. Further, the film closes with the Christian admoni-tion not to meddle in God's affairs. Yet to Douglas, *I Was A Teenage Werewolf* was "scandalous and immoral." To keep Senator Douglas's criticism in mind as one watches the movie in the second decade of the twenty-first century is to be jolted almost physically by the changes that have been made in scandal and immorality; we have reached summits that previously would have been thought unattainable. The film now seems almost inno-cent. But not then.

As for Arkoff, the more he composed himself and thought about Doug-las's complaints, the more he seems to have considered devising a new series of ads, these featuring quotes from Douglas. Arkoff knew that his audience was comprised mostly of adolescents, and that they would be drawn virtually to any film censured by one of the country's leading authority figures. You couldn't buy that kind of publicity! Maybe the ad even could feature a sketch of Douglas with fangs, dragging a teenage beauty off to her fate.

But giving the senator's letter more thought, Arkoff decided that a more mature response was in order. He was sure he knew what had happened. Douglas had kept his letter short and had made no specific criticisms of scenes in the movie; in fact, his language was general enough to apply to scores of more highly regarded films, certainly including James Dean's classic *Rebel Without a Cause*, Marlon Brando's *The Wild One*, and '57's box office bonanza, *The Guns of Navarone*.

Understanding this, it was but a short step for Arkoff to realize that Douglas had not seen the movie. He was just reacting to constituents, most of whom probably had not seen the movie either. The senator simply was playing politics, keeping the voters happy. More than likely, he hadn't even written the letter himself, assigning it to a staff member and merely attaching his signature to the finished product.

So Arkoff decided to play his own brand of politics, responding to Douglas's letter in the manner of an adult—a reflective one at that.

"Please do not be overly influenced by the advertisement for the movie," he began, writing the missive himself. "As you know, there is a tendency among American businesses to be enthusiastic about their products. Perfume manufacturers hold out the promise of seduction in their ads, yet every time a woman uses a few drops, she isn't automatically seduced. Keep that in mind when you read the ads for *I Was a Teenage Werewolf*."

The analogy, of course, does not quite work. Even the most virtuous of women prefer to be seduced more often than they want to be shredded to death and their remains consumed by a monster. Nonetheless, Arkoff sounded reasonable, all the more so when he offered to arrange a private screening for Douglas and anyone he might want to bring with him.

As he expected, Arkoff never heard from the senator again. He could not have handled the budding crisis better.

At a later point, however, Arkoff would hear indirectly from Jason Jones, writing for the website classic-horror.com. He probably spoke for a majority of those who saw the motion picture: "After finally sitting down and watching *I Was a Teenage Werewolf*, I can honestly say it's just about as crappy a movie as you'd expect it to be. It's poorly scripted," Jones said, "over acted, over simplified, largely boring and sometimes just plain trite. Even with these major league strikes against it, I still really enjoyed this drive-in classic and I'm not alone. If you mention this 1957 bargain basement cheese fest to a person of the right age, they smile."

That *I Was a Teenage Werewolf* was not one of the twenty top-grossing movies of 1957 left Samuel Z. Arkoff untroubled. That it probably was the year's only film to earn the enmity of a United States senator did not bother him either. In fact, nothing bothered him about the production, not after the accountants did their calculations and determined that *Teenage Werewolf*, after having been made on a budget of $82,000, had enriched American Independent by $2 million, a return of more than 2,000 percent on its investment. And in this day, when the salaries of movie stars often exceed the annual budgets of small African countries, Arkoff paid Michael Landon a mere $1,000 for six days of labor.

In the long run, though, Landon exceeded his investment by even more than Arkoff and Nicholson did. Two years after his low-rent horror film, he went on to land a starring role in the western *Bonanza*, one of the most popular television programs of its time. From there it was on to another leading role in TV's adaptation of the Laura Ingalls Wilder novel, *Little House on the Prairie*, and then a third starring role in the small screen big hit, *Highway to Heaven*.

In the latter, Landon played an angel demoted to earth for a probationary period, and in one of the episodes paid homage to his first big break. "I Was a Middle-Aged Werewolf," this particular episode of the show was called, and "Writer/director Landon has the proverbial field day spoofing his infamous 1957 role, going so far as to be made up as the titular beast, snarling and terrorizing" his best friend, Mark.

Near the end of the program, Mark is watching a late-night movie called *I Was a Teenage Werewolf* and comments to Jonathan Smith (Landon's character in *Highway to Heaven*) that this Tony Sanders guy looks a lot like a young Jonathan. Landon squints into the screen, shrugging. Apparently the resemblance eludes him.

In all of Landon's major TV roles he played wholesome individuals, in the third of them even a divine character. And so successful was he, so much did his non-werewolf parts enable him to demonstrate his innate charm, that he appeared on the cover of *TV Guide* twenty-two times, second only to Lucille Ball.

In an online publication called ComingSoon.net, Chris Fowler, who has written both music for and books about movies, often second-string horror movies, explains why he believes *I Was a Teenage Werewolf* deserves to be considered, borrowing the title of Dreiser's classic novel, "An American Tragedy."

As was the case after the first World War, Fowler believes, the young people are most emotionally dislocated; they must cope with the shattered beliefs in the wisdom of their elders to find their country's government and ethical structure.

Writes Fowler:

Truth. If it wasn't for World War II, there would be no French New Wave, no Godzilla. And no I Was a Teenage Werewolf. The latter-mentioned 1957 horror film is seldom discussed in terms of its socio-political significance, but I can think of no other American genre of the period that so taps into the anxieties and cynicism of the burgeoning U.S. youth culture, fueled as it was by rock 'n' roll and rebellion. And in [director] Gene Fowler, Jr.'s scrappy, cheap and innovative flick that bile came in the form [of] a toothy, drooling and merciless and hormonal and merciless menace.

Chris Fowler goes on to say that the critics who condescended to review the film, invariably snickering at its simple-minded dialogue and plot devices, not to mention its almost comical special effects, "had no idea what the movie was really about and rejected the concept of teenage angst as being just a laughable rite of passage, totally ignorant that the sort of angst that was swelling around them would birth a generation of intensely political, angry, and aware kids whose minds and hearts would affect the world." In its finest moments, Fowler concludes—and other critics notwithstanding, he believes it had many—I Was A Teenage Werewolf brims with "primal, urgent and heartbreaking energy, that it is "a remarkable and important movie from a transitional time in movie history."

Truth. Does Fowler speak it in his essay on the film? Perhaps, but only to a point. Fowler presents a tenuous form of veracity, all the more so when he overstates the movie's virtues. But his analysis of Teenage Werewolf is worth considering. There were reasons aplenty for the youthful disaffection produced by World War II and the Korean War and the generation of leaders that had steered the United States into them—in the former case, it should be added, of necessity. And Fowler was right when he opined that I Was a Teenage Werewolf reflects some of the reasons for the postwar malaise among young Americans.

More evidence for this point of view comes from other monster movies made at this time. To name the most popular among dozens: Creature from the Black Lagoon, The Beast from 20,000 Fathoms, and The Blob, starring a young Steve McQueen. There must be a reason that the fifties were the peak period for monster movies, that no other decade even comes close to it. Fowler's reason seems to me as valid as any other. His reference to "a transitional time in movie history" is only logical, considering that the fifties were a transitional time in American history.

Even though I Was a Teenage Werewolf is only the thirty-first best monster film of the fifties according to ranker.com, it might be, even now, the era's best known.

Most of those who know the movie and enjoy it at present do not do so for sociopolitical reasons. In fact, "today the film is largely regarded as a source of camp humor, and while at the time of release the idea of an adult human being turning into a monster was nothing new, the idea of a teenager doing just that in a movie was considered avant-garde—and even shocking—in 1957."

And so in homage to that distant year, there is still the rare midnight showing of *I Was a Teenage Werewolf* in an indoor theater; the movie's posters still sell modestly, both online and in nostalgia shops, especially the poster that shows streams of blood running *upward* from a set of fingernails; and *Teenage Werewolf* T-shirts may be purchased in both long- and short-sleeved versions. Appropriate Halloween costumes are available, in both adult and children's sizes, and action figures of Tony Rivers have been for sale, so malleable that he may be bent into poses Michael Landon never could have achieved in life.

And on the vinyl LP *Songs the Lord Taught Us*, released in 1980 by a punk rock group known as the Cramps, is a song the Lord *hadn't* taught them.

> I was a teenage werewolf
> Braces on my fangs
> I was a teenage werewolf
> And no one even said thanks
> And no one made me stop.

Thus, the movie has achieved cult status. As the late mystery writer John D. MacDonald once said to me, "If you hang around long enough, they'll get tired of pummeling you and start looking for elements in your work that they can praise. And damned if they don't find them!"

In *I Was a Teenage Werewolf*, they were indeed found. The movie without a name that finally was named so memorably has achieved a respectable old age, in the process having survived the ridicule of its gimcrack days and gone on to become an Edsel of sorts of motion pictures.

PART FIVE

The United States Finally Takes Off

15

The Successes of Failure

Three weeks after Sputnik was launched, its battery ran out of juice, and the satellite stopped beeping. The sound that had so frightened Americans when we first heard it, the alarm that we feared was the signal for doomsday, had faded into celestial silence, its tiny power source not having lasted as long as that of a child's toy. The battery was declared officially dead on October 26 by Radio Moscow; actually, it had lasted a day longer than three weeks.

But before the beep officially had perished, American military and intelligence agencies had figured it out. It was, as previously surmised, telemetry, powered by a "one-watt, battery-operated transmitter . . . placed inside the aluminum shell [of the satellite] simply so that it could be tracked." And that was the sole purpose of the sound: nothing more ominous than a means of following the satellite's path. Because the path was the same each time it looped around the Earth, three weeks was more than enough time to establish a pattern, and one watt was more than enough energy.

But questions *still* remained—except that now they were about the satellite, not the sound.

Sputnik continued to orbit for more than seventy days without a peep. However, its low Earth trajectory kept getting lower and lower until it finally reentered the atmosphere and burst into flame, reduced to metallic ashes early in the new year.

"Sputnik 1," it was concluded, "burned up on January 4, 1958. It fell from orbit upon re-entering earth's atmosphere after traveling about 60 million km (37 million miles) and spending 3 months in orbit."

However, another version of the satellite's demise caught the attention of National Public Radio, which in turn brought it to the attention of millions of Americans who liked a good story. The star of this one was a fellow named Bob Morgan, who earned his living by renting Jet Skis near Santa

229

Barbara, California. Morgan said that when his father, with whom he shared a home, woke up on the morning of December 8, 1957, the old man was astounded to see "a glowing object in their yard." The younger Morgan continued: "[My father] looked out the back window and there was something that was so bright in the back yard, he couldn't look at it."

The something in the Morgans' yard was several things, a few pieces of metal and a few plastic tubes—objects seldom known for being too bright on which to focus. All were of different shapes, and none seemed sufficiently damaged to have survived the heat of reentry to the Earth's atmosphere. Yet for no discernible reason, the Morgans and their neighbors concluded that the scraps belonged to Sputnik that had come loose and fallen off in transit. So certain were they, in fact, that they began searching for more fragments, as diligent in their pursuit as children scouring a lawn for Easter eggs. But they found no more than the original pieces.

Eventually, the Morgans turned them over to the Air Force, which carefully examined them, then returned the debris to the Morgans, but without an explanation. So what *were* those items that had been found on a southern California lawn? What was their purpose? And what, if anything, had military scientists learned from them? Were they in fact the remains of the world's first successful man-made satellite? Or were they . . . *what*?

Not only did the Air Force not comment at the time; it has not commented since. To many, the Morgans notable among them, the lack of a reaction was suspicious, tacit admission that their lawn had been Sputnik's final resting place. Some of the scraps, it is believed, now rest in a safe deposit box in the Morgans' bank, although that is not known for certain. They, too, are not commenting.

But the family's story contains many inconsistencies. Primary among them are the dates. Because scientists believed that Sputnik achieved oblivion in the first week of the new year, it is unlikely that it took almost a month—remember, the Morgans made their discovery on December 8—for the satellite to deteriorate. Scientists explained their belief by stating that an object with the weight, mass, and dimensions of Sputnik would have been destroyed within seconds of reacquainting with the atmosphere. The logical conclusion, then, is that the money the Morgans are spending on their safe deposit box could better be spent on mortgage payments, groceries, or vacuum cleaner bags.

Beyond whatever telemetric information the Soviet satellite might have gathered—and it seems to have been a meager amount—the purpose of Sputnik, the first object ever launched into low Earth orbit, remains unknown. Unless that is, you accept the notion that the secret of Sputnik is that there is no secret. And that is probably the truth; that is, the likelihood is that Sputnik probably wasn't even a test of Sputnik, not for the most part. It was, rather, a test of the R-7 rocket and its launch capabilities.

If that is so, it passed superbly, and with more improvements certain to be made—that is to say, with the continuing evolution of the R-7, the rocket might soon be able to propel larger and more sophisticated objects into orbit: navigation satellites, research satellites, weather satellites.

Even military satellites.

The Western world, then, would not be surprised when more R-7-launched devices were flung heavenward, nor when those devices far exceeded the distance and flight time the Sputnik I orbit achieved. What *did* surprise us was that the process began so quickly. In fact, Sputnik II was launched one day short of a month after its predecessor, thereby joining Sputnik I in orbit for a while. And whereas Sputnik I was virtually empty, Sputnik II had an occupant.

America's first meaningful response to the Soviets having blasted a second satellite into orbit came not on the testing grounds or launch pads, but in the houses of Congress. While our engineers tried to get us off the ground, our legislators took a longer view by creating the National Defense Education Act, the second word juxtaposed with the third as a warning to the Soviet Union that we were determined not to be caught off guard militarily in the future because we were deficient scientifically. We would be deficient no more.[1]

Nor would we lack for sufficient financial backing. "What [the NDEA] did was provide a billion dollars for students of math, science and languages, subjects that, within a few years, became obsessions. Because by the early 1960s, we Americans had come to believe that we should pursue education the way that our most admired football coach pursued NFL championships: by mastering the fundamentals. John Dewey was dead; long live Vince Lombardi!"

But no less important than the space program to Americans was the nascent computer industry, as the former would be stillborn without the latter. If there had been a computer race, the United States would probably have been ahead in 1957, but for us to maintain our lead, we would need more properly trained men and women to develop them, and at the time we were suffering from a scarcity of mathematicians. The hard drives were there, but not nearly enough operators.

Nor were there enough programmers, the people capable of constantly improving computers, making them more creative, as well as capable of performing with speed and accuracy of calculation that would forever be beyond the reach of humans. The government now sought to find these men and women and pay them well for the expertise they would develop.

---

1. Note that the word "Defense" also had been added to the Eisenhower Highway Act. As was the case with the NDEA, it was primarily a means of placating the more military-minded legislators.

There never had been a piece of legislation like the NDEA. It was "a historic break with twentieth-century practice," writes Brown University scholar James T. Patterson, "which had assigned education spending primarily to states and localities. As its title indicated, however, the NDEA was sold as a defense measure, not as endorsement of a broader principle of federal aid to schools or universities. In fact, individuals who received money under the act [teachers and students] had to sign a clause affirming loyalty to the United States and to swear that they had never engaged in subversive activities."

The loyalty clause was a sop to McCarthyism that would have been a major source of controversy just a few months earlier. But with the senator now resting eternally, legislators saw the clause not as an infringement on the personal right to privacy and self-expression, but as a means of appeasing the far right, which was not powerful enough to employ it as ruthlessly as it had when McCarthy was alive.

As a result, the NDEA easily passed through the House and Senate, and members of both chambers could assure constituents that they had voted for defense spending as well as the eradication of communism. But in reality, as at least some lawmakers seemed to know, education in the United States needed funding much more than defense.

In 1957, only 60 percent of American high schools were offering foreign languages. Less than 50 percent of high school graduates were going to college. And the United States was graduating only half as many scientists and engineers as the Soviet Union, for the most part students who were not nearly as well trained; the average Soviet student had at least ten years of mathematics, including trigonometry; five years of physics, including introductory quantum theory; four years of chemistry; and at least one of astronomy. On a typical night, the average Soviet had four hours of homework. The average American spent an equal amount of time with his favorite new toy, the television.

But the NDEA was remarkably effective in helping us close the gap. Within seven years of its passage, the number of students in American institutions of higher learning had increased by 50 percent, and within a decade, by 100 percent. Says historian Geoffrey Perrett, "By the early 1960s, the Federal government was providing aid to education in various ways at a cost of $3 billion a year, ten times the level of Federal assistance in 1945." So successful was the NDEA in promoting science that, by the late sixties, we had too many physicists for the jobs available. The NDEA was not the only reason for such a boom, but that it ranked near the top cannot be denied.

And so successful was the NDEA in promoting foreign languages that, in addition to the presence of some eight thousand language laboratories in public schools, "Berlitz schools, phonograph-record lessons and other commercials aids to quick-study for prospective overseas travelers had a vogue."

That the quality of American education has declined so markedly in the years since is not a subject for this book. But it is worth pointing out that, according to the Pew Research Center's most recent study, in 2015, the United States, although ranking first in expenditures on young minds, ranked thirty-eighth out of seventy-one countries in achievement in math and twenty-fourth in science. It is an appalling performance by a country that possesses the greatest resources in the world for academic accomplishment, yet chooses to use so much of them elsewhere.

In his prototypical novel of the fifties, *The Man in the Gray Flannel Suit,* Sloan Wilson wrote that students "had been smothered with anxious concern, softened with lack of exercise, seduced with luxuries, then overfed and underworked. They have too much leisure and too little discipline." Responsible for such woeful children, Sloan believed, were parents who meant well but who, having suffered through the Depression, were determined to give their offspring a far less rigorous and worrisome life than they had known.

It was only natural then, according to Wilson's analysis, that America's boys and girls would be undereducated and insufficiently motivated. Only natural that substandard performances in the classroom would be the result not of a lack of intelligence so much as a lack of incentive. Natural that, as inherent idlers, children were expecting the best in life to be delivered to them rather than earned by hard work, rigorous study, or both. And natural that they were students not of a curriculum, but of the popular culture, scholars of the inconsequential, in search of diversion more than edification.

The floodgates were now open for such masters of the aphorism as financier and statesman Bernard Baruch . . .

"If America ever crashes, it will be in a two-tone convertible."

. . . and historian William Manchester: "Sputnik I dealt the *coup de grace* to Ford's fading Edsel, which had been introduced the month before, and which was now widely regarded as a discredited symbol of the tinny baubles America must thrust aside."

In addition to the NDEA, our country reacted to the Sputniks by giving birth to the National Aeronautics and Space Administration, and its period of gestation was remarkably fast. NASA was up and running less than a year after Sputnik I was up and orbiting. It was headed by civilians, President Eisenhower's way to show the Soviets that his country wanted peace in the heavens, not war.

Of course, NASA's great triumph was still more than a decade away. On July 20, 1969, astronaut Neil Armstrong became the first human being to walk on the moon. It was, as Armstrong famously said, "one small step for a man, one giant leap for mankind." A few minutes later, Armstrong was joined on the moon by fellow astronaut Buzz Aldrin. The third member of the crew, Michael Collins, remained in the command module, supervising the complicated technology that enabled Armstrong and Aldrin to gambol about with only a minimum of gravity to hold them in place.

Eventually, ten other men would step on the moon, a dozen altogether, and every one of them was an American. Russian footsteps have remained firmly planted on Earth.

But moonwalking no longer remains a NASA priority. We have long since mastered it and moved on to greater challenges. In fact, according to James Webb, NASA's second administrator, who served from 1961 to 1968, the agency's priority always had been more than just a first-place finish in the space race. Despite his civilian status, he believed that "the space program required nothing less than the mobilization of the nation to a war footing in peacetime. Society (as he later wrote) had 'reached a point where its program and even its survival increasingly depend upon our ability to organize the complex and do the unusual. We cannot do these things except through large aggregations of resources and power.'"

Webb insisted that Americans must be engaged "by all means possible, in an endless search for new food for thought processes, new information and knowledge," and that because of this, the work of NASA was indispensable. "It is not too much to say," he declared, "that in many ways the viability of representative government and of the free enterprise system in a period of revolutionary changes based on science and technology is being tested in space."

Webb wrote the preceding late in the sixties. But back in '57, when we Americans were taking our first steps toward the creation of the NDEA and NASA, as well as instituting other programs to make sure that we would never again receive a surprise of Sputnik's magnitude; when we were simultaneously assigning blame for the Soviet orb, especially with the army blaming the navy and vice versa; when we were trying to inspire ourselves to greater triumph by remembering how quickly we had prepared ourselves for World War II, converting an industrial nation to a war machine in a mere blur of time; when we now began to think of ways to master the skies with the same speed and technological acuity that we had demonstrated in the early forties—back when all of this was happening, we were failing to make "revolutionary changes based on science and technology." We succeeded only in humiliating ourselves while the whole world watched, snickering at the arrogance of capitalism.

16

Muttnik

At first, she was called Kudryavka, a name that means "Little Curly" and sounds as if it belongs to a character in a Soviet version of *Little Rascals*. But Kudryavka was not curly; rather, her hair lay flat against her, matted on her head and body, clump against clump, while flies hovered around her, landing, sucking in the filthy scent of her. The little dog's hangouts were the low places of Moscow, where she ate scraps of food from the garbage and slept wherever she happened to fall when she was tired. She had no home, no friends, was too suspicious a sort for that. She looked at the world through frightened eyes.

So, on the day when a couple of men—nobody knows who they were—tried to capture her, she probably was an elusive target. But worth the effort, they would have believed; as a creature of the streets, she was used to extremes: cold weather, hot weather, pain, hunger approaching starvation. Granted, it does not sound like a promising background, but considering the job that Soviet officials had in mind for her, she was perfect. Once she was apprehended, she was only a few weeks from being the most famous dog in the world, not to mention one of its most easily recognized faces.

She was not the only candidate for celebrity, however. Originally, she was one of ten, a semifinalist, so to speak, with the other nine being dogs who shared Kudryavka's lifestyle. The whole of them were put through a battery of tests to measure their health, intelligence, and disposition.

The results were carefully watched, tabulated, and then came the finals, the candidates now winnowed down to three. Joining Kudryavka were Muhka and Albina, and they were subjected to even more detailed and demanding appraisals. For instance, to simulate the kickback of rocket launch, they went for rides in centrifuges, which provided jolts such as the three dogs had never known before, even when kicked in their sleep by a drunk. To simulate the noises of a spacecraft, the animals were blasted with so many decibels that they squeezed their paws over the flaps of their ears. As a result of such trials, these and others, the dogs' blood pressure shot up, and their pulse rates almost doubled. It hardly needs to be said that the poor animals had no idea what was happening to them. Nor would any layman who had happened by at the moment.

If the dogs *did* know, they might have felt a measure of consolation, because all three would have a role in the final project; Sergei Korolev, who oversaw the program, referred to it as "Simple Sputnik 2," but it was a masterpiece of complexity for its time.

The test results for Muhka showed that she cared least for being banged around and deafened, and so she finished last among the three finalists; her assignment, thus, was to test equipment on the ground. Albina was the runner-up and would be put through the same preparations as the winner in case something happened to her; she was, in other words, the star's understudy for the upcoming production. And the winner, finishing first in the trials, was Kudryavka. She would be dead long before the other two.

Her name was hard to pronounce, and so many people would be uttering it, even after she was killed. So the Soviets changed it. No longer Little Curly, she was now Laika (*Lie*-ka), "one who barks." A creature of many breeds, one was a Samoyed terrier, a handsome animal when well groomed. But like her, and probably like her parents, grandparents, great-grandparents, and generations even further back, Laika was a street prowler, not groomed at all, and there was no way of knowing what other nationalities had gone into her composition.

However, the men who worked for the Soviet space program didn't care. Once she was scrubbed and brushed, and the fleas and parasites were removed from her, she was ready for her closeups. A cute little dog—scrawny, not exactly Asta, for she had not eaten much in her three-year life span—she was nonetheless photogenic enough for her purpose.

Still, Soviet engineers thought she would not only look better but could better cope with the rigors of what lay ahead if she were fattened up a bit. But only a bit; launch time was fast approaching, and by the morning of her ascension, despite having been crammed with calories, she had arrived at a mere fourteen pounds. It was not ideal, but it would have to do.

When she wasn't eating, Laika was training, which is to say that she was repeating the torment of the centrifuge, loudspeaker, and other devices of technological sadism. It was unlikely that she got used to either the force-feeding or the pummeling, but she was a dog and had no choice other than to put up with the vicious whims of the humans who studied her carefully, filling notebooks with their observations.

Floyd Patterson, the heavyweight champion of the world, did not train harder than Laika, the Moscow mongrel. And such a trooper was she that, by the time she had gone through all of her preflight preparations, she had won the hearts of most of those in charge of her. One of them, Dr. Vladimir Yazdovsky, even took her home one night to play with his children. His youngsters were delighted; their guest captivated them. "Laika was quiet and charming . . . I wanted to do something nice for her. She had so little time left to live."

Thirty days after Sputnik had been launched, beepless but still in orbit, the Soviets deepened the wounds in America's pride by sending their next satellite into space. Two now for the Soviets, none for their supposed superiors.

Some people had expected the Soviets' second venture in space to be a moon landing, but their program was not nearly that advanced yet. Nonetheless, what they accomplished on November 3, 1957, was impressive in several different ways.

Rather than a tiny spherical object like its predecessor, Sputnik II was large and cone shaped, thirteen feet high with a diameter of six and a half feet at its base. Aesthetically, it was a sleek and pleasing structure. It weighed 1,118 pounds, the same "as a four-door full-size Detroit sedan," and six times more than the first Sputnik.

Inside was a small animal shivering with fright, unaware of the history she was making. The United States and Soviet Union previously had sent dogs into brief, suborbital flights. Laika, however, would be the first to achieve low Earth orbit, and she would pay the highest possible price for her accomplishment.

Muttnik, as her satellite came inevitably to be called, had been modified for her. There was no way to make the upcoming flight safe, but at least Laika could be comforted in her last few hours of life. "The padded, pressurized cabin on Sputnik II allowed enough room for her to lie down or stand. An air-regeneration system provided oxygen, while food and water were dispensed in gelatinized form. Laika was fitted with a harness, a bag to collect waste, and electrodes to monitor her vital signs. Early telemetry indicated Laika was agitated but eating her food."

A primitive television camera was installed in the dog's quarters; she was under constant observation, and from the beginning of the flight provided a heartrending show. Her agitation was so great that her intake of nutrition was minimal. She could barely keep her balance long enough to bite, and after a few seconds, she gave up. Or fell over, depending on your point of view. She never got up again.

At that point, of course, Soviet scientists had no further need to watch her on television; in fact, for them to do so, it would have been macabre to sneak looks at the body of a dead dog spinning around the Earth. Many of the scientists, though, reportedly did just that.

They and their engineer colleagues had gone through a lot of trouble for a short period of time. Laika, whose face had been plastered on almost every newspaper front page and magazine cover in both the Soviet Union and United States, gave up her life four days after rising from the Earth. At least the Soviets insisted on that figure at the time; later research into their archives indicates that the dog probably lasted only a few hours.

As for the flight itself, the end did not come quickly, at least not compared to Sputnik I. Sputnik II stayed aloft for more than five months, tumbling to Earth with its cargo, a dog in a horrible state of decomposition, on April 14, 1958.

The difference between responses in the United States to the two Soviet flights was extraordinary. The first one filled us with dread, the second with sympathy for the mission's poor passenger. And, among animal-rights advocates, the sympathy was laced with rage; they did everything they could to show their feelings for Muttnik—a term they never used, by the way, finding it belittling—and to persuade the Soviets not even to consider committing such a heinous act again.

Picket lines were set up in front of both the Soviet Embassy in London and the United Nations in New York. In Britain, "the National Canine Defence League called on all dog owners to observe a minute's silence, while the Royal Society for the Prevention of Cruelty to Animals (RSPCA) received protests even before Radio Moscow had finished announcing the launch." An animal adoption group in New York sent a telegram to the Soviet Embassy in Washington, calling the treatment of Laika "an atrocity," and heavily publicized their condemnation. Other groups, as well as individuals, named their puppies "Laika."

There didn't seem to be protests of any significance in the Soviet Union. But Oleg Gazenko, an esteemed member of the Soviet space team and one of the men most directly responsible for the ascent of Sputnik II, *did* protest, and in terms almost exactly the same as those of the ASPCA. "Work with animals is a source of suffering to all of us. We treat them like babies who cannot speak. The more time passes, the more I'm sorry about it. We shouldn't have done it . . . We did not learn enough from this mission to justify the death of the dog."

A complaint of a different sort came from people with a fundamentalist religious bent, who insisted that it would not do to have a dead dog orbiting the Earth for whatever the new satellite's term in orbit turned out to be. Such an act would make a mockery of what God had created; they demanded that the Soviets retrieve the carcass immediately. Which could be done, of course, only by aborting the mission. And it hardly needs to be said that that was not going to happen.

With each orbit, the world seemed to take [the deceased] Laika closer to heart. A radio station in Blackfoot, Idaho, claimed to have recorded her barking. The

British press gave her all sorts of affectionate nicknames, including, "the Hound of Heaven," and a *New York Times* editorial lapsed into pathos and called her the "shaggiest, handsomest, saddest dog in all history."

Clearly unprepared for the uproar, the Russians began hinting that the dog might come back by parachute, but this bit of nonsensical disinformation was floated when Laika was dying or dead. In 1965, when Eisenhower wrote his memoir of the period, it still amused him that for many the dog's death overshadowed the stunning feat of getting her up in the first place.

Something that a few people—but only a few—believed, and fewer still made public, was what we would today call a conspiracy theory. They suspected that the CIA was responsible for the animal-rights protests—some of them, at any rate—because our intelligence community was trying to divert attention from the inability of the United States to launch a satellite. Better to have the world railing at the Soviets for barbarism than laughing at the Americans for incompetence. But even if the conspiracy theorists were correct, their plan didn't work. Despite all of the uproar over Laika, plenty was left for the U.S. space program, which had not even scheduled a launch yet.

Laika's premature demise excepted, the Soviets got precisely what they wanted out of their second mission, both politically and scientifically. Muttnik "not only provided Soviet scientists with the first data on the behavior of a living organism in the space environment but appeared to cement their dominance of the heavens. American leaders were chagrined that the Soviets seemed almost blasé about Sputnik II, which was much larger and more sophisticated than anything on America's drawing boards."

As far as dominating the heavens is concerned, no argument could be made; at least for the time being, the skies belonged to the sons of Stalin. Among other things, the Soviets now had information about the effects of low Earth orbit on dogs, information their American rivals did not possess. But a majority of non-Soviet scientists, although impressed by the length of Sputnik II's journey, thought of Laika's presence on board as more of a publicity stunt than a means of gathering information. Humans are altogether different creatures from canines, with different body structures and psychological needs. We have different shapes, different weights, different means of reacting to both pleasure and discomfort. Perhaps we have a little in common with dogs in such situations, but *so* little that we could not know what was relevant and what wasn't. Which is all to say that Laika might well have given her life to tell us something we had no need to know.

Finally, though, the United States could stop fretting about the competition, concentrating instead on its own performance. Finally, a bare two-months after the first Sputnik tipped the world from its axis, Americans were ready to ascend from the drawing boards, to attempt the leap to launching pad, and from there into orbit, and from there to glory.

But that is not exactly the way our space program started out.

17

Kaputnik

The date was December 6, 1957.

Early that morning, when the sky was still as dark as a vampire's cape, the United States Naval Research Center's Test Vehicle 3, or TV3, was driven to its Cape Canaveral launch pad. In a few hours, it would be shot into space, making this the day for which American rocketeers had been preparing for decades and the country's population had been clamoring for two months. This was the day when the space race would become a race, when the heavens would no longer be the private property of America's Cold War foe.

Later in the morning, when one of the technicians was asked whether all of the preliminary checks had been made, he said no. He said *more* than all checks had been made. TV3, which would initiate America's Vanguard program, was the first three-stage rocket ever built[1] and thus the most powerful. Having been checked and double-checked, it was now ready to test the effects of a satellite lift-off and its orbits on the environment. It was ready to obtain geodetic measurements (pertaining to the Earth's shape, its orientation in space, and its gravitational field) through the analysis of its flight trajectory. And, of course, it was ready to compare itself to the accomplishments of Sputniks I and II. These were the goals of the TV3, and if the rocket were a success, it would contribute more to the scientific knowledge of space than the two Soviet spacecrafts and one canine passenger put together.

---

1. Had the Vanguard program kept to its original schedule, it would have blasted off nine months earlier, preceding the first Sputnik by more than half a year. But "[t]he first stage lacked sufficient thrust, the second had to be redesigned, and the third was too heavy." These problems would be rectified. More would arise in the week closer to ignition, but these, too, would seem to be solved.

American scientists were optimistic. "The days leading up to launch were marked by surprisingly few problems. The second stage engine was replaced when a crack was found during an inspection. The first two stages passed static fire tests on the ground. The electronics and instrumentation were examined and found to be in flawless condition. All preflight operations proceeded without major hiccups." Or even minor hiccups. With the exception, that is, of a delay because of uncooperative weather.

Still, the men responsible for the launch were troubled. "It was less than ideal for the Vanguard team," wrote the knowledgeable Amy Shira Teitel, "who, in the early era of rocketry, would have much preferred to carry out a test of a new system without the nation and the world following along in person or by radio and television broadcasts." In fact, "[r]eporters from around the world converged on Cape Canaveral and cranked up suspense. A spotlight shown down on the United States simply because it was the United States."

Scores of sightseers joined the journalists outside the fence ringing the launch pad—some standing, some sitting on lawn chairs, others remaining in their cars, not just to be more comfortable, but because it was a colder morning than usual for a Florida December. Winds were biting, and some of the engineers wondered whether they might be strong enough to blow the rocket off course. Unlikely, they decided, and tried their best to believe it.

Most of those watching, inside their vehicles and out, had draped binoculars around their necks. But how soon would they be able to use them? The spectators were in their places early, when the morning was still night. The Vanguard TV3 was in its place on time. Due to the weather, though, the launch was late. In fact, it was several hours late. The TV3 was supposed to have lifted off shortly after daylight. Instead, it sat there, an unmoving monolith, until noon approached. By that time, the spectators were reeling from both tedium and tension.

But at 11:44:55 a.m., after having outwaited both the thawing of a frozen valve and the taming of the winds, it was time for blast-off.

And blast off it did, as pathetically as if the NASA scientists had gathered around the rocket and tried to pick it up and heave it manually. The TV3 reached a height of four feet in a journey that lasted all of two seconds. At that point, too early for distant spectators even to have realized the rocket had ignited, the spacecraft "shuddered slightly, buckled under its own weight, burst into flames and collapsed." Within seconds the TV3 disappeared into the flames, such an enormous cloud of them that it seemed "as if the gates of hell had opened up."

After the two seconds that TV3 spent wobbling off the ground, "the rocket settled uneasily on its engines before falling against the firing structure. The tanks ruptured as the rocket toppled, spilling its fuel and oxidizer into the line of fire, sparking an inferno." After a few more seconds, the rocket's nose fell off, tipping through the fiery wall that had consumed the TV3 after years of planning and work. The American space program lay in debris at the feet of the Vanguard rocket, which was itself fast becoming debris. "It was a spectacular failure," wrote Teitel, "and the world had seen it all."

The late Tom Wolfe would later write a typically brilliant book on the program that succeeded Vanguard, Project Mercury. He would call it *The Right Stuff*, and he was among those watching that morning when everything went wrong. He described the disaster as only he could. "The first stage, bloated with fuel, explodes, and the rest of the rocket sinks into the sand beside the launch platform . . . very slowly, like a fat man collapsing into a Barcalounger. . . . This picture—the big buildup, the dramatic countdown, followed by the exploding cigar—was unforgettable."

The aftereffects of the explosion began as soon as people could get over their numbness and accept the reality of what they had just seen. This was not the beginning of the American space program after all; it was more like the end, or at least a giant step backward, not only for Project Vanguard but for Wall Street as well. By 11:50 a.m., a mere five minutes after the catastrophe on the launch pad, so many sell orders for stock in the Glenn L. Martin Company, Vanguard's prime contractor, had been phoned in to brokers that the New York Stock Exchange was forced to suspend trading in the firm.

In the afternoon newspapers of December 6, and journals published the following morning, the world would read all about it. To the distress of American officials, U.S. papers had the most fun with the catastrophe, an unseemly reaction to a failure of such magnitude for the home team. "The *Los Angeles Herald and Examiner* headlined: '9-8-7-6-5-4-3-2-1-Pfft.' 'Oh dear' was the *New York Daily Mirror*'s caption for the Vanguard pictured toppling into the roiling flames on the Florida beach. 'The Pearl Harbor of the Cold War,' cried the *San Francisco Daily News*. 'Alibis are worthless,' commented the *Rocky Mountain News*."

Americans with even the slightest of patriotic strains were not merely embarrassed for their country but horrified. The Soviet Union had two satellites in low Earth orbit while we, on the other hand, had opened the gates of Hell. *What would it mean? What was the future to hold?*

From the point of view of Vanguard officials, the *Des Moines Register* made the most salient point, as it wrote without clever headlines or hyperbole that "Soviet newspapers have not told us whether any failures preceded the first success of the Sputniks. That's the difference between the free government of the people and the suppressive power of the police state."

But emotional reactions overwhelmed reasoned responses, and not just the American press leaped onto the bandwagon of ridicule. Newspapers in

Britain, Canada, and, of course, *Pravda*, the official organ of the Soviet state, thought of the TV3 as the straight man for a wide variety of punch lines: The Americans had launched "Kaputnik," "Flopnik," "Goofnik," "Sputternik," "Stayputnik," "Ike's Phutnik." And as for "Ike's Sputnik," it was "a Dudnik."

For the British, our closest friends in the international community, it was not enough to insert one or two of these nik-names into its headlines. The BBC, the radio network owned by the Crown and known for a respectability that bordered on stodginess, got word that a calypso singer named Rory McEwen had written a song about the Vanguard calamity. He was invited to perform it on the air, and it included the following couplet:

> They've been pressing the button for a month or more,
> But they can't get the blighter off the floor.

"But this was just the beginning," wrote Paul Dickson. "On the same morning, at the United Nations headquarters in New York City, the Soviet delegation formally offered financial aid to the United States as part of a program of technical assistance to backward nations. America's humiliation was complete."

Epilogue

The Return of the Preacher Man

It might have been complete, but it was not enduring.

On January 31, 1958, at 10:48 p.m., the United States rocket Juno I soared into space "like a Roman candle in the dark, lighting up the swamps of the Banana River [flowing alongside Cape Canaveral] . . . free from the humbling competition of God's own sunshine." In a matter of seconds, the rocket had almost disappeared; the vertical part of the mission had been a success. Now for the horizontal, which is to say, the orbital.

Anxiety mounted by the minute, and the minutes mounted until they had exceeded an hour. And then someone rose from his chair in the control room and handed a slip of paper to Secretary of the Army Wilbur M. Brucker, also seated in the control room. Explorer I, the satellite propelled by Juno I, had achieved orbit. The United States had achieved pride.

Brucker took a moment to digest the news, then read the message aloud, whooped, and passed it around. The engineers and scientists surrounding the secretary cheered like baseball fans who had just watched their team win the World Series. Everyone rose to his feet; pens were thrown, countertops pounded, coffee cups accidentally knocked over—all of it in sheer exuberance. Grown men "yahooed" and "yippied" and hugged each other and pounded each other's backs. Suddenly Americans were living in a different world, a world in which they had not only equaled the Soviets but surpassed them.

At 1:30 a.m., in the great Hall at the National Academy of Sciences in Washington, D.C., NASA officials held an impromptu press conference. The Explorer's success was announced to a hundred or more journalists from a dozen or more nations. Its orbit was official.

President Eisenhower's comment revealed restraint as much as pleasure. "That's wonderful," the chief executive said, learning of the launch, "I surely feel a lot better now." Then he paused briefly. "Let's not make too great a hullabaloo over this."

Typical Ike.

But the country, of course, *did* make a hullaballoo, and *should* have done so, as Juno and Explorer had combined to exceed the accomplishments of the first two Sputniks by every conceivable standard. Including the aesthetic. Explorer I was long and glossy and shaped like an enormous bullet, as if to pierce the firmament more easily. It was eighty inches from top to bottom and a little more than six inches in diameter. As far as the batteries used for telemetric purposes were concerned, they would not stop beeping for 105 days.

By that time, though, the satellite no longer needed them. Explorer I was airborne for the virtually inconceivable total of twelve years, reentering the Earth's atmosphere over the Pacific Ocean on March 31, 1970. On its journey it had looped the planet more than fifty-eight thousand times and been joined in space by several other satellites, both Soviet and American. But this first of the American vessels was the flagship, as it "made about twelve and a half orbits per day, collecting scientific information and sending the data back to Earth (including data about radiation belts that surround the planet)."

The vast, eternal void that covered the Earth with an alternating canopy of light and darkness was no longer such a lonely place.

The next two American attempts to join Explorer I and Sputnik II in orbit were failures, but the Vanguard satellite launched on March 17, 1958, was the beginning of a series of almost entirely successful, and constantly more ambitious, space missions. Vanguard led to Mercury, the first series of manned missions, and then came Gemini and Apollo, with the eleventh of the latter missions landing men on the Moon.

And then Americans went beyond, stretching the boundaries of beyond by the amazing long-distance accomplishments of Voyager.

Nineteen fifty-seven, the most nightmarish year to date for the U.S. space program, had led to a glistening future, one that still shows no signs of weakening. Rather, every indication is that an American satellite, one of which has already passed Jupiter and Saturn, continuously playing music from the Earth on its passage, will go ever farther, its limit probably dictated only by the limit of mankind's ambition.[1]

---

1. Among the selections are such totally unrepresentative pieces of music from our planet as songs from Java, Senegal, Zaire, Bulgaria, Peru, the Navajo Indians, the Solomon Islands, the aborigines of Australia, and the bagpipes of Azerbaijan. Three numbers from Bach are included and two from Beethoven. Two American blues songs are on the menu (one, fortunately, from Louis Armstrong), yet the Beatles are excluded; the only rock 'n' roll song beamed down to Jupiter and Saturn was Chuck Berry's "Johnny B. Goode." A good choice, but where are the others? Where is

But our space programs have not just been competitions that we won for sport, or to wave banners of self-promotion and inner-galactic experimentation. Even including the Vanguard TV3 failure, they have comprised, however inadvertently, the largest, most successful research and development program in our country's history.

In preparing for its various launches and our eventual Moon landing and journeys beyond, NASA applied technology more creatively than any government agency or private enterprise has done before or since. In fact, a case can be made for saying that NASA helped to *create* technology, and the results are as varied as they are numerous: the invention of inorganic paints, food sticks, police radios, insulation material, heart-rate monitors, the Jarvik artificial heart, LASIK eye surgery, water filters, smoke detectors, freeze-drying, cordless tools, pocket calculators, invisible braces, anti-inflammable fabrics such as Kevlar, various biomedical instruments, GPS systems, fuel cell mechanisms, communication systems that enable doctors manning remote-control monitoring devices at large urban hospitals to communicate with paramedics in the jungles of Africa and South America.

Add memory foam for pillows and mattresses, improved firefighting equipment, improved radial tires, improved artificial limbs, enriched baby food, sensors to regulate water flow to flower beds and gardens, and tennis rackets, golf clubs, and fishing poles made from composite graphite fibers.

It is remarkable to contemplate that we might never have landed on the Moon had we not first figured out how to make enriched baby food, pocket calculators, and invisible braces, just as it is depressing to contemplate life on Earth without the products that resulted from our quest for the Moon.

It took a while for Little Richard to come around. Not until 1962 did he feel safe enough under the world's skies, which is to say, secure enough about the American space program, to make his return to rock 'n' roll—and even then, it doesn't seem to have been his intention. Initially, he was tricked by circumstance.

Thinking he was going to sing gospel music, the only kind of songs he had been singing for the past five years, he agreed to tour Europe, with Sam Cooke as his opening act. At his first concert, he was a flop. With his old rock songs still popular across the Atlantic, no one wanted to hear an evening's worth of church music. The audience was polite—the songs, after all, were paeans to the glory of God—but ticket buyers had not spent money

---

Gershwin's "Rhapsody in Blue"? Where are the big bands and any one of their hundreds of memorable melodies? "You Go to My Head," for instance. Appalling omissions.

Do the life forms at the far reaches of the solar system really need three Bachs? Or even one ditty from the Solomon Islands?

to hear a restrained Rev. Richard Penniman singing without a beat, without sexual innuendo, and without any jolly nonsense syllables. They had not paid their money to see him standing on a stage, behaving like a perfect gentleman.

Before the second concert on the tour, he was warming up backstage with the famed rock organist and onetime "fifth Beatle," Billy Preston. They were playing one of Richard's old hits, although without any particular intensity. "Good golly Miss Molly / Sure like to ball / Good golly Miss Molly / Sure like to ball / When you're rockin' and rollin' / Can't hear your mama call." Just warming up, noodling around, that's all.

They almost started a riot.

"I'd heard so much about the audience reaction that I thought there must be some exaggeration. But it was all true. He drove the whole house into a complete frenzy. . . . I couldn't believe the power of Little Richard on stage. He was amazing." That was what Mick Jagger said about the pre-Sputnik Little Richard. But it also applied to Richard that night overseas, the night of his resurrection.

He had not yet stepped into the footlights, was not yet straining his vocal cords, yet the audience could hear him, and its juices were flowing. It was on its way to that "complete frenzy" that the crowd was soon to reach, even exceed, and Richard could feel the stirring, hear the foot stomping, on the other side of the curtain. His adrenaline began to rise, to surge, to boil over until he could resist his impulses no longer.

The audience wanted the old hits? Well, he supposed it was time. He would *give* them the old hits, the old days. Sputnik no longer existed, Laika was long deceased, and Little Richard was feeling alive again. He and Preston looked at each other, smiling. After Richard told the backup musicians there would be a slight change in the program, he bounded onto the stage—very un-preacher-like, ready for his second act in American life.

Little Richard Penniman dedicated the performance to his Lord, hoping He would understand.

Act two, though, was not nearly as successful as the first one. When he returned to the United States, he began to write and record new rock 'n' roll songs. But times had changed; the music did not have the same effect that it had had in the fifties. Although Little Richard was the same dynamo he had always been, American audiences had gotten used to his absence, and only a single song that he laid down in the post-Sputnik era made the *Billboard* "Top 100," with "Bama Lama Bama Loo's" climbing no higher than number 87, just barely creeping onto the charts.

A few years earlier, the tune would have been a smash, as it showed off the same beat, the same manic melody, and the same jabberwocky as his previous hits. It fit perfectly into the Penniman canon, which had begun to assemble itself in 1955. In the world of rock 'n' roll, though, seven years is a long time to wait from first hit to comeback. Now the charts belonged to Chubby Checker, Ray Charles, Bobby Vinton, and Phil Spector's "Wall of Sound." Not to mention the Colonel's version of Elvis. An eclectic blend of music, headed nowhere in particular; it was an interim period, as the Beatles, Rolling Stones, and others gathered steam across the ocean.

But imagine, just imagine, what it would have been like if that first hit of Little Richard's had been roaring through speakers in mission control as the space program's first hit began soaring through space. Imagine, in other words, a flight of fancy to accompany the flight of reality. Secretary of the Army Brucker announces that Explorer I has begun to explore the reaches of the solar system, and the needle drops on a 45 rpm record with the Specialty label—yellow, white, and black. Everything already is chaos in the control room, which is to say that Little Richard blends right in. He is made for chaos. He makes chaos more chaotic.

> Bop-bopa-a-lu bop a wop bam boo
> Tutti frutti, oh Rudy
> Tutti frutti, wooooo
> Tutti frutti, oh Rudy
> Tutti frutti, oh Rudy
> Tutti frutti, oh Rudy
> A whop-bopa-a-lu-bop a wop bam boo.

It never happened, of course, but what a scene it would have been—the incongruously jubilant NASA nerds shimmying and shaking amid the technological hoodoo they had so brilliantly constructed, the present having been launched like a torpedo into the future! And then that music, oh that music: the pulse-pounding beat, the crashing piano keys, the howling voice . . . and as for the lyrics, well, who needs sense when emotions are running so high?

Yes, just a fantasy. Mere illusion. Thirteen months of 1957 finally had come to a glorious climax at January's end in '58—and Little Richard among the missing, singing "Amazing Grace" in church rather than "Tutti Frutti" in stadiums. But Buddy Holly and the Everly Brothers were among those moving ahead, flavoring rock 'n' roll with country; and the Coasters were blasting yakety saxes into their melody lines; and the Platters were enlivening the sweetness of their ballads with unaccustomed drumbeats. And far more dramatic changes were just ahead, musically and otherwise, as the United States, with a constantly evolving soundtrack, began making its way, sometimes splendidly, sometimes tragically, toward the century in which we live now.

Acknowledgments

The acknowledgments section of a book is, I suspect, little read. Yet, despite its brevity, it is in some ways the most important of a book's pages. This volume, for instance, could have been written without the assistance of those I am about to name. But it would not be nearly as good (I hope, of course, that the reader finds "good" an appropriate description for my efforts), not nearly as detailed, not nearly as well analyzed, and would have taken twice as long to write. So this is what the following people have helped me avoid: an inferior product that took an extra year or more to create.

As is always the case, my researcher, Carolyn Zygmont of the Westport Public Library in Westport, Connecticut, heads the list of indispensables. Westport's library, under the superb stewardship of Bill Harmar, is the finest institution of its size in the country; Carolyn is, as far as I'm concerned, the finest researcher in a library of any size. Sometimes I ask her for information, and it takes her five minutes to get back to me. Other times I tweak her and say, "There's something I need to know and I'm afraid it might be too esoteric even for you to dig up." In that case, it takes her ten minutes.

Thank you, Carolyn, for your skills and your constant willingness to make me sound more knowledgeable than I am.

Other librarians who provided much needed information include Susan Luchars of Connecticut's Sacred Heart University, who helped me better understand the noble Winthrop Rockefeller; and Dr. Wendy Richter, professor and archivist at the Riley-Hickenbotham Library and Special Collections on the campus of Ouachita Baptist University in Arkadelphia, Arkansas, who provided needed background on her state's racial politics in the fifties.

I know very little about cars. I care even less. But it was crucial that I pass myself off as at least passably erudite on the 1957 Chevy Bel Air, and for that I heartily thank Christo Datini, the managing archivist at the General Motors Heritage Center/General Motors Media Archive.

John Shoup and Daniel Rodriguez of the South Norwalk Branch of the Norwalk, Connecticut, Library filled in several holes for me—Carolyn can't do everything!

My biggest challenge in writing this book was acquainting myself with George Metesky. His is, I believe, an engaging tale, but history justly regards him among the most minor figures. I was able to meet the challenge through a variety of sources, none more valuable than Michael M. Greenburg's superbly researched book *The Mad Bomber of New York*. On one occasion, finding myself particularly vexed by something about Metesky, I tracked down Greenburg, an attorney near Boston, and talked to him on the phone. He could not have been more helpful, nor his book more insightful.

Brian Ross, whom I am proud to call a friend, brought three decades of credit to ABC News, where he was the chief investigative correspondent. Brian is a man of unique diligence, unique perception. He caught an error in the manuscript that would have made me look quite foolish. I'm very grateful, Brian.

And then there's Ashton Hawley. An author is dependent on so many people when he writes; Ashton is an IT wizard, not only keeping my computer in working order, but teaching me how to use the damn thing. I write on a Dell desktop with the latest version of Microsoft Word, easily one of the worst inventions ever by a major American corporation. Nothing is as clear, as user friendly, as the Word programs of a decade ago and more. The latest Microsoft abomination is so preposterously esoteric, its functions disguised so brilliantly, that I once had to call Ashton to ask him how to number my pages. I'd rather drive an Edsel.

On behalf of myself, I thank you, Ashton. On behalf of Microsoft, well, I have said enough.

At Rowman & Littlefield, where but a few people did the work of many, I would especially like to thank senior executive editor Jonathan Sisk, assistant managing editor Karen Ackermann, editorial assistant Dina Guilak, publicist Garret Bond, and the artist whose rendering of a Chevy Bel Air on the cover looks as if it is ready for lift-off.

Eric Burns
March 2020

Bibliography

NEWSPAPERS, MAGAZINES, DOCUMENTS

BB Billboard, December 1957.

EA Lawson, Stephen F., and Charles Payne, eds. *Debating the Civil Right Movement, 1945–1968*. "Dwight D. Eisenhower's Radio and Television Address to the American People on the Situation in Little Rock." Lanham, MD: Rowman & Littlefield, 1998.

JET "Alabama Radio Station Smeared with KKK Signs," *Jet*, March 8, 1956.

JM Farber, Samuel, "Cuba before the Revolution," *Jacobin*, September 6, 2015.

LAT Los Angeles Times, October 15, 1957.

MCR McClellan Committee, Report No. 1139.

NR Schlamm, William. "Arts and Manners: Elvis Presley and the Mozart Year," *National Review*, July 11, 1956.

NY New Yorker, October 25, 1957.

NYDN New York Daily News, November 15, 1957.

NYH New York Herald, May 21, 1893.

NYHT New York Herald Tribune.

NYJ-A New York Journal-American, December 26, 1956.

NYP New York Post.

NYT New York Times, various dates.

PAR Shearer, Lloyd, "Elvis Presley," *Parade*, September 30, 1956.

PRT "Exploration of Cosmic Space with Reactive Devices," in *Pioneers of Rocket Technology*, Moscow, 1964.

SEP Bigart, Homer. "Will the Law Ever Get Hoffa?," *Saturday Evening Post*, March 30, 1983.

SDU San Diego Union, November 20, 1958.

RNL Richmond New Leader, February 22, 1960.

SM Geiling, Natasha. "Before the Revolution," *Smithsonian*, July 31, 2007.

ST Burns, Eric. "Sputnik and Its Times," a four-part series about Sputnik on the satellite's twenty-fifth anniversary. The reports were broadcast on NBC News's *Today* program September 28–October 1, 1982.
WP Washington Post.

BOOKS

Allen, Oliver E. *New York, New York: A History of the World's Most Exhilarating & Challenging City*. New York: Atheneum, 1990.

Ambrose, Stephen E. *Eisenhower: The President*. New York: Simon & Schuster, 1984.

———. *Nixon: The Education of a Politician, 1913–1962*. New York: Simon & Schuster, 1987.

———. *Undaunted Courage: Meriwether Lewis, Thomas Jefferson, and the Opening of the American West*. New York: Simon & Schuster, 1996.

Anderson, John. *Parallel Motion: A Biography of Nevil Shute Norway*. Kerhonkson, NY: Paper Tiger, 2011.

Anonymous. *Everyman and Other Miracles and Morality Plays*. Mineola, NY: Dover, 1995.

Asbury, Herbert. *The Great Illusion: An Informal History of Prohibition*. New York: Doubleday, 1950.

Axelrod, Alan. *The Gilded Age: 1876–1912: Overture to the American Century*. New York: Sterling, 2017.

Barone, Michael. *Our Country: The Shaping of America from Roosevelt to Reagan*. New York: Free Press, 1990.

Bashe, Philip. *Teenage Idol: The Complete Biography of Rick Nelson*. New York: Hyperion, 1992.

Berliner, Michael S., ed. *Letters of Ayn Rand*. New York: Dutton, 1995.

Berry, Chuck. *Chuck Berry: The Autobiography*. New York: Harmony Books, 1987.

Bertrand, Michael. *Race, Rock, and Elvis*. Urbana: University of Illinois Press, 2000.

Beschloss, Michael R. *May-Day: Eisenhower, Khrushchev and the U-2 Affair*. New York: Harper & Row, 1986.

Boorstin, Daniel. *The Americans: The Democratic Experience*. Norwalk, CT: Easton Press, 1965

Braden, Barbara. *The Passion of Ayn Rand: A Biography*. Garden City, NY: Doubleday, 1986.

Bruns, Roger A. *Preacher: Billy Sunday & Big-Time American Evangelism*. New York: Norton, 1992.

Burns, Eric. *Invasion of the Mind-Snatchers: Television's Conquest of America in the Fifties*. Philadelphia: Temple University Press, 2010.

———. *The Spirits of America: A Social History of Alcohol*. Philadelphia: Temple University Press, 2004.

Burns, Jennifer. *Goddess of the Market: Ayn Rand and the American Right*. New York: Oxford University Press, 2011.

Caro, Robert. *The Power Broker: Robert Moses and the Fall of New York*. New York: Knopf, 1974.

————. *Working: Researching, Interviewing, Writing.* New York: Knopf, 2019.

————. *The Years of Lyndon Johnson: Master of the Senate.* New York: Knopf, 2002.

Castro, Fidel, and Ignacio Ramonet. *Fidel Castro: My Life: A Spoken Autobiography.* New York: Scribner, 2006.

Clarke, Gerald. *Capote: A Biography.* New York: Simon & Schuster, 1988.

Coleman, Rick. *Blue Monday: Fats Domino and the Lost Dawn of Rock 'n' Roll.* New York: Da Capo, 2006.

Coltman, Leycester. *The Real Fidel Castro.* New Haven, CT: Yale University Press, 2003.

Consumer Guide, Auto Editors. *Chevrolet: The Complete History.* Lincolnwood, IL: Publications International, 1996.

Crichton, Michael. *Travels.* New York: Knopf, 1988.

DeStefano, Anthony M. *Top Hoodlum: Frank Costello, Prime Minister of the Mafia.* New York: Citadel Press, 2018.

Dickens, Charles. *A Tale of Two Cities.* Norwalk, CT: Easton Press, 1981.

Dickson, Paul. *Sputnik: The Shock of the Century.* New York: Walker & Company, 2001.

————. *Timelines: Day by Day and Trend by Trend from the Dawn of the Atomic Age to the Close of the Cold War.* New York and Reading, MA: Addison-Wesley, 1990.

Dietz, Dan. *The Complete Book of 1950s Broadway Musicals.* Lanham, MD: Rowman & Littlefield, 2014.

Diggins, John Patrick. *The Proud Decades: America in War and Peace, 1941–1960.* New York: Norton, 1988.

Doss, Erika. *Elvis Culture: Fans, Faith, & Image.* Lawrence: University Press of Kansas, 1999.

Dundy, Elaine. *Elvis and Gladys: The First Revealing Look at How the King's Mother Shaped His Life.* New York: Macmillan, 1985.

English, T. J. *Havana Nocturne: How the Mob Owned Cuba . . . and Then Lost It to the Revolution.* New York: William Morrow, 2007.

Finch, Christopher. *Highways to Heaven: The AUTO Biography of America.* New York: HarperCollins, 1992.

Folsom, Robert G. *The Money Trail: How Elmer Irey and his T-Men Brought Down America's Criminal Elite.* Lincoln, NE: Potomac Books, 2010.

Fox, Richard Wightmam, *Lincoln's Body: A Cultural History.* New York: Norton, 2015.

Fox, Stephen. *Blood and Power: Organized Crime in Twentieth-Century America.* New York: William Morrow, 1989.

Frady, Marshall. *Billy Graham: A Parable of American Righteousness.* Boston: Little, Brown, 1979.

Franco, Joseph (Joe), with Richard Hammer. *Hoffa's Man: The Rise and Fall of Jimmy Hoffa as Witnessed by His Strongest Arm.* New York: Prentice-Hall, 1987.

Goldman, Albert. *Elvis.* New York: McGraw-Hill, 1981.

Goodall, Howard. *The Story of Music: From Babylon to the Beatles, How Music Has Shaped Civilization.* New York: Pegasus, 2013.

Goodwin, Richard N. *Remembering America: A Voice from the Sixties.* Boston: Little, Brown, 1988.

Gordon, Lois, and Alan Gordon. *American Chronicle: Six Decades in American Life, 1920–1980.* New York: Atheneum, 1987.

Gray, Francis Clayton, and Yanick Rice Lamb. *Born to Win: The Authorized Biography of Althea Gibson*. New York: Wiley, 2004.

Greenburg, Michael. *The Mad Bomber of New York: The Extraordinary True Story of the Manhunt That Paralyzed a City*. New York: Union Square Press, 2011.

Greenland, David R. *Michael Landon: The Career and Artistry of a Television Genius*. Albany, GA: BearManor Media, 2014.

Guralnick, Peter. *Last Train to Memphis: The Rise of Elvis Presley*. New York: Little, Brown, 1994.

———. *Sam Phillips: The Man Who Invented Rock 'n' Roll*. New York: Little, Brown, 2015.

Hale, Edward Everett. *The Brick Moon and Life in the Brick Moon*. London: Douglas McIntosh, 2012.

Hardesty, Von, and Gene Eisman. *Epic Rivalry: The Inside Story of the Soviet and American Space Race*. Washington, DC: National Geographic, 2007.

Hart, Jeffrey. *When the Going Was Good! American Life in the Fifties*. New York: Crown, 1982.

Halberstam, David. *The Fifties*. New York: Villard, 1993.

Heller, Anne. *Ayn Rand and the World She Made*. New York: Doubleday, 2007.

Hilburn, Robert. *Paul Simon: The Life*. New York: Simon & Schuster, 2018.

Hitchcock, William I. *The Age of Eisenhower: America and the World in the 1950s*. New York: Simon & Schuster, 2108.

Ingrassia, Paul. *Engines of Change: A History of the American Dream in Fifteen Cars*. New York: Simon & Schuster, 2012.

Jackson, John A. *Big Beat Heat: Alan Freed and the Early Years of Rock & Roll*. New York: Schirmer Books, 1991.

Jacoway, Elizabeth. *Turn Away Thy Son: Little Rock, the Crisis That Shocked the Nation*. New York: Free Press, 2007.

Jennings, Dean. *We Only Kill Each Other: The Life and Bad Times of Bugsy Siegel*. New York: Prentice-Hall, 1968.

Johnson, Curt, and R. Craig Sautter. *The Wicked City: Chicago from Kenna to Capone*. Boston: Da Capo, 1994.

Jowitt, Deborah. *Jerome Robbins: His Life, His Theater, His Dance*. New York: Simon & Schuster, 2004.

Kay, Jane Holtz. *Asphalt Nation: How the Automobile Took Over America and How to Take It Back*. New York: Crown, 1997.

Keefe, Rose. *The Man Who Got Away: The Bugs Moran Story: A Biography*. Nashville, TN: Cumberland House, 2005.

Kerouac, Jack. *On the Road*. New York: Viking Press, 1957.

Kirby, David. *Little Richard: The Birth of Rock 'n' Roll*. New York: Continuum, 2009.

Kobler, John. *Capone: The Life and World of Al Capone*. New York: Putnam, 1971.

Lacey, Robert. *Little Man: Meyer Lansky and the Gangster Life*. Boston: Little, Brown, 1991.

Larson, Edward J. *Summer for the Gods: The Scopes Trial and America's Continuing Debate Over Science and Religion*. New York: BasicBooks, 1997.

Laymon, Sherry. *Fearless: John L. McClellan, United States Senator*. Mustang, OK: Tate Publishing, 2011.

Lepore, Jill. *These Truths: A History of the United States*. New York, Norton, 2018.

Lipsyte, Robert. *SportsWorld: An American Dreamland*. New Brunswick, NJ: Rutgers University Press, 2018.

Manchester, William. *The Glory and the Dream: A Narrative History of America, 1932–1972*. Boston: Little, Brown, 1974.

Marcus, Greil. *Dead Elvis: A Chronicle of a Cultural Obsession*. New York: Doubleday, 1991.

Marsh, Peter, and Peter Collett. *Driving Passion: The Psychology of the Car*. Boston: Faber and Faber, 1986.

McCallum, John D. *Dave Beck*. Mercer Island, WA: Writing Works, 1978.

McCullough, David. *Truman*. New York: Simon & Schuster, 1992.

McDougall, Walter A. *The Heavens and the Earth: A Political History of the Space Age*. New York: Basic Books, 1985.

Mellow, James R. *Hemingway: A Life Without Consequences*. Boston: Houghton Mifflin, 1992

Moldea, Dan E. *The Hoffa Wars: Teamsters, Rebels, Politicians and the Mob*. New York: Paddington Press, 1978.

Miller, Donald L. *Lewis Mumford: A Life*. New York: Weidenfeld & Nicolson, 1989.

Miller, Douglas T., and Marion Nowak. *The Fifties: The Way We Really Were*. Garden City, NY: Doubleday, 1977.

Miller, Merle. *Plain Speaking: An Oral Biography of Harry S. Truman*. New York: Putnam's, 1974.

Mordden, Ethan. *On Sondheim: An Opinionated Guide*. Oxford, UK: Oxford University Press, 2016.

Murray, Bruce. *Journey into Space: The First Thirty Years of Space Exploration*. New York: Norton, 1989.

Neff, James. *Vendetta: Bobby Kennedy Versus Jimmy Hoffa*. New York: Little, Brown, 2015.

Norman, Philip. *Rave On: The Biography of Buddy Holly*. New York: Simon & Schuster, 1996.

Oakley, J. Ronald. *God's Country: America in the Fifties*. New York: Dembner, 1986.

Ohlin, Mancy. *Blast Back: The Space Race*. New York: Little Bee, 2017.

Patterson, James T. Brown v. Board of Education: *A Civil Rights Milestone and Its Troubled Legacy*. New York: Oxford University Press, 2001.

———. *Grand Expectations: The United States, 1945–1974*. New York: Oxford University Press, 1996.

Patton, Phil. *Open Road: A Celebration of the American Highway*. New York: Simon & Schuster, 1986.

Pegg, Bruce. *Brown Eyed Handsome Man: The Life and Hard Times of Chuck Berry*. New York: Routledge, 2002.

Perrett, Geoffrey. *A Dream of Greatness: The American People, 1945–1963*. New York: Coward, McCann & Geoghegan, 1979.

Peyser, Joan. *Bernstein: A Biography*. New York: William Morrow, 1987.

Raab, Selwyn. *Five Families: The Rise, Decline, and Resurgence of America's Most Powerful Mafia Empires*. New York: St. Martin's, 2005.

Rand, Ayn. *Atlas Shrugged*. Norwalk, CT: Easton Press, 1989.

————. *The Fountainhead*. Norwalk, CT: Easton Press, 1989.

Reed, Roy. *Faubus: The Life and Times of an American Prodigal*. Fayetteville: University of Arkansas Press, 1997.

Reeves, Thomas C. *The Life and Times of Joe McCarthy*. New York: Stein and Day, 1982.

Remnick, David, ed. *Life Stories: Profiles from the* New Yorker. "Wunderkind," A. J. Liebling. New York: Random House, 2000.

Reppetto, Thomas. *American Mafia: A History of Its Rise to Power*. New York: Henry Holt, 2004.

Rhodes, Richard. *Dark Sun: The Making of the Hydrogen Bomb*. New York: Simon & Schuster, 1995.

Roberts, Gene, and Hank Klibanoff. *The Race Beat: The Press, The Civil Rights Struggle, and the Awakening of a Nation*. New York: Knopf, 2006.

Ross, Alex. *The Rest Is Noise: Listening to the Twentieth Century*. New York: Farrar, Straus and Giroux, 2017.

Roth, Philip. *Portnoy's Complaint*. New York: Vintage International, 1994.

Sale, Kirkpatrick. *The Fire of His Genius: Robert Fulton and the American Dream*. New York: Free Press, 2001.

Schlesinger, Arthur M. *The Dynamics of World Power: A Documentary History of the United States Foreign Policy, 1945–1973*. New York: McGraw-Hill, 1973.

Schlesinger, Arthur M., Jr. *Robert Kennedy and His Times*. Boston: Houghton Mifflin, 1978.

Shaw, Arnold. *The Rockin' 50s*. New York: Hawthorn Books, 1974.

Shute, Nevil. *On the Beach*. New York: William Morrow, 1957.

Silverman, Al, and Brian Silverman, eds. *The Twentieth Century Treasury of Sports*. New York: Viking, 1992.

Smith, Julian. *Nevil Shute (Nevil Shute Norway)*. Boston: Twayne Publishers, 1976.

Smith, Page. *America Enters the World: A People's History of the Progressive Era and World War I, Volume Seven*. New York: McGraw-Hill, 1985.

Solberg, Carl. *Riding High: America in the Cold War*. New York: Mason & Lipscomb Publishers, 1973.

Stratton, W. K. *Floyd Patterson: The Fighting Life of Boxing's Invisible Champion*. Boston: Houghton Mifflin Harcourt, 2012.

Szulc, Tad. *Then and Now: How the World Has Changed Since WWII*. New York: Morrow, 1990.

Talese, Gay. *The Gay Talese Reader: Portraits and Encounters*, "The Loser." New York: Walker, 2003.

Teitel, Amy Shira. *Breaking the Chains of Gravity: The Story of Spaceflight before NASA*. New York: Bloomsbury Sigma, 2016.

Viertel, Jack. *The Secret Life of the American Musical: How Broadway Shows Are Built*. New York: Farrar, Straus and Giroux, 2016.

Walvin, James. *Sugar: The World Corrupted: From Slavery to Obesity*. New York: Pegasus, 2018.

Ward, John. *The Arkansas Rockefeller*. Baton Rouge: Louisiana State University Press, 1978.

Warren, Earl. *The Memoirs of Earl Warren*. Garden City, NY: Doubleday, 1977.

Weesner, Theodore. *The Car Thief.* New York: Grove Press, 1972.

Weiss, Gary. *Ayn Rand Nation: The Hidden Struggle for America's Soul.* New York: St. Martin's Press, 2012.

White, Charles. *The Life and Times of Little Richard: The Quasar of Rock.* New York: Harmony Books, 1985.

Willson, Quentin. *Cars: A Celebration.* London: Dorling Kindersley, 2001.

Wolf, Stacy. *Changed for Good: A Feminist History of the Broadway Musical.* Oxford, UK: Oxford University Press, 2011.

Notes

PROLOGUE

Sputnik 1

2 "It is important that the orbit," Dickson, 105.
3 "the most haunting evocation," https://enwikipedia.org/wiki/On_the_Beach -(novel)#Reception.
4 " 'Nausea,' the chemist said," Shute, 158.
4 "the sound that forevermore separates," quoted in Dickson, 1.
4 "chirping in the key of A-flat," ibid., 1.
5 "There were ten days," quoted in ibid., 92.
5 "The CIA, Defense Intelligence Agency," Dickson, *Sputnik*, 113.
5 "The opening of the Space Age," McDougall, 143.
6 "It looked as though," quoted in White, 91–92.
6 "as far as the satellite," quoted in Ambrose, *Eisenhower*, 430.
7 "Eisenhower's first response," ibid., 427.
7 "White House advisers," Dickson, *Sputnik*, 111.
7 "the key men in Washington," quoted in ibid., 120.
7 "Sputnik Could Be Spy-in-the-Sky," *WP*, October 7, 1957, 1.
7 "What is at stake," quoted in ibid., 116.
7 "lost a battle more important," quoted in ibid., 117.
7 "Don't be surprised, my friends," quoted in ibid., 115.
8 "The news was a bombshell," Goodwin, 94.
8 "If the U.S. government," ibid., 96–97.
9 "The first R-7 exploded," Dickson, 95.
9 "The Soviet is likely to beat," *NYT*, September 8, 1957, 1.
9 "I thought of the rocket," quoted in ibid., 58.

PART ONE
CHAPTER ONE

The Mad Bomber of New York

16 "a length of iron pipe," Greenburg, 1.
16 "a flashlight bulb," ibid., 5.

16 "CON ED CROOKS," quoted in ibid., 1.
17 "crazy house," and, "roundly thought of," ibid., 19.
17 "It worked great, too," quoted in ibid., 31.
18 "the Eisenhower of psychotics," quoted in ibid., 242.
19 "I wrote 900 letters," quoted in https://enwikipedia.org/wiki/George_Metesky.
19 "Feeling superior to his fellow students," ibid., 17.
19 "Well, he was a strange one," ibid.
20 "The boiler room filled," ibid., 21.
21 "When a motorist injures a dog," http://www.enwikipedia.org/wiki/George_Metesky, 8.
21 "I WILL MAKE NO MORE," quoted in ibid., 4.
21 "an official service classification," Greenburg, 18.
21 "boys or pranksters," Bellow, Alan. "Ghoulish Acts & DastardlyDeeds," www.damninteresting.com.
22 "HAVE YOU NOTICED," http://www.enwikipedia.org/wiki/George_Metesky/
22 "AN OPEN LETTER," *NYJ-A*, p. 1.
23 "[e]xpert in civil or military ordnance," quoted in *NYJ-A*, December 25, 1956."
23 "A thirty-six-year-old postal clerk," Greenburg, xi.
24 "Bow-tied," quoted in ibid., 68.
25 "Sensing a possible confession," ibid., 155.
26 "Fair Play," ibid.
26 "his demeanor instantly transformed," ibid.
26 "timing devices," and following quotes about throat lozenges, author interview with Michael M. Greenburg, February 9, 2018.
26 "the entrenched and evil," and, "cult-hero," and, "epitomizes the futility," Greenburg, 241.
27 "The story of the century," quoted in Greenburg, 165.

CHAPTER TWO

The Committee
29 "thundering voice," Laymon, 15.
30 "John McClellan did not have," ibid., 25.
30 "raised by people," quoted in ibid., 24.
30 "His Christian upbringing," ibid.
30 "the breakup of his first marriage," Fox, 322.
31 "had begun to distance himself," Franco with Hammer, 92.
31 "the astringent, disapproving demeanor," quoted in Fox, 322.
32 "to construct [Beck's] private home," Moldea, 70.
33 " 'Do you,' asked Chairman McClellan," McCallum, 119.
34 "I'll be able to come out of this," quoted in ibid.
35 "the men of the family," Moldea, 22.
36 "thick legs, heavy shoulders," ibid., 23.
36 "The 'Strawberry Boys,' " ibid.
37 "Our cars were bombed out," quoted in Fox, 200–201.
37 "The police were no help," quoted in ibid., 201.

37 "arrested, released, back to the line," ibid.
38 "Hoffa behaved as many Teamsters," Franco with Hamilton, p. 91.
39 "conflicts of interest," Fox, 324.
39 "his dynamic leadership," quoted in Neff, 43.
39 "the Catholic bishop of Chicago," ibid., 43–44.
40 "was candid with Ragano," Raab, 149.
41 "Well, I don't know," quoted in Neff, 93.
41 "[T]hat spoiled brat," *SEP*, 68.
41 "There were no services," quoted in Neff, 99.
41 "As Teamster boss," *SEP*, 68.
42 "To the best of my recollection," Neff, 103.
42 *"disremembrance,"* quoted in AmericanMafia.com/Feature/Articles_458.html.
42 "Let's have order," 192.
42 "faced Kennedy and the senators," Franco with Hammer, 129.
42 "the most convenient *forgettery,*" quoted in AmericanMafia.com/Feature/Articles_458.html.
43 "charged with thirty-four," Moldea, 80.
43 "There were a lot of," quoted in Fox, 324.
43 "The United States is being run," quoted in www.nashvillescene.com/test/article/13006945/the-people-vs./jimmy/hoffa/part-1.

CHAPTER THREE

From Apalachin to Havana

49 "How to keep younger," *WP*, A10.
49 "The cops arrested," Fox, 326.
49 "The sight of all those gangsters," Moldea, 89.
50 "50 had arrest records," *MCR*, 487.
50 "symptomatic of the growing power," ibid., 509.
50 "Well, I hope you're satisfied," quoted in Fox, 326.
51 "carried wads of money," and, "[W]ithout evidence," Raab, 118.
51 "made," quoted in ibid., 326.
51 "obviously well-heeled bums," *NYDN*, 2.
52 "The FBI didn't know anything," quoted in Neff, 118.
54 "Prime Minister," quoted in https://themobmuseum.org/notable_names/frank-costello/.
54 "Over at Toots Shor's saloon," DeStefano, 8–9.
55 "liked to start off their day," Lacey, *Lansky*, 91.
55 "clean," quoted in ibid., 90.
55 "with black hair brushed straight back," and, "His nose was," Wolf with DiMona, 137.
56 "His apartment was a seven-room penthouse," ibid.
56 "husky and rasping," ibid.
57 "a washed up boxer," and, "rushed through the door," and "held in his right hand," and "fire a single shot," DeStefano, 242.
57 "This is for you, Frank," quoted in Wolf with DiMona, 253.

57　"By flinching and turning," DeStefano, 242.

57　"I didn't see no one," and, "I don't know who," quoted in ibid., 254.

58　"Boss of all Bosses," quoted in https:/enwikipedia.org/wiki/Vito-Genovese.

59　"What's an Italian boy," Raab, 109.

59　"who earned fame," DeStefano, 7.

60　"the Mad Hatter," and, "Lord High Executioner," quoted in https:// enwikipedia .org/wiki/Albert_Anastasia.

60　"by his psychopathic enjoyment," Raab, 68.

61　"the one who got away," ibid., 194.

62　"with the division of spoils," English, 189.

62　"his number one boy," Moldea, 87.

63　"walked to the nearby Park-Sheraton," ibid.

64　"He had no list," Lepore, 551.

64　MCCARTHY WAS MURDERED," quoted in ibid.

65　"officials listed the cause," Reeves, 671.

65　"reported unequivocally that Joe," ibid., 672.

66　"The most fascinating young man," quoted in Fox, 156.

67　"The Flamingo," quoted in www.history.com/this-day-in-history/bugsy-siegel -opens-flamingo-hotel.

67　"Benny Siegel was alive," Lacey, 156.

68　"smash in Benny's left eye," ibid., 157.

68　"El Mulatto Lindo," quoted in English, 61.

70　"a mistress of pleasure," quoted in *SM*, www.smithsonianmagazine.com/his tory/before-the-revolution-159682020/.

70　"a country known mainly," quoted in ibid.

71　"The country's most precious resources," English, xiv.

71　"It is true," ibid.

72　"told the story of how," ibid., 60.

72　"The corruption of the Government," Schlesinger, *Dynamics*, 512.

74　"We'd made slingshots," quoted in Castro and Ramonet, 57.

75　"[h]e showed no great signs," English, 112.

75　"To the mobsters," ibid., 113.

75　"a minor affair," ibid.

77　"Matthews was no neophyte," quoted in ibid., 199.

77　"Early in December 1958," Lacey, *Lanksy*, 249.

78　"While most mobsters dashed back," Raab, 144.

78　"a charm offensive," https://enwikipedia.org/wiki/Fidel-Castro#Provisional_ government-1959.

79　"not only out of," *NYT*, April 19, 1959, E7.

79　"Viva Castro," ibid., April 16, 1.

79　"Rather than seek out," Ambrose, *Education*, 516.

79　"did not give," and "The real question," ibid., E7.

79　"One of the first decisions," quoted in Lacey, *Lansky*, 252.

80　"confiscated sugar estates," Walvin, 166.

81　"In the end," quoted in Coltman, 322.

82　"The gambling casinos," English, xix.

82 "conversation with the gods," https://enwikipedia.org/wiki/Mambo_(dance).

83 "the violin executes rhythmic cords," https://enwikipedia.org/wiki/Mambo_(music).

PART TWO
CHAPTER FOUR

Highways to Everywhere

87 "the road system," Ambrose, *Eisenhower*, 250.

87 "Except for the Pennsylvania Turnpike," ibid.

87 "Bridges cracked and were rebuilt," www.enwikipedia.org/wiki/Federal_Aid_Highway_Act_of-_1956.

88 "been impressed by Hitler's system," Ambrose, *Eisenhower*, 250.

88 "No river or ravine," Kay, 231.

88 "that would, according to Eisenhower," ibid.

88 "Our national flower," quoted in Miller, 378.

88 "were required to have," Finch, 227.

89 "gas taxes would be spent," Hitchcock, 264.

89 "The Interstate system was," Patton, 94.

90 "sixteen cities engaged," Kay, 251.

90 "worse was to come," ibid.

90 "would move enough earth," Patton, 92.

91 "developed an original," Fox, 208.

91 "ascendancy could not have come," Franco with Hammer, 93.

93 "Oh public road," https://www.poetryfoundation.org/poems/48859/song_of_the_open_road.

93 "As new and greater road systems," quoted in Patton, 127.

CHAPTER FIVE

The Design of an Era

94 "Small cars from overseas," Dickson, *Timelines*, 104.

95 "If any single car," *Consumer Guide*, 74.

95 "Not until years later," ibid., 74.

95 "Seventeen exterior colors," gmheritagecenter.com/docs/gm-heritage-archive/historical-brochures/Chevrolet_Engineering_Features/reduced/Chevrolet-Engineering-Features-19 57.

96 "the Bel Air is one of the most," Willson, 126.

96 "junior Cadillac," ibid., 126.

96 "[e]very detail," gmheritagecenter.com/docs/gm-heritage-archive/historical-brochures/Chevrolet_Engineering_Features/reduced/Chevrolet-Engineering-Features-19 57.

96 "peppy 'small block' V-8 engine," Ingrassia, 342.

96 "as much a symbol," https://www.wired.com/2010/12/classic_airliners_gallery/.

97 "The '57 Bel Air sums up," Willson, 129.

97 "In easy fantasies," Weesner, 10.
98 "The automobile business," Miller and Nowak, 138.
98 "In King Farouk's case," ibid., 138.

CHAPTER SIX

The Vagina in the Grille

101 "The tragic disappointment," Brinkley, 577.
101 "Over my dead body," quoted in Collier and Horowitz, 265.
101 "1. The name should be short," quoted in ibid., 577.
102 "the Special Products Division," ibid., 577–78.
102 "[he] went out," and, "three fingers," Collier and Horowitz, 313.
102 "A man periodically swept," Collier and Horowitz, 265.
102 "By the late summer 1955," ibid.
103 "a grape tendril," by William Carlos Williams, quoted in poets.org/poet/
       marianne-moore.
103 "on its dashboard," Gordon and Gordon, 359.
103 "a grape tendril/ties a knot," quoted in www.poemhunter.com/poem/poetry/
       #content.
104 "the Resilient Bullet," Lacey, *Ford*, 482.
104 "The Executive Committee," ibid., 483.
104 "the biggest business failure," Perrett, 514.
105 "Behind-the-scenes tension," Lacey, *Ford*, 489.
105 "But by November," Collier and Horowitz, 277.
106 "The amount of shake," quoted in ibid., 277.
106 "Quality control over the new Edsel," www.readex.com/readex-report/ford
       -fiasco-tracking-rise-and-fall-edsel-americans-newspaper-archives.
106 "was based on the most," Perrett, 514.
107 "market researchers [were sent out]," Lacey, 484.
107 "was compared to a man," Collier and Horowitz, 276.
108 "Ford Motor Co. Drops Edsel Line," and following article, *SDU*, 1.
108 "As John Brooks calculated," Brinkley, p. 579.
108 "gentle epitaph," ibid.
108 "maybe it means," quoted in ibid.
108 "Edselcade," quoted in ibid., 580.
109 "decided in 1998 to prove," ibid.

CHAPTER SEVEN

Highways to Nowhere

110 "a brand new Buick," Kerouac, 233.
110 "his old Chevy," ibid., 152.
110 "a '39 Chevy," ibid., 90.
110 "his Texas Chevy," ibid., 142.
110 "a put-together jalopy," ibid., 21.

110 "his old Ford coupe," ibid., 38.
110 "a '37 Ford sedan," ibid., 265.
110 "a '47 Cadillac limousine," ibid., 224.
110 "a mud-spattered '49 Hudson," 109–10.
110 "a fag Plymouth," ibid., 206.
110 "a souped-up rod," ibid., 79.
110 "toolshack on wheels," ibid., 18.
110 "mule wagon," ibid., 113.
110 "weird, crazy Nebraska," ibid., 23.
110 "a brand new pickup truck," 80.
110 "farmer-cars, and once in a while, ibid., 22.
112 "In a freshman game," Hart, 275.
113 "isn't writing at all," quoted in Clarke, 315 n.
113 "I'd often dreamed of going West," Kerouac, 3.
113 "actually was born," quoted in Axelrod, 3.
113 "cheated, robbed," quoted in Halberstam, 301.
115 "we turned our faces to Mexico," Kerouac, 275.
115 " 'More Mambo Jambo," quoted in ibid., 287.
116 "the road is life," Kerouac, 211.
116 "three times married," ibid., 305.

PART THREE
CHAPTER EIGHT

Whites against Blacks

NOTE: In a previous book—little read, I am sad to say—I wrote about *Brown v. Board of Education* and the hateful occurrence three years later, when Arkansas governor Orval Faubus defied the Supreme Court and refused to allow black students to enter Little Rock's Central High School. As might be expected, some of what I said, though certainly not all, fits into the context of this chapter almost perfectly. Thus, I saw no reason to change my wording merely for the sake of variety. I wrote and analyzed as well as I could back then; I have put the same best foot forward in the present volume. In a few places.

119 "had to leave home," Patterson, 32.
120 "On winter mornings," Perrett, 367.
120 "he came to believe," Patterson, 34.
121 "been on the bench," Manchester, 735.
121 "Racial segregation," www.ourdocuments.gov.doc.php?flash = true&doc = 87.
121 "perhaps the single most important," Halberstam, 423.
122 "[o]ne of the most significant events," Szulc, 176.
122 "The *Brown* decision," Barone, 272.
122 "The improvement of race relations," quoted in Patterson, 81.
122 "The States in North America," https://sageamericanhistory.net/Jeffersonian/documents/JeffOnStatesRight.htm.
122 "I think it makes no difference," quoted in Ambrose, *Eisenhower*, 338.
123 "no word of support," quoted in ibid., 289.

123 "excited and racist-minded." quoted in Warren, 289.

123 "first muted, then infuriated," Diggins, 279.

123 "Sometimes it's a hassle," quoted in www.kansascity.com/latest-news/article206918919.html.

124 "assessment [was] that Arkansas," quoted in Ward, vii.

124 "that there was a world beyond the borders," ibid.

124 "heavy drinker known for his playboy life style," http://www.encyclopediaofarkansas.net/encyclopedia/entry-detail/aspx?entryID = 122.

125 "He had helped open," and, "had helped Arkansas," Reed, 163.

125 "at the very least," ibid.

125 "a 47-year-old army veteran," Hitchcock, 362.

126 "I'm sorry, but I'm already committed," quoted in ibid., 800.

126 "despicable behavior," Ward, vii.

126 "argued against [it] to the very end," ibid., vii–viii.

126 "popularity was waning," ibid., 800.

127 "There was no indication," quoted in ibid.

127 "mostly to Negro youths," quoted in ibid., 801.

128 "that sputtering sputnik," quoted in Lepore, 587.

128 "Their 500-page report," Ward, 801.

128 "Keep the niggers out!" quoted in Halberstam, 674.

129 "wanted to be a lawyer," Jacoway, 1.

130 "Here she comes," quoted in Jacoway, 4.

130 "Go home, you burr head!" quoted in Manchester, 801.

130 "Go home, you bastard," quoted in Halberstam, 675.

130 "Go home before you get hurt," quoted in Jacoway, 4.

130 "No nigger bitch," and, "Lynch her," quoted in Halberstam, 675.

131 "Television news cameras," Roberts and Klibanoff, 160.

132 "Are you going to go to school," quoted in ibid., 161.

132 "The girl did not," and "frozen in fear," ibid.

132 "You don't care to say," quoted in ibid.

132 "cruel inquisition," ibid.

133 "Don't let them see you cry," quoted in Jacoway, 5.

133 "helped the frightened child," ibid.

133 "She's scared," quoted in ibid., 5–6.

133 "[Chancellor] had watched," Halberstam, 676.

134 "The trouble in Little Rock," quoted in Manchester, 803.

135 "thwarted by the governor," quoted in Halberstam, 802.

135 "there could be only one outcome," quoted in Ambrose, *Eisenhower*, 416.

135 "The very basis of our individual rights," *EA*, 62.

136 "Retreating, they were pursued," Manchester, 803.

136 "Most of the white students," ibid.

136 "[t]he Russians [to use]," Dickson, 132.

137 "*fau-bus* (faw-bus)," quoted in Manchester, 799.

138 "Thurmond held the floor," Caro, 998.

138 "He read a Supreme Court decision," www.businessinsider.com/longest-filibuster-in-history-strom-thurmond-rand-paul-2013–13.

138 "great achievement," Caro, 999.

139 "it was better than nothing," ibid., 1001.

CHAPTER NINE

Whites *with* Blacks

140 "Used to be so easy," www.youtube.com/watch?v = s-qXrj2JkzU.

140 "I'm gonna buy me," en.wikipedia.org/wiki/Traditional_blues_verses.

141 "In the forties and fifties," Dundy, 157.

141 "After years of enduring," Bertrand, 24.

141 "Poor we were," quoted in Guralnick, 29.

141 "DA," Dickson, 103.

142 "While still in high school," Doss, 170–71.

142 "He sat there mesmerized," Guralnick, 47.

142 "the stately harmonies," ibid.

144 "If I could find," quoted in Marcus, 52.

144 "extols the virtues," Goodall, 299.

144 "There'll be 15 Minutes," quoted in https://genius.com/The-Dominoes-sixty -minute-man-lyrics.

144 "hear-your-own-voice," quoted in Marcus, 52.

145 "noting his name, vocal style," ibid.

145 "couldn't have been further," Guralnick, 64.

146 "I really would like to open," quoted in Bashe, 249.

146 "his onstage body movements," Doss, 172.

146 "for a young white boy," quoted in Bertrand, 203.

147 "During the program," quoted in ibid.

147 "I had this great big head," quoted in Kirby, 31.

147 "began with piano-driven rock," Kirby, 99.

147 "It would be standing-room-only," quoted in ibid., 186.

148 "Aided by the affluence of the time," Oakley, 279–80.

148 "You guys have any special arrangements," and following conversation, quoted in Bashe, 68.

148 "Nelson's hits never sold," Coleman, 171.

149 "Fats had co-written," Bashe, 70.

149 (n) "it didn't work," quoted in Jackson, 80.

149 "[a]n anemic version," White, 62n.

150 "police had the nearly impossible task," Bertrand, 176.

150 "When Carl Perkins came on," quoted in ibid., 24.

150 "a Columbia University professor," Gordon and Gordon, 359.

150 "[l]eads to hell and damnation," quoted in Mellow, 22.

151 "voluptuous, sensible embrace," quoted in Bruns, 142–43.

152 "I got a girl," quoted in www.songlyrics.com/larry-williams/bony-Moronie -lyrics/.

152 "The bulk of the ninety minutes," quoted in Oakley, 281.

153 "The first couple of shows," Norman, 138.

153 "When we just couldn't get through," quoted in ibid.

154 "[H]e recalled that during a southern tour," Bertrand, 174.
154 "jungle bunnies," quoted in *RNL*, 8.
154 "white nigger," and, "nigger trash," quoted in ibid.
154 "Perhaps no entertainer in history," *PAR*, 8.
155 "an unspeakably untalented," and, "Where do you go from Elvis Presley," quoted in Shaw, 151.
155 "music or madness?" quoted in ibid., 16.
155 "May the Lord," quoted in *NR*.
155 "Turn on your radio," quoted in Bertrand, 172.
155 "plunges men's minds," quoted in ibid., 101.
155 "knocked black [radio] station," *Jet*, 63.
155 "Beware Elvis Presley," and other newspaper headlines, quoted in Bertrand, 194.
156 "The screaming, idiotic words," quoted in ibid., 164.
156 "concerned white citizen," Bertrand, 54.
156 "brainwashing the adolescent mind," quoted in ibid.
156 "Segregation now," quoted in https://enwikipedia.org/wiki/Asa_Earl_Carter.
156 "the best way," quoted in Bertrand, 163.
156 "The effect was explosive," Hart, 131.
156 "*The Kinsey Report* set to music," ibid.
156 "'Twas brillig," quoted in https://poetsfoundation.org/poems/42916/jabberwocky.
157 "1. All Shook Up," *BB*.
157 "In the social atmosphere?" and, "Did this musical," Bertrand, 235.
158 "Rhythm and blues," quoted in ibid., photo section, between 124 and 125.
158 "White and black," quoted in Fox, 89.
159 "There was an integration problem," quoted in ibid., 41.
159 "Just let me hear some," quoted in https://www.genius.com/Chuck-berry-rock -and-roll-music-lyrics.

PART FOUR
CHAPTER TEN

Moving Stories
163 "It's like being in love," quoted in Remnick, ed., 302.
163 "Floyd Patterson was one of the heroes," quoted in Stratton, 92.
164 "When my mother asked," quoted in ibid., 6.
164 "a tall, straight stick," Remnick, 303.
165 "It's not a *bad* feeling," quoted in Talese, 66.
165 "Indeed, among contemporary boxers," quoted in Stratton, xiii.
165 "I remember the glimpse," quoted in ibid., 152.
166 "He considered himself socially superior," Lipsyte, 68.
167 "I'm not going to work out," quoted in Talese, 69.
167 "so his voice went soft," ibid.
168 "He went to the floor," *NYT*, July 30, 1957, 27.
168 "lost in dementia's fog," Stratton, 210.

171 "[t]he trials of Larry Doby," Lipsyte, 30.

171 "and it determined that an Auburn assistant," www.al.com/sports/index.ssf/ 2017/11/auburns_1957_national-championship.html.

172 "She is one of the greatest players," quoted in Gray and Lamb, 214.

173 "Baseball is Heaven's gift to morals," quoted in www.baseball-Almanac/ quotes/george_will_quotes.shtml.

173 "and the farther I had to run," Roth, 70, 71.

173 "In Ebbets Field," quoted in Silverman and Silverman, 363.

174 "Ebbets Field was a great place," Hirsch, Paul. "Walter O'Malley Was Right," https://sabr.org/research/walter-omalley-was-right, 2.

174 "By 1957," ibid.

175 "On the last Wednesday," ibid.

176 "seventeen outdoor swimming pools," Allen, 273.

176 "was building gigantic," Caro, *Working*, 24–25.

176 "moses turned the big Packard limousine," Caro, *Moses*, 226.

177 "[t]o build his expressways," Caro, *Working*, 34.

177 "to keep many city officials," Caro, *Moses*, 14.

178 "A city never grows," quoted in Newman, Mark. "Wyman reflects on bringing Dodgers to LA," https://www.mlb.com/news/rosalyn-wyman-on-dodgers-mov ing-to-la-in-1957, 1–2.

178 "Dear Mr. O'Malley," quoted in ibid., 2.

180 "I'm still ticked," quoted in *NYT*, May 29, 2018.

180 "It was a disaster," quoted in ibid.

180 "Am I Blue," and following songs, ibid.

180 "supreme performing art," quoted in Lipsyte, 42.

180 "We just suffered," quoted in https://nypost.com/2012/10/28/lasting-love-of -long-gone-dodgeres-shows-devotion-of-brooklynfans.

180 "I always kind of related," ibid.

181 "Brooklyn fans still don't like me," quoted in Newman, Mark. "Wyman reflects on bringing Dodgers to LA," https://www.mlb.com/news/Rosalyn-wyman-on -dodgers-moving-to-la-19 57, 3.

CHAPTER ELEVEN

The Man Who Believed in God

184 "America's Pastor," and, "national clergyman," quoted in https://christianityto day.com/ct/2018.bill-grah/died-billy-graham-obituary.htm.

184 "was perhaps the most significant," ibid.

186 "black starless mornings," Frady, 45.

186 "as soon as I could walk," quoted in ibid.

186 "He grew up," ibid., 48.

186 "a great thrower," Bruns, 50–51.

186 "Wide-eyed," ibid., 78.

186 "with the shyest hint," ibid., 113.

187 "his head hung," ibid., 112–13.

188 "Billy Graham drew over," Manchester, 484.

188 "over 1,100 social-sounding organizations," quoted in Patterson, *Expectations*, 237.

188 "It used to be," quoted in Miller, Merle, 363.

189 "I will never forget," quoted in https://billygraham.org/gallery/bill-graham-pastor-to-the-presidents/.

189 "Billy Graham: Six things he believed," https://www.bbc.org./news/world-us-canada-43144752.

189 [Graham] came with the office," quoted in ibid.

190 "it's supposed to be the obligation," quoted in ibid., 249–50.

190 "by the time," quoted in ibid., 308.

190 "the name of Jesus Christ," quoted in ibid., 293.

190 "For his part, Graham not began casting," ibid.

191 "Sonja Henie, Pearl Bailey," ibid., 298.

191 "100,000 Fill Yankee Stadium," and, "One hundred thousand Persons," *NYT*, July 21, 1957, 1.

192 "The only open space," ibid.

192 "83,150 sports fans," ibid.

192 "Mickey Mantle hit two home runs," Frady, 291.

193 "For all of his anticipatory," ibid., 299–300.

CHAPTER TWELVE

The Woman Who Believed in Man

195 "In a 1991 survey," Heller, xii.

196 "the largely abandoned class," quoted in Heller, 287.

196 "In a certain sense," and, "In order to define," quoted in www. aynrand.org/about/about-ayn-rand.

197 "the property-seizing principle," quoted in Lipsyte, 44.

198 "Rand didn't agree," Heller, 19.

199 "I swear—by my life," ibid., 1069.

199 "The Mind on Strike," quoted in Branden, 220.

199 "Men do not live," Rand, 1010.

201 "The road is cleared," Rand, 1168.

201 "It takes the total," quoted in Branden, 246.

202 "The need to communicate," quoted in ibid.

202 "It was in a case," ibid., 236.

203 "[As] loudly as Miss Rand," quoted in Heller, 282.

203 "Is it a novel?," *LAT*, B5.

203 "the globe's two billion," *NY*, 195.

203 "Miss Rand," quoted in Branden, 297.

203 "I had told Bennett," Heller, p. 275

204 "vibrant and powerful novel," quoted in Heller, 283.

204 "Ayn Rand is destined," quoted in ibid.

204 "black agony of depression," Branden, 303.

204 "As always in Ayn's professional cover," Branden, 204.

204 "the most creative thinker alive," quoted in Burns, Jennifer, 2.

205 "August 21, 1948, Dear Mimi," quoted in Berliner, ed., 405–6.
205 "Ayn, nobody's going to read that," quoted in Branden, 292.

CHAPTER THIRTEEN

Gang Wars on Broadway

207 "the classic and the hip," https://en.wikipedia.org/wiki?West_Side-Story.
208 "cut the frabba-jabba," from the book to *West Side Story*.
208 "Just as Tony and Maria," quoted in *NYHT*, August 4, 1957.
209 "Dear kindly Sergeant Krupke," quoted in www.metrolyrics.com/gee-officer -krupke-lyrics-westside-story-html.
209 "truly epochal," Dietz, 290.
209 "the most savage, restless and electrifying," quoted in ibid.
209 "it was the danced narrative," quoted in Jowitt, 266.
210 "No previous Broadway musical," ibid.
210 "one of the most prodigiously talented," quoted in Henahan, Donal, *NYT*, October 15, 1990.
211 "the American musical idiom," quoted in ibid., 290.
211 "a charming, gifted boy," quoted in Secrest, 24.
211 "could not have different more sharply," ibid., 46.
211 "gave him nothing to play with," ibid., 46.
212 "profoundly moving," and following excerpts, quoted in ibid., 290.
212 "freshness," quoted in Viertel, 130.
212 "the main theme," Ross, 408.
213 "Instead of glamour," quoted in Peyser, 270–71.
213 "Columbus, Ohio," quoted in ibid., 209–10.
214 "Jerry [Robbins] loves our gang idea," quoted in ibid., 210.

CHAPTER FOURTEEN

The Youngest Monster

Much information about the movie *I Was a Teenage Werewolf* is provided by the author, who viewed the film on YouTube on July 16, 2018.

215 "I guess I lost my head," from film.
216 "I burn easy," from the film.
216 "by the sound," Arkoff, 63.
217 "famed in World War II movies," and, "but it wasn't a pain-killer," Crichton, 45.
219 "Upon dying," and "man interfering in the realms," from the film.
219 " 'Listen to this one,' " quoted in Arkoff, 61.
220 "To take first things first," quoted in ibid., 62.
220 "[S]till weeks before the movie was shot," ibid., 62–63.
221 *"I Was A Teenage Werewolf,"* quoted in Arkoff, 65.
221 "Another in the cycle," V.

221 "An American Tragedy," www.comingsoon.net/horror/features-why-1957s
    -I-was-a-teenage-werewolf-is-an-american-tragedy.

223 "Please do not be overly influenced," quote in Arkoff, 55–56.

223 "*I Was a Middle-Aged Werewolf*," and, "Writer/producer Landon," Greenland,
    138.

224 "Truth. If it wasn't for WWII," ibid., Fowler.

224 "had no idea," ibid.

224 "primal, urgent, and heartbreaking energy," ibid.

224 "today the film is largely regarded," https;//en.wilipedia.org/wiki/I_Was_a
    -Teenage-Werewolf.

225 "I was a teenage werewolf," quoted in https://genius.com/The-cramps-I-was-a
    -teenage-werewolf-lyrics.

PART FIVE
CHAPTER FIFTEEN

The Successes of Failure

229 "one watt," www.answers.com/Q/When/did/sputnik/die.

229 "Sputnik I burned up," ibid., 114.

230 "a glowing object," and, "He looked out the back window," www .npr.org/tem
    plates/story.php?storyId=14949891, 2.

231 "What [the NDEA] did," *ST*, September 30, 1982.

232 "a historic break," Patterson, 421.

232 "By the early 1960s," Perrett, 466.

232 "Berlitz schools, phonograph-record lessons," Solberg, 352.

233 "had been smothered," Wilson, 232.

233 "If America ever crashes," quoted in ibid., 139.

233 "Sputnik I dealt the *coup de grace*," Manchester, 791.

234 "the space program required," McDougall, 381.

234 "by all means possible," quoted in ibid.

234 "It is not too much to say," quoted in ibid, p. 381.

234 "the viability of representative government," quoted in ibid.

CHAPTER 16

Muttnik

237 "as a four-door full-size," Dickson, *Sputnik*, 142.

237 "The padded, pressurized cabin," ibid., 141.

238 "an atrocity," quoted in ibid., 144.

238 "With each orbit," ibid., 144.

239 "not only provided," ibid., 141.

CHAPTER SEVENTEEN

Kaputnik

242 "The days leading up," Teitel, 242.

242 "[t]he first stage," ibid., 11.

242 "[r]eporters from around the world," McDougall, 154.

242 "It was less than ideal," Teitel, 242.

242 "shuddered slightly," Dickson, *Sputnik*, 156.

242 "the rocket settled uneasily," Teitel, 242.

242 "as if the gates of Hell," quoted in McDougall, 154.

243 "It was a spectacular failure," ibid., 243.

243 "The *Los Angeles Herald and Examiner*," quoted in Solberg, 342.

243 "Soviet newspapers have not told us," ibid.

244 "Kaputnik," "Flopnik," and "Stayputnik," quoted in Dickson, *Sputnik*, 158–59.

244 "They're been pressing the button," quoted in ibid., 159.

244 "But this was just the beginning," ibid.

EPILOGUE

The Return of the Preacher Man

245 "like a Roman candle," McDougall, 168.

245 "That's wonderful," quoted in ibid.

246 "made about twelve and a half orbits," Ohlin, 55.

248 "I'd heard so much," quoted in White, 119.

248 "Bama lama bama loo," www.metrolyrics.com/bama-lama-bama-loo-little
-richard.html.

Index

Fowler, Gene, Jr., 224
Fox, Stephen, 37
Frady, Marshall, 189–91
Francis, Connie, 145
Friendly Persuasion (film), 10
From the Earth to the Moon (Verne), 9
Fuller, Buckminster, 178n2
Fuller, Charles, 186
funk music, 147

Gable, Clark, 66
Gallo, Joseph, 63
Gallo, Larry, 63
Gambino, Carlo, 47
García Lorca, Federico, 173
Gardner, Ava, 70
Gazenko, Oleg, 238
General Motors, 98–99
Gennaro, Peter, 210
Genovese, Vito, 47, 58
Giancana, Sam, 47–48, 50
Gibson, Althea, 172
Gigante, Vincent, 57, 58, 63
Gillespie, Dizzy, 70
Gilliam, Jim "Junior," 170
Ginsberg, Alan, 113n1
Gladwell, Malcolm, 107
Glenn L. Martin Company, 243
Globe Theatre, 208
Golden Gate Quartet, 142
golf, 172
Gonzalez, Lina Ruz, 73
Goodding, Gladys, 180
Goodman, Shirley, 150
Goodwin, Richard, 8
Gordon, Alan, 150
Gordon, Lois, 150
gospel music: Little Richard with, 6,
    247; rock 'n' roll from, 142–43,
    146–47
Gotti, John, 83
Grable, Betty, 66
Graham, Billy: conversion of, 186–87;
    legacy of, 184–85, 189; politics and,
    188–90, 188n1, 192; popularity of,
    11, 205; with religious crusades, 184,

190–93; at Yankee Stadium, 190–92,
    195
Grant, Ulysses S., 9
Green, Ernest, 137
Greenburg, Michael, 21, 26
"groundlings," 208
Guinness Book of Records, 138
Gwynn, Tony, 182

hairstyles, "DA," 141–42, 141n1
Halberstam, David, 121–22, 133
Hale, Edward Everett, 9
Hall of Fame, 142n2, 169, 172, 173
Hamilton, Roy, 142
Hammarskjold, Dag, 10
Hammerstein, James, 211–12
Hammerstein, Oscar II, 211, 212
Handy, W. C., 140
Hanson, Ted, 166–67
Hargis, Billy James, 189
Harriman, W. Averell, 175
Hart, Jeffrey, 156
Havana, Cuba: culture in, 70–71,
    82–83; organized crime and, 62–63,
    70–72, 75, 76–78, 80, 81
Heinsohn, Tom, 172
Heller, Anne, 196, 198
Hemingway, Ernest, 70, 150–51
Henie, Sonja, 191
Henry, Robert, 142
Henry's Record Shop, Memphis, 142
high fidelity, 148
highways, 89–92
Highway to Heaven (television show),
    223
Hill, Virginia "The Flamingo," 67–68
Hines, Earl "Fatha," 142
Hitchcock, Alfred, 208
Hitchcock, William I., 89
Hitler, Adolf, 44, 88, 203–4
Hodges, Gil, 170
Hoffa, James P., Jr., 43n1
Hoffa, James Riddle, 11; Beck and,
    38–39; crimes of, 36, 37, 39, 40, 44;
    disappearance of, 45, 45n2; Eisen-
    hower Highway Act and, 91; with
    Havana, Cuba, 81; IBT and, 35,